NEW MERMAIDS

General editor: Brian Gibbons
Professor of English Literature, University of Münster

Drawing of an early twentieth-century proscenium stage
by C. Walter Hodges

NEW MERMAIDS

OSCAR WILDE

AN IDEAL HUSBAND

edited by Russell Jackson

Director, Shakespeare Institute, University of Birmingham

A & C Black • London
WW Norton • New York

Second edition 1993
Reprinted 1996, 1998, 2000
Reprinted with new cover 2003
A & C Black Publishers Limited
37 Soho Square
London W1D 3QZ
www.acblack.com

ISBN 0-7136-6687-0

First New Mermaid edition published 1983
as part of *Two Society Comedies*,
combined with *A Woman of No Importance*
by Ernest Benn Limited

Published in the United States of America by
W. W. Norton & Company Inc.
500 Fifth Avenue, New York, NY 10110

ISBN 0-393-90068-1

CIP catalogue records for this book are available
from the British Library and the Library of Congress

Printed in Great Britain by
Bookmarque Ltd, Croydon, Surrey

CONTENTS

PREFACE

This revised edition of *An Ideal Husband* supersedes that published in the New Mermaid Drama Series in 1983 in the volume *Two Society Comedies*. Like Ian Small's revised New Mermaid edition of *A Woman of No Importance*, it has a new introduction to the play, and the section on the play's composition takes account of recent work. Apart from the correction of minor errors, the text itself and the footnotes remain unaltered. The two revised editions share a biographical note on Wilde by the present writer and a section on the theatrical and intellectual background to the 'society comedies' written jointly with Ian Small.

I am grateful to Merlin Holland, the author's grandson, for permission to quote from unpublished drafts, and to the following institutions for access to materials in their possession: Birmingham Public Library; the Bodleian Library; the British Library; the William Andrews Clark Memorial Library, University of California; the Harvard Theatre Collection; New York Public Library at Lincoln Center; the Theatre Museum, London. Mrs S. Bruce, secretary general of the Women's Liberal Association, responded kindly to enquiries concerning the organisation's early history. I have benefitted from the encouragement and advice of Brian Gibbons, Ian Small and John Stokes, and I am especially grateful to Joel H. Kaplan, editor of the play for the forthcoming Oxford English Texts Edition, for information concerning the recently discovered typescript of the play. My greatest single (and continuing) debt remains that to my wife, Linda Rosenberg.

Birmingham, February 1993   RUSSELL JACKSON

ABBREVIATIONS

References to *An Ideal Husband* (abbreviated to *Husband* in the annotation) are to the line numbering of this edition; *The Importance of being Earnest* (*Earnest*) and *Lady Windermere's Fan* (*LWF*) are cited in the respective New Mermaid editions by Russell Jackson (1980; 4th impression, 1992) and Ian Small (1980). *A Woman of No Importance* is referred to by the line numbering common to the edition by Ian Small in *Two Society Comedies* (1983) and his revised edition (1993). Reference to *The Picture of Dorian Gray* (abbreviated to *Dorian Gray* or *DG*) is to the edition by Isobel Murray (Oxford, 1974), and Wilde's other fiction is cited from the same editor's *Complete Shorter Fiction of Oscar Wilde* (*CSF*) (Oxford, 1979). Other works are referred to by the title of the volume in which they appear in Robert Ross's edition of the *Works* (1908). For convenience of reference I have also given page numbers from the Collins *Complete Works* (1979), which is designated *CW*. *The Letters of Oscar Wilde*, edited by Sir Rupert Hart-Davis (1963), is abbreviated to *Letters*.

The drafts and texts of the play are referred to as follows:

MS   Manuscript drafts of the four acts (including two versions of Act II): British Library, MS Add. 37946.

BLTS   Typescripts of the four acts, with manuscript revisions: British Library, MS Add. 37947.

C   Typescripts of the four acts, with manuscript revisions: William Andrews Clark Memorial Library.

HTC   Typescript of Act I, with manuscript revisions: Harvard Theatre Collection (uncatalogued).

LC   Typescript of the four acts, submitted to the Lord Chamberlain's Office: British Library, MS Add. 53566(A).

F   Typescripts of the four acts, the fourth with manuscript stage-directions (not in Wilde's hand), used by Daniel Frohman: New York Public Library at Lincoln Center, N.C.19-/NCOF.

Pbk   Typescript of Act I, apparently marked as a prompt book (some revisions in hand(s) other than author's): Harvard Theatre Collection (uncatalogued).

PR   Page-proofs of the first edition, with Wilde's manuscript revisions: William Andrews Clark Memorial Library, Finzi 2456.

1st Ed.   *An Ideal Husband, by the author of 'Lady Windermere's Fan'* (London: Leonard Smithers, 1899).

Other abbreviations
OED   *Oxford English Dictionary.*
s.d.   stage direction(s).

In the notes the names of some characters are abbreviated to initials.

INTRODUCTION

THE AUTHOR

ANDRÉ GIDE DESCRIBES Oscar Wilde as he appeared in 1891, when 'his success was so certain that it seemed that it preceded [him] and that all he needed do was go forward and meet it':

> . . . He was rich; he was tall; he was handsome; laden with good fortune and honours. Some compared him to an Asiatic Bacchus; others to some Roman emperor; others to Apollo himself – and the fact is that he was radiant.[1]

The melodramatic contrast between this triumphant figure and the pathetic convict serving two years' hard labour was drawn by Wilde himself in *De Profundis*, the letter written from prison to his lover, Lord Alfred Douglas. He described his transfer in November 1895 from Wandsworth to Reading Gaol, little care being taken for his privacy:

> From two o'clock till half-past two on that day I had to stand on the centre platform at Clapham Junction in convict dress and handcuffed, for the world to look at. I had been taken out of the Hospital Ward without a moment's notice being given to me. Of all possible objects I was the most grotesque. When people saw me they laughed. Each train as it came up swelled the audience. Nothing could exceed their amusement. That was of course before they knew who I was. As soon as they had been informed, they laughed still more. For half an hour I stood there in the grey November rain surrounded by a jeering mob.[2]

Wilde insisted that his life was as much an artistic endeavour as his works – in *De Profundis* he claimed to have been 'a man who stood in symbolic relations to the art and culture of my age', and in conversation with Gide he remarked that the great drama of his life lay in his having put his talent into his works, and his genius into his life.[3] For an author who returned as often as Wilde to the proposition that art transforms and is the superior of Nature, such claims were more than boasting – they were an affirmation of faith.

---

[1] André Gide, 'In Memoriam' from *Oscar Wilde*, translated Bernard Frechtman (New York, 1949): quoted from the extract in Richard Ellmann, ed., *Oscar Wilde: A Collection of Critical Essays* (Englewood Cliffs, N.J., 1969), pp. 25–34. The principal sources for the present account of Wilde's career are H. Montgomery Hyde, *Oscar Wilde* (1975), Richard Ellmann, *Oscar Wilde* (1987) and Rupert Hart-Davis, ed., *The Letters of Oscar Wilde* (revised ed., 1963). Subsequent references to Wilde's *Letters* are to this edition.
[2] Wilde, *Letters*, pp. 490–1. This long letter was written in Reading Gaol in January–March 1897. An abridged version was published by Robert Ross in 1905 as *De Profundis*: the most reliable edition is that contained in *Letters*, pp. 423–511.
[3] Wilde, *Letters*, p. 466; Gide, 'In Memoriam', ed. cit., p. 34.

Oscar Wilde was born in Dublin on 16 October 1854, second son of Sir William and Lady Wilde. The father was an eminent surgeon, the mother a poetess and fervent Irish nationalist who wrote as 'Speranza'. To medical distinction Sir William joined notoriety as a philanderer.[4] Both parents were enthusiasts for the study of Irish legend, folk-lore and history, an interest reflected in the first two of the names given to their son, Oscar Fingal O'Flahertie Wills Wilde. He was educated at Portora Royal School and Trinity College, Dublin, where he became a protégé of the classicist John Pentland Mahaffy. In 1875 he won a scholarship – a 'Classical Demyship' – to Magdalen College, Oxford, where he subsequently took first-class honours in the final school of *Literae Humaniores* (Greek and Roman literature, history and philosophy). He picked up a reputation for wit, charm and conversational prowess. Most important, he came under the influence of two eminent writers on art and its relation to life, John Ruskin and Walter Pater. Ruskin, the most distinguished contemporary art critic, championed the moral and social dimensions of art, and its ability to influence men's lives for the better. Under Ruskin's supervision, Wilde and a few other undergraduates had begun the construction of a road near Hinksey, as a practical demonstration of the aesthetic dignity of labour and the workmanlike qualities essential to the labours of the artist. From Pater, Wilde learned a conflicting interpretation of art as a means to the cultivation of the individual, an idea which received its most notorious statement in the 'Conclusion' to Pater's book *The Renaissance*. There the fully-developed sensibility is claimed as the expression of a full existence: 'To burn always with this hard, gem-like flame, to maintain this ecstasy, is success in life'.[5] These two theories of the relation between art and life were to dominate Wilde's writing. The arguments of the painter James McNeill Whistler against the conservative critics' insistence on moral significance and pictorial verisimilitude in art also influenced Wilde deeply.[6] The close of his Oxford career was marked by two triumphs – his first-class degree and the Newdigate Prize for his poem 'Ravenna' – and two failures. Wilde was not given the Chancellor's English Essay Prize for his essay 'The Rise of Historical Criticism' and he was not offered a fellowship at Magdalen.

---

[4] On Sir William and Lady Wilde see Terence de Vere White, *Parents of Oscar Wilde* (1967).

[5] Walter Pater, *The Renaissance* (1873; Library ed., 1910), p. 236. This 'Conclusion' was omitted in the second edition (1877) and restored, in a modified form, in the third edition (1888).

[6] Whistler later quarrelled with Wilde, accusing him of plagiarism. Some of their exchanges appeared in Whistler's *The Gentle Art of Making Enemies* (1890) and in *Wilde vs. Whistler* (1906).

Moving to London, Wilde set about making himself a name in the capital's fashionable artistic and literary worlds. He had enough poems to make a collected volume, published at his own expense in 1881, and he was seen at the right parties, first nights, and private views. Occasionally he wore the velvet coat and knee-breeches, soft-collared shirt and cravat, that became fixed in the popular imagination as 'aesthetic' dress (and which derived from a fancy-dress ball he had attended when an undergraduate). In December 1881 he embarked on a lecture-tour of the United States organised by the impresario Richard D'Oyly Carte. This was a shrewd back-up to the tour of Gilbert and Sullivan's comic opera *Patience*, but it was also a simple exploitation of the American appetite for being lectured to. Although *Patience*, which satirised the Aesthetic Movement, featured rival poets dressed in a costume closely resembling that adopted by Wilde, the lecturer was taken seriously as a prophet of the 'new renaissance' of art. In his lectures he insisted on comparing the new preoccupation with life-styles with the aspirations of the Italian Renaissance and the Romantic Movement – this was 'a sort of new birth of the spirit of man', like the earlier rebirth 'in its desire for a more gracious and comely way of life, its passion for physical beauty, its exclusive attention to form, its seeking for new subjects for poetry, new forms of art, new intellectual and imaginative enjoyment . . .'[7] The blend of aesthetic theory and enthusiasm for reform of design and colouring in dress and decorative art was derived from a variety of sources, not all successfully synthesized. In addition to Ruskin, Pater and Whistler, Wilde had absorbed the ideas of William Morris and the architect E. W. Godwin. The lectures were exercises in *haute vulgarisation* and not all the sources were acknowledged. Japanese and other oriental art, eighteenth-century furniture, distempered walls in pastel colours, stylised floral motifs – all had made their appearance in English art before Wilde became their advocate. But the influence of his popularising talents was, for all that, considerable. 'In fact,' wrote Max Beerbohm in 1895, looking back on 1880 as though it were a remote historical period, 'Beauty had existed long before 1880. It was Mr Oscar Wilde who managed her *début*'.[8]

As well as establishing him as a popular oracle on matters of art and taste, Wilde's lecture-tour made him a great deal of badly-needed money – he had no prospect of inheriting a family fortune, and would have to make his own way. On his return the velvet suits

---

[7] Wilde, 'The English Renaissance of Art', in Ross's edition of his *Essays and Lectures* (1909), pp. 111f. The text was edited by Ross from four drafts of a lecture first given in New York on 9 January 1882.

[8] Max Beerbohm, *Works* (1922), p. 39.

were discarded, and his hair, worn long and flowing in his 'Aesthetic' period, was cut short in a style resembling the young Nero. The
figure described by Gide was beginning to emerge. After a holiday
in Paris, Wilde moved into rooms at 9 Charles Street, Grosvenor
Square. He returned briefly to New York for the first performance
of his melodrama *Vera; or, the Nihilists* and then prepared for an
autumn lecture-tour of the United Kingdom. On 26 November he
became engaged to Constance Lloyd, and they married on 29 May
1884. In January 1885 they moved into a house designed by
Godwin at 16 Tite Street, Chelsea. Two sons, Cyril and Vyvyan,
were born in 1885 and 1886 respectively. In the early years of his
marriage Wilde was working hard as a journalist. He contributed
reviews to magazines (including the *Pall Mall Gazette* and the
Dramatic Review) and even for a while undertook the editorship of
one, *Woman's World*, which he hoped to turn into 'the recognised
organ through which women of culture and position will express
their views, and to which they will contribute'.[9] By and by
Constance came into a small inheritance, but money was never
plentiful. The life of a professional journalist was laborious and
demanded a high degree of craftsmanship, but it offered a training
from which Wilde, like Shaw, Wells and many others, profited
immensely. Wilde became a fastidious and tireless reviser of his
own work, and his reviews show him as an acute critic of others'.

In 1891 four of Wilde's books appeared, all consisting of earlier
work, some of it in a revised form: *Intentions*, a collection of critical
essays; *Lord Arthur Savile's Crime and Other Stories*; *The Picture of
Dorian Gray*, considerably altered from the version published in
Lippincott's Magazine in 1890; and a collection of children's stories,
A House of Pomegranates. In the same year a verse tragedy written
in 1882, *The Duchess of Padua*, was produced in New York by
Lawrence Barrett under the title *Guido Ferranti*. Like *Vera* it was
poorly received, but Wilde was already turning away from the
pseudo-Elizabethan dramatic form that had preoccupied so many
nineteenth-century poets and contemplating a newer, more com-
mercially acceptable mode. In the summer of 1891 he began work
on the first of a series of successful plays for the fashionable theatres
of the West End: *Lady Windermere's Fan* (St James's, 20 February
1892), *A Woman of No Importance* (Haymarket, 19 April 1893), and
An Ideal Husband (Haymarket, 3 January 1895). The refusal of a
performance licence to the exotic biblical tragedy *Salomé* (in 1892)
proved a temporary setback: acclaim as a dramatic author confirmed Wilde's career in what seemed an irresistible upward curve.

The summer of 1891 was also remarkable for the beginning of an

---

[9] Wilde, *Letters*, p. 202 (to Mrs Alfred Hunt, August 1887).

association that was to be the direct cause of his downfall: the poet Lionel Johnson introduced him to 'Bosie', Lord Alfred Douglas, third son of the Marquess of Queensberry. Wilde appears to have been already a practising homosexual, and his marriage was under some strain. The affair with Douglas estranged him further from Constance, and the drain it caused on Wilde's nervous and financial resources was formidable. Douglas was happy to let Wilde spend money on him after his father stopped his allowance; more seriously, he made ceaseless demands on the time set aside for writing. In *De Profundis* Wilde described his attempts to finish *An Ideal Husband* in an apartment in St James's Place:

> I arrived . . . every morning at 11.30, in order to have the opportunity of thinking and writing without the interruptions inseparable from my own household, quiet and peaceful as that household was. But the attempt was vain. At twelve o'clock you drove up, and stayed smoking cigarettes and chattering till 1.30, when I had to take you out to luncheon at the Café Royal or the Berkeley. Luncheon with its *liqueurs* lasted usually till 3.30. For an hour you retired to White's [Club]. At tea-time you appeared again, and stayed until it was time to dress for dinner. You dined with me either at the Savoy or at Tite Street. We did not separate as a rule till after midnight, as supper at Willis's had to wind up the entrancing day.[10]

This was in 1893. A year later Wilde was working on what was to prove his last play, *The Importance of Being Earnest*, the first draft of which had been composed during a family holiday (largely Douglas-free) at Worthing. In October, Constance had returned to London with the children. Wilde and Douglas stayed together in Brighton, first at the Metropole Hotel, then in private lodgings. Douglas developed influenza and Wilde nursed him through it. He in turn suffered an attack of the virus, and Douglas (by Wilde's account) more or less neglected him. The result was what seemed like an irrevocable quarrel, with Douglas living at Wilde's expense in a hotel but hardly bothering to visit him. In hindsight Wilde claimed that this cruelty afforded him a moment of clear understanding:

> Is it necessary for me to state that I saw clearly that it would be a dishonour to myself to continue even an acquaintance with such a one as you had showed [*sic*] yourself to be? That I recognised that ultimate moment had come, and recognised it as being really a great relief? And that I knew that for the future my Art and Life would be freer and better and more beautiful in every possible way? Ill as I was, I felt at ease.[11]

But reconciliation followed.

10 Wilde, *Letters*, p. 426.
11 Wilde, *Letters*, p. 438.

On 3 January 1895 *An Ideal Husband* was given its first performance. Meanwhile George Alexander, actor-manager of the St
James's Theatre, had turned down the new comedy. It found a
taker in Charles Wyndham, who intended to bring it out at the
Criterion. Then Alexander found himself at a loss for a play to replace Henry James's *Guy Domville*, which had failed spectacularly.
Wyndham agreed to release *The Importance of Being Earnest* on the
condition that he had the option on Wilde's next play, and it was
put into rehearsal at the St James's. At first Wilde attended rehearsals, but his continual interruptions made Alexander suggest that
he might leave the manager and his company to their own resources. He agreed with good grace and left with Douglas for a holiday in Algeria. There they encountered André Gide, who was told
by Wilde that he had a premonition of some disaster awaiting him on
his return.[12] Although his artistic reputation was beyond question,
and he was shortly to have two plays running simultaneously in the
West End, Wilde was already worried by the activities of Douglas's
father. Queensberry was a violent, irrational man, who hated his
son's lover and was capable of hurting both parties. Bosie insisted
on flaunting his relationship with Wilde to annoy his father and he
was reckless of the effect of this public display of unconventional
behaviour. Homosexuality was no less a fact of life in 1895 than it is
now: moreover, the artistic and theatrical world accommodated it
better than society at large. It had a flourishing and varied subcul-
ture and a number of sophisticated apologists. The double life that
it entailed was by no means a simple matter of deceit and guilt for
Wilde: it suited the cultivation of moral independence and detachment from society that he considered essential to art. None the less,
if his affair with Douglas should ever come to be more public, and if
the law were to be invoked, Wilde would be ruined. There had
been scandals and trials involving homosexuals of the upper
classes, which had to a degree closed their ranks to protect their
own. But Wilde had made powerful enemies in a country whose
leaders, institutions and press seemed devoted to Philistinism and
where art itself was always suspect as constituting a threat to the
moral fibre of the nation. *Dorian Gray* in particular had aroused
violent mistrust, especially in its original form, and a satirical novel
by Robert Hichens, *The Green Carnation* (1894), had hinted at a
homosexual relationship between two characters obviously based
on Wilde and Douglas. Queensberry had made his feelings about

---

12 'I am not claiming that Wilde clearly saw prison rising up before him; but I do assert
that the dramatic turn which surprised and astounded London, abruptly turning Wilde
from accuser to accused, did not, strictly speaking, cause him any surprises' (Gide, 'In
Memoriam', ed. cit., p. 34).

his son's private life well known in Clubland. On the first night of *The Importance of Being Earnest*, which opened on 14 February 1895, he tried to cause a disturbance at the theatre, but was thwarted by the management. The play was a great success – according to one of the actors, 'The audience rose in their seats and cheered and cheered again'.[13] As it settled down to what promised to be a long run, Wilde's career was at its height.

A fortnight later, on 28 February, Queensberry left a card at the Albemarle Club 'For Oscar Wilde posing as a somdomite' [*sic*]. The club porter put the card in an envelope, noting on the back the time and date, and Wilde was given it when he arrived at the club later that evening. The events that followed ruined him within a few months. Urged on by Douglas, but against the advice of most of his friends, Wilde sued Queensberry for criminal libel. The case went against Wilde, who found himself answering charges under the 1885 Criminal Law Amendment Act, which made both private and public homosexual relations between men illegal. Significantly, the accusations against him did not include his affair with Douglas: he was alleged to have committed acts of gross indecency on a number of occasions and to have conspired to procure the committing of such acts. The men involved were 'renters', young, lower-class, male prostitutes, and there was a strong sense in the proceedings that Wilde was being tried for betraying his class's social as well as sexual ethics. Much was made of the alleged immorality of his works, especially *Dorian Gray*. The jury at what was effectively the second trial of Wilde (after the hearings in his charge against Queensberry) failed to agree, and a retrial was ordered. Finally, on 25 May 1895, Wilde was convicted and sentenced to two years' imprisonment with hard labour. In the autumn he was declared bankrupt and all his effects were auctioned, including drafts and manuscripts of published and unpublished works. On 19 May 1897 he was released, and took up residence in France. During his imprisonment he had composed a long, bitter letter to Douglas, later published under the title *De Profundis*. Shortly after his release he completed a narrative poem, *The Ballad of Reading Gaol*. These and a few letters to the press on prison reform apart, Wilde published nothing new after his imprisonment. He did manage to arrange for the publication of *The Importance of Being Earnest* and *An Ideal Husband*, which appeared in 1899. Projects for further plays came to nothing. The affair with Douglas was taken up again and continued sporadically. They led a nomadic life on the continent, Wilde often chronically in debt despite the good

[13] Allen Aynesworth, quoted by Hesketh Pearson, *The Life of Oscar Wilde* (1946), p. 257.

offices of his friends. His allowance from Constance was withdrawn when he resumed living with Bosie. His plays were not yet being re-vived in England and his published works brought in little by way of royalties.

Wilde died on 30 November 1900 in Paris, from cerebral menin-gitis which set in after an operation on his ear. The day before he had been received into the Roman Catholic Church. He was buried at Bagneux, but in 1909 his remains were moved to the Père Lachaise cemetery, where they now rest under a monument by Jacob Epstein.

R.J.

THE SOCIETY COMEDIES AND THEIR BACKGROUND

Wilde's society plays, written and performed between 1892 and 1895, are products of a period when authors and critics viewed the state of the London theatre with a degree of optimism – qualified, however, with misgivings as to the direction in which development was to be desired. On one side the advance guard of the New Drama clamoured for social commitment and psychological ver-isimilitude; on the other, conservative critics, anxious not to lose the newly-regained support of the middle classes, mounted a last ditch defence of sentimental idealism; meanwhile puzzled, earnest craftsmen like Arthur Wing Pinero and Henry Arthur Jones sought out the middle ground in order to occupy it in the name of good sense and moderation.

By the 1890s the distinct genres of the earlier decades of the cen-tury had undergone some modification, corresponding both to changes in the social composition of audiences and to the size of the theatres. The values represented in melodrama became more overtly middle-class; from extravaganza, farce and comic opera the musical comedy evolved; pantomime began to accommodate more and more music-hall performers, adapting itself to the display of their talents. Although 'purer' examples of the old-style melo-dramas, farces and burlesques survived, it was to the new, hybrid forms that aspiring dramatists turned. Of these the 'society play' offered settings in a fashionable *milieu*, literate and witty dialogue and the opportunity to discuss manners and morals. It had the appeal of topicality and a glamour that reflected its audience's tastes. More often than not, it concerned itself with the discrimina-tion between acceptable and unacceptable behaviour, the qualifica-tions for entry into 'society' – particularly those concerned with sexual *mores* – and the requirements of public duty. The sentimen-talism of Tom Robertson in the 1860s was supplanted by a smart, ironic perception of the ways of the world, but there was still scope for the impassioned defence of a cherished principle: Pinero or Jones could allow themselves redeeming patches of earnestness. The stylish, well-made French plays from which British dramatists learned (and which they not infrequently copied) provided technical devices and set a high standard of urbane dialogue. References to sexual misdemeanours that provided motivation in French plays usually became less explicit in their British imitations. Adultery was likely to become flirting or – so as to remove all but the slightest suspicion of error – thinking about flirting. Too often it was the machinery of the well-made play – information 'fed' carefully to the audience, surprising revelations which arrive by post, telegram or word of mouth in time for each act to end on a point of suspense – that survived the channel crossing. Grace, wit and sophistication did not travel so easily.[14]

The stage's endorsement of its audience's values took appropriate forms. The *couturière*, tailor and interior decorator often took over from the theatrical costumier and property-maker, and insisted upon receiving their proper credit. Some women's magazines carried reviews of the dresses worn on stage by actresses, as though they constituted a fashion-show. The area formerly occupied by the benches of the pit – cheap seats, occupied by knowing, enthusiastic but not necessarily well-to-do playgoers – now accommodated the *fauteuils* of the stalls, offering drawing-room comfort to those prepared to dress formally and pay their half-guinea. The long, cheap playbill with its bold black type and ink that came off on the hand had been superseded by a small programme, more like an invitation or greeting-card and sometimes perfumed by Rimmel. The air of the auditorium was no longer heavy with the smell of gas – cooler, safer electric lighting had taken over in the mid-1880s and the standards of ventilation and safety had been improved. The producers of Wilde's society plays, George Alexander, Herbert Beerbohm Tree and Lewis Waller, were members of a new breed of actor managers. In the stalls and

---

[14] For a useful account of the genre, see John Russell Taylor, *The Rise and Fall of the Well-Made Play* (1967). Wilde's borrowings from French dramatists are discussed by E. H. Mikhail, 'The French Influences on Oscar Wilde's Comedies', *Revue de Littérature Comparée*, 42, 2 (1968), 220–33; Charles B. Paul and Robert D. Pepper, 'The Importance of Reading Alfred: Oscar Wilde's Debt to Alfred de Musset', *Bulletin of the New York Public Library*, 75 (1971), 506–42; Katharine Worth, *Oscar Wilde* (1983); and Kerry Powell, *Oscar Wilde and the Theatre of the 1890s* (1990). For further accounts of Wilde's transactions with French thought and literature, see Ruth Temple, *The Critic's Alchemy: A Study of the Introduction of French Symbolism into England* (1953); Christophe Campos, *The View of France from Arnold to Bloomsbury* (1965); Malcolm Bradbury and Ian Fletcher, eds., *Decadence and the 1890s* (1979); Patricia Clements, *Baudelaire and the English Tradition* (1985); and Peter Raby, *Oscar Wilde* (1988).

dress-circles of their theatres, the audience found entertainment and hospitality that comforted and confirmed their own way of life: sophisticated, in good taste, moving and thought-provoking only to a degree that they found acceptable. For this state of affairs the Bancrofts could claim some responsibility. Their management of The Prince of Wales's Theatre (1865–80) and collaboration with Tom Robertson 'rendered a public service by proving that the refined and educated classes were as ready as ever to crowd the playhouses, provided only that the entertainment given there was suited to their sympathies and tastes'.[15]

To the modern reader or spectator the serious plays of this theatre rarely seem adventurous or unconventional. In, for example, Pinero's *The Second Mrs Tanqueray* or Jones's *The Case of Rebellious Susan*, it is the patterns derived from melodrama and the conservatism of the dramatists' conclusions that strike us. Compared with Ibsen and Strindberg – or even with their less penetrating French contemporaries – the British authors now seem timid and reactionary, hinting at problems, vaguely suggesting the possibility of a radical solution but rarely pushing matters to it, and, indeed, sometimes resorting to sleight of hand to avoid controversy. It is odd therefore to find the British 'society play' attacked in its own day as a cynical conspiracy *against* morality, and to discover the work of a rank sentimentalist like Charles Haddon Chambers at the centre of a 'dirty plays' controversy. This dispute and the larger debate about the morality of literature (of which it formed part) illustrate the pressures under which playwrights of Wilde's generation wrote. The terms are relevant to his own fight against reactionary opinion and the immense conservatism of theatrical institutions.

In the autumn of 1894 *The Times* reviewed Haddon Chambers's play *John-a-Dreams*, produced by Herbert Beerbohm Tree at the Haymarket. Its plot concerned a 'reclaimed' woman-with-a-past and the struggle between two friends (one an opium addict) for her hand in marriage. Kate Cloud, the heroine, possessed (said *The Times*) 'something of that *virginité de l'âme* of which the author of *La Dame aux Camélias* [Dumas *fils*] speaks'. Mrs Patrick Campbell managed 'to impart a certain plausibility to this aspect of the character'. She was 'gentle and winning, with the chastened look of suffering nobly borne'. The reviewer reflected that it was 'impossible not to be struck at least with the freedom with which the *femme perdue* and her interests are now discussed on the English

[15] Sir Squire and Lady Bancroft, *The Bancrofts: Recollections of Sixty Years* (1909), p. 83. Although Bancroft modestly ascribes this effect to the dramatist's work, the achievement can be credited to the management as well as to Robertson.

stage'. The play was mildly praised and the tone of the notice was more thoughtful than controversial.

A letter quickly followed from a reader signing himself 'X.Y.Z.' in which Chambers's plot was attacked as representing 'the lowest type of sickly immorality', dealing as it did with 'a partially-reclaimed harlot and an opium-drinking sot'. *John-a-Dreams* was compared with the 'immoralities' of *The Second Mrs Tanqueray* and 'the deadly dull and not always moral vulgarities' of Jones's *The Masqueraders*. A number of replies were published, including Tree's defence of the play he had produced and acted in, and the paper itself contributed a leader on the general principles of the case. This editorial offers a concise statement of the conservative opposition to the New Drama: such plays are not a true reflection of life, as they deal only in exceptional cases; they are merely artificial vehicles for modish didacticism.

> The leading doctrine of the New Woman school, which contains a certain number of effeminate males, is that the thing worth living and working for is the free discussion of unsavoury subjects by men and women . . . The one excuse for dealing in public with themes usually excluded from conversation is to be found in the masterly treatment which lifts the whole subject up to a plane far above that of common life. That excuse cannot be pleaded for even the best of these problem plays. Nor has the best of them that inevitable character which in great tragedy redeems and ennobles the treatment of the most appalling crimes.

The combining of cultural conservatism with anti-feminism (with a sidelong glance at 'effeminate males') and the appeal to a higher stratum of works ('great tragedy') in which the treatment of 'unsavoury' subjects is dignified – these are common characteristics of reactionary comment on the 'New Drama' of the 1890s. The conservative critic Clement Scott argued that plays like *John-a-Dreams* were profoundly unrealistic, in that they treated pathological oddities rather than 'average human nature'. Scott urged Tree to seek his themes in this area rather than consult 'the experience of the specialist in moral diseases'.[16]

In fact this debate about realism and morality in the theatre was only the latest turn of a very long debate about art – particularly literature – its audience and its ideology that had its origins in the reception of the work of the Pre-Raphaelite and Aesthetic movements. The subjects and the leading voices in the debate changed, but the terms within which it was conducted remained virtually unaltered. In the *Contemporary Review* in 1871 Robert Buchanan

---

[16] Clement Scott, 'The Modern Society Play', *The Theatre*, 4th series, 23 (January 1895), pp. 6–10. The leader in *The Times* appeared on 12 December 1894.

had accused Dante Gabriel Rossetti of a 'morbid deviation from healthy forms of life'. Algernon Swinburne had suffered the same sort of criticism several years earlier, and the arguments that Buchanan had employed – the decadence of new ideas about morality and the decadence of new forms of art which opposed themselves to a socially responsible art – were appropriated virtually wholesale by the critics of Aestheticism a decade later. Walter Pater and Wilde himself were subjected to a range of censure, from the mild reproofs of George Du Maurier's cartoons in *Punch* to violent condemnation by conservative critics in the periodical press. The line of argument picked out the 'unhealthiness' and 'élitism' inherent in certain forms of literature, and isolated a propensity to social and moral corruption – a term which, like 'effeminacy', usually referred to homosexuality – as their most debilitating feature. In the 1890s the treatment of sexuality provided the clearest focus of interest. The controversy about the way in which sexuality and sexual *mores* ought to be represented in art could encompass a *succès de scandale* like Grant Allen's novel *The Woman Who Did* (1895); the hostile reception in England of much French Impressionist painting (and in particular the work of Degas); and works of sociology and psychology like Max Nordau's *Degeneration* (published in Britain in 1895) which branded both as manifestations of the pathologically deviant and so politically subversive currents in contemporary society. Moreover the two most famous casualties of the controversy over 'dirty' or 'subversive' art occurred in the middle of the decade. After the chorus of adverse criticism that followed the publication of *Jude the Obscure* (1895), Thomas Hardy chose to stop writing fiction. Earlier in the same year the controversy claimed its biggest casualty, the career of Wilde himself.

Indeed for several years Wilde had been under attack and had been obliged to defend a number of his works, notably *The Picture of Dorian Gray*. The whole of his critical writings and, indeed, his entire way of life were opposed to the assumptions embedded in such criticism as Clement Scott's. In *The Soul of Man under Socialism*, first published in 1891, Wilde singled out some of the epithets used pejoratively by critics like Scott, arguing that their meaning had been misapplied or perverted: 'unintelligible', 'immoral', 'exotic', 'unhealthy' and 'morbid'. Popular art-criticism suffered from 'the natural inability of a community corrupted by authority to understand or appreciate Individualism'. British journalists had 'nailed their own ears to the keyhole' and sat in unworthy and illegitimate judgment on the affairs of public figures. 'The private lives of men and women should not be told to the public. The public have nothing to do with them at all'.[17] Of course,

[17] *Intentions*, pp. 307–10, 313/*CW*, pp. 1092–4, 1095.

paradoxically no one had made fuller use than Wilde of the attentions of journalism; no one took better advantage of the press's ability to create 'personalities'.[18] This was merely one of the large contradictions that Wilde's career encompassed. In addition, he could proclaim the importance of the artist's work as a transformation of his life and yet at the same time canvass his right to privacy, his essential individualism. In his critical writing Wilde maintained that the critic's reading of a work should be an act of creation in its own right, but at the same time he rebuked the press and public for their inability to reflect anything other than their own inadequacies in judging his work. There were further complexities: Wilde would present himself at one and the same time as both a great teacher and an enemy of authority, unstinting in his advice on art and life but insisting (in the words he gives Lord Goring in *An Ideal Husband*) that the only thing to do with good advice is to pass it on – 'It is never of use to oneself'. The ironic, nonchalant manner, frequent references to 'masks' and 'poses' and continual use of the opposition's vocabulary were a means of keeping the public guessing, of avoiding being fixed, and so 'known'. Jack Worthing, in *The Importance of Being Earnest*, has a hatred of cocksure 'cleverness' as energetic as any expressed by conservatives like Clement Scott:

> I am sick to death of cleverness. Everybody is clever nowadays. You can't go anywhere without meeting clever people. The thing has become an absolute public nuisance. I wish to goodness we had a few fools left.   (I, 630)'

In a passage drafted for the same play but later transferred in an adapted form to *An Ideal Husband*, Lord Goring's father asks him whether he really understands what he says, and receives the thoughtful reply, 'Yes, father, if I listen attentively' (III, 136). The watchwords of the reactionaries are used with a sincere and earnest wrongness. 'Healthy' and 'morbid' are misapplied in this way: Mrs Marchmont in *An Ideal Husband* complains that her husband, 'painfully unobservant', has never once told her she is morbid. At its best – in *The Importance of Being Earnest* – this technique results in a tightly-controlled play on notions of sincerity and triviality, a heightened awareness of the necessary but arbitrary judgments made continually by those who take themselves seriously and abjure facile 'cleverness'. It is entirely appropriate in this respect

---

[18] For classic accounts of the popular press in late nineteenth-century Britain, see John Gross, *The Rise and Fall of the Man of Letters* (1969) and Raymond Williams, *The Long Revolution* (1961); for a discussion of Wilde's relationship with the power of the press, see Regenia A. Gagnier, *Idylls of the Marketplace: Oscar Wilde and the Victorian Public* (1987) and John Stokes, *In the Nineties* (1989).

that Wilde should have wavered between subtitling his last comedy 'A Serious Comedy for Trivial People' or 'A Trivial Comedy for Serious People'. The interchangeability of terms is, in the world of the play, exhilarating and liberating.[19]

Although Wilde takes his plots seriously, and appears to invest them with some of his own preoccupations and experiences, he takes care to treat at least one of the solemn moments in each play with a degree of irony, extending the principle of paradox to the 'strong' situations required by the *genre* in which he is working. In *Lady Windermere's Fan* Mrs Erlynne renounces her claims as a mother in a passage which modulates from a sincere and moving account of the experience that has changed her intentions ('Only once in my life have I known a mother's feelings. That was last night. They were terrible . . .') to the flippancy of a Wildean dandy:

> I thought I had no heart. I find I have and a heart doesn't suit me, Windermere. Somehow it doesn't go with modern dress. It makes one look old. (*Takes up hand-mirror from table and looks into it*) And it spoils one's career at critical moments. (IV, 239–43)

Presently she is lecturing Lord Windermere on the difference between life and fiction: 'I suppose . . . you would like me to retire into a convent or become a hospital nurse, or something of that kind as people do in silly modern novels.' Repentance, she points out, 'is quite out of date'. In a similar kind of reversal in *A Woman of No Importance*, Mrs Arbuthnot pleads with her son not to pursue his intention of forcing Lord Illingworth to marry her and insists that it is her shameful secret and the consciousness of it which has kept them together:

> Oh, don't you see? don't you understand? It is my dishonour that has made you so dear to me. It is my disgrace that has bound you so closely to me. It is the price I paid for you – the price of body and soul – that makes me love you as I do. Oh, don't ask me to do this horrible thing. Child of my shame, be still the child of my shame! (IV, 255–60)

In *An Ideal Husband*, Sir Robert Chiltern rebukes his wife for having made an idol of him, effectively destroying his career by her insistence on a high-minded rejection of the blackmailer's terms:

> The sin of my youth, that I had thought was buried, rose up in front of me, hideous, horrible, with its hands at my throat. I could have killed it for ever, sent it back into its tomb, destroyed its record, burned the one witness against me. You prevented me. No one but you, you know it.

---

[19] For further discussion of Wilde's attempts to revalue the significance of terms such as 'immoral', 'unhealthy' and 'morbid', see Jonathan Dollimore, 'Different Desires: Subjectivity and Transgression in Wilde and Gide', *Textual Practice*, 1, 1 (1987), 48–67.

Now he faces 'public disgrace, ruin, terrible shame', for which (somewhat perversely we may think) he holds her responsible:

> Let women make no more ideals of men! Let them not put them on altars and bow before them or they may ruin other lives as completely as you – you whom I have so wildly loved – have ruined mine! (II, 803–14)

Each of these passages represents a turning-point in its respective play. In each case Wilde makes the moving factor the character's understanding of a point of view that is a complete inversion of the convention: a mother recognises and sets aside the natural feelings of a parent; a mother insists on remaining unmarried because of the intimacy brought about by sin; a man rebukes a woman for setting him on a pedestal. The ancient motif of affinity between kin revealing itself – *la voix du sang* – is evoked and rejected by Mrs Erlynne and Mrs Arbuthnot. The familiar figure of a fallen woman becomes in Chiltern a fallen man. At the same time there is no doubt that the passages are to be taken seriously – Wilde rarely uses lightly words like 'horrible' or 'terrible' – and the outbursts of both Mrs Arbuthnot and Chiltern are meant to be vivid and chilling. Wilde regarded the crisis in Act III of *A Woman of No Importance* as the 'psychological' act, and Goring's references to a 'psychological experiment' in *An Ideal Husband* point to the same interest. To Wilde, 'psychology' seems to denote the investigation of abnormal states of mind by novelists (like Paul Bourget, Emile Zola, J.-K. Huysmans and Dostoevsky) and the investigations into criminality conducted by Lombroso and others. The objective examination of sexuality (for example by Havelock Ellis) also involved 'psychology'. The word has suggestions of scientific analysis, as distinct from moral interpretation, of what would seem aberrations to the 'normal' man or woman. In Chapter IV of *The Picture of Dorian Gray* Lord Henry Wotton reflects on the 'scientific' spirit in which he contemplates Dorian's personality: 'It was clear to him that the experimental method was the only method by which one could arrive at any scientific analysis of the passions; and certainly Dorian Gray was a subject made to his hand, and seemed to promise rich and fruitful results'.[20] This is a more obviously sinister equivalent of Lord Goring's 'psychological experiment' in *An Ideal Husband*. In Wilde himself the 'psychological' approach involves finding the moment at which a reaction or change of behaviour occurs, and in the attempt to produce character subtly differentiated from conventional theatrical 'types'. He may not convince us in the accounts of the mentality of his characters, but we can recognise the implicit argument that their behaviour is true to something other than the

[20] *Dorian Gray*, p. 58/*CW*, p. 56.

'type' by which the world has hitherto judged such men or women in such situations, or the theatrical convention by which it affirms a moral code. Here the peculiarly elusive nature of the plays is once more in evidence. The rhetoric of the dialogue is sending out one set of signals – orthodox, familiar – but the action is developing in a way that would seem perverse to a conservative critic of the period. The modern reader picks up the conventional element, but the contemporary reviewer of *A Woman of No Importance* finds the play 'Ibsenish'.   R.J. and I.S.

AN IDEAL HUSBAND

Is it possible for a modern audience to find *An Ideal Husband* 'Ibsenish' – in the sense of dramatising social problems and ethical dilemmas? For directors, actors and audiences the abiding problem of the society plays that preceded *The Importance of Being Earnest* lies in the melodramatic structure and the 'serious' moral dilemmas that seem to provide the pretext for the witty repartee that is so highly valued and which, it has to be admitted, keeps them in currency today. Wilde liked to claim that he wrote quickly, but it is clear from the drafts of his plays that he revised carefully and at length and that he took great care with the mechanics of construction and stagecraft. Perhaps to a modern audience the plays seem to exemplify the formulae of the 'well-made play' that in their time they sought to subvert.

The resolution of the plot of *An Ideal Husband* depends on the discovery of evidence that will incriminate and thus vanquish the blackmailing Mrs Cheveley. Wilde was well into the play's composition before – perhaps with his actors' help – he decided on the most economical means of effecting this reversal: the bracelet, found by Mabel Chiltern in Act I (see pp. xxxv–xliii, 'The Play's Composition and Publication'). The structure places crucial points of plot strategically among supportive material that establishes a sense of *milieu* and character. (The structure is analysed in Appendix III below.) It is arguable that this is the best-plotted and executed of the plays staged before *The Importance of Being Earnest*. Nevertheless, the 'well-made' play's mechanisms, however skilfully engineered, have long been out of favour, and the later comedy has been influential in establishing the sense of a 'Wildean' view of the drama of the time. It makes sport with the mechanisms of the serious dramas and novels of its time: family secrets – and relatives – lost and found, 'stock' characterisations carefully distorted, poetic justice achieved and guyed in the final scenes, arbitrary but crucial changes of direction brought about through the arrival of news by telegram and letter and the discovery of lost mementoes. In the three-volume novel (of more than usually sickening sentimentality) that the governess, Miss Prism, had misplaced, the good ended happily and the bad unhappily: 'That is what fiction means'. Wilde's final and most popular play relentlessly inverts the familiar rules by which conduct is assessed, guys the customary inquisition into a prospective husband's 'past', and makes hay with the clichés of rural innocence and urban sophistication and of idealism and materialism. It establishes a comic world in which, at the moment of revelation, a young man can declare to his prospective bride that 'it is a terrible thing for a man to find out suddenly that all his life he has been speaking nothing but the truth' and ask her earnestly whether she can forgive him, and she can reply: 'I can. For I feel sure that you are sure to change' (III, 477–80).

Audiences of the 1990s who come to *An Ideal Husband* with *The Importance of Being Earnest* in mind can hardly be blamed for baulking at a play whose final moments deal as follows with the dishonest but providentially unpunished Sir Robert Chiltern and his naively idealistic wife:

> *They all go out except* SIR ROBERT CHILTERN. *He sinks into a chair, wrapt in thought. After a little time* LADY CHILTERN *returns to look for him*
> LADY CHILTERN (*Leaning over the back of the chair*)
>   Aren't you coming in, Robert?
> SIR ROBERT CHILTERN (*Taking her hand*)
>   Gertrude, is it love you feel for me, or is it pity merely?
> LADY CHILTERN (*Kisses him*)
>   It is love, Robert. Love and only love. For both of us a new life is beginning.
>   CURTAIN
>   (IV, 551–5)

A recent London production provided a subtext of earnestness for this and other moments (notably the end of Act I) by bringing up the strains of Elgar, *nobilmente*, under the stage-picture, but it is open to question whether the seriousness of the moment can or should be redeemed in this way.[21] It is quite conceivable that Wilde intended audiences to feel uncomfortable, and that the final moments should register as the restatement of an unresolved problem rather than as the prospect of unclouded happiness. The career of Sir Robert Chiltern has been based on the profits from an act of dishonesty and pursued in ignorance of his wife's true capabilities

[21] Directed by Sir Peter Hall for the Peter Hall Company, Globe Theatre, London, 4 November 1992.

and with priggish readiness not to forgive the faults of others. At the end of Act I Gertrude Chiltern insists that her husband maintain the high moral standard she has worshipped in him and refuse Mrs Cheveley's demand that he should support a fraudulent scheme: at the end of the next act he turns on her with an extraordinary tirade against women's folly in idealising men. In Act III, at Goring's house, he is abject in his requests for help in extricating himself from the blackmailer's grasp and then melodramatically severe in refusing to hear any explanation when he finds Mrs Cheveley in an adjoining room. In Act IV he is naively self-absorbed in his reactions to the news that the incriminating letter has been burned and almost childish in his reluctance to do 'the right thing' and refuse to take Cabinet office. Then, as the play approaches its finale, when Sir Robert tells Lord Goring that he cannot countenance his marriage to Mabel, he has the gall to preach a sermon on love and marriage:

> . . . Loveless marriages are horrible. But there is one thing worse than an absolutely loveless marriage. A marriage in which there is love, but on one side only; faith, but on one side only; devotion, but on one side only, and in which of the two hearts one is sure to be broken.   (468–72)

In *Earnest* it is made clear that 'a high moral tone can hardly be said to conduce very much to one's health or one's happiness' (I, 207–9), but here the dramatist seems to expect its adoption to seem appropriate. Or does he? If Wilde is treating Chiltern with a degree of irony, has the fact been concealed too effectively from the audience?

In all this an ethical and a technical problem are intertwined. The ethical difficulty consists of two elements: the fact that the formulations of the issues at stake are those current in the 1890s; and the indisposition of a modern audience to find Chiltern worth saving. The first is discussed with admirable thoroughness by Kerry Powell in his *Oscar Wilde and the Theatre of the 1890s*: 'The late Victorian stage was crowded with Sir Robert Chilterns',[22] and argument for the equality of status between the sexes was often formulated in terms of the need to produce improved, 'ideal' men, as well as the requirement that the understanding and horizons of women should be altered. The alleged impossibility of this was a commonplace of worldly comedy and journalism. However, the positively Tennysonian terms used by Wilde's Lady Chiltern – 'We needs must love the highest when we see it' (I, 803n) – are far re-

[22] Kerry Powell, *Oscar Wilde and the Theatre of the 1890s* (Cambridge, 1990), p. 90. See also Russell Jackson, ed., *The Importance of Being Earnest* (New Mermaid Drama Series, London, 4th impression, 1992), pp. xx–xxvii. The 'ideal husband' is discussed at some length in Act II of *A Woman of No Importance* (ed. Ian Small, New Mermaid Drama Series, London 1993, II, 59–231).

moved from those employed in late twentieth-century debates on the 'new man'. Without being accustomed to the habitual Victorian formulations of the 'ideal woman' it is difficult for an audience or reader to appreciate the impact of Wilde's ironic inversion of them at the end of the play's first act. This is a point of 'psychology' of the kind he prided himself on – and which has been discussed in the preceding section of this introduction (see p. xxiii).

In this sequence of the play and elsewhere Wilde uses a rhetoric of idealism that would have seemed less stilted – or at least more appropriate – to contemporaries. Now it is likely to suggest that he is simply pompous. But even when such allowances are made, it can hardly be denied that Chiltern manages to behave in a stiffly unsympathetic manner. He is unlikely to win hearts by his refusal, thinking that Goring has been conducting an affair with Mrs Cheveley, to let him marry Mabel, even if it can be explained in terms of the prevailing moral and social assumptions of the period. The technical problem lies in the stage-management of these scenes of crisis, and in fact cannot be separated from the ethical difficulties they embody. The first act is made to climax on the conflict between Gertrude Chiltern's absurd idealism and her husband's secret guilt; the third act has a hide-and-seek staginess that seems too close to farce for the seriousness of the situation; the fourth act seems equally contrived; and throughout Chiltern and his wife speak in a tone of strenuous moral concern. Also of a technical nature – being fictional and theatrical clichés of the period – are the unconvincing nature of Chiltern's political life (in which the Prime Minister can suddenly send a letter of appointment by a conveniently influential old Peer) and the novelletish world of the sinister Baron Arnheim and the showy adventuress who is to be Chiltern's nemesis. Chiltern seems a thoroughly bad character in terms of both the 'ideal husband's' morality and the dramatist's stagecraft. Although he is supposed to be an exemplary politician, we never learn what opinions he has on any topic of the day (although this would probably not have been permitted by the Lord Chamberlain's Office, which censored plays rigorously for any hint of political controversy). In her own comic vein Lady Markby has more to say on politics than he does. Moreover, as a dramatic character Chiltern is reactive rather than active. Bad news is brought to him, he is put into awkward situations and he responds, but it is Goring who takes positive action. It is also remarkable that Mrs Cheveley, whose career as an adventuress has distinct (and conventionally) sexual overtones, has never been connected personally to Chiltern's indiscretions: she was Arnheim's mistress and once before attempted to entrap Goring in marriage. Chiltern does not even have the appeal of a passionate romantic or sexual past to recommend him. Can it be argued that the difficulties are dramatised by Wilde, and have a function in the play's strategy rather than simply being symptoms of the confusions we may think it shares with its age?

For help one might turn to Wilde's elaborate stage direction describing Chiltern on his first entrance (I, 84 etc.). This was added, with others of the same kind, when the play was prepared for publication in 1899: it seeks to make Chiltern as enigmatic as possible, and also to make him 'nervous' to the point of neurosis. It might be claimed that this is a more interesting personality than the one Wilde has dramatised, but the character-sketch is especially valuable because it brings Chiltern closer to a real-life character – Wilde. Comparison with the account Wilde gave of himself at the height of his fame – 'a man who stood in symbolic relations to the art and culture of my age' – suggests the same insistence on the figure's representative nature. Chiltern is described in terms of a tension between suppressed romanticism and political logic. Lord Goring, as described in another stage direction (I, 198), also seems like another formulation of Wilde's attitude in the mid-1890s: 'He plays with life, and is on perfectly good terms with the world. He is fond of being misunderstood. It gives him a post of vantage'. In the stage direction at the beginning of Act III, Goring 'stands in immediate relation to modern life, makes it indeed, and so masters it', and is 'the first well-dressed philosopher in the history of thought'. The butler Phipps is no less formidable, 'a mask with a manner', and also seems a shadow of Wilde's successful self. As well as being of interest because they were written by Wilde after the disastrous events that showed the disadvantages of being misunderstood, these stage directions point to one of the narrative patterns that absorbed him as a writer: that of the young man who sells his integrity to an older, persuasive mentor and then pays terribly for the success he achieves. The relationship between Chiltern and Arnheim, described in Act II, resembles that of Dorian Gray and Lord Henry Wotton.

> I remember so well how, with a strange smile on his pale curved lips, he led me through his wonderful picture gallery, showed me his tapestries, his enamels, his jewels, his carved ivories, made me wonder at the strange loveliness of the luxury in which he lived; and then told me that luxury was nothing but a background, a painted scene in a play, and that power, power over other men, power over the world was the one thing worth having, the one supreme pleasure worth knowing, the one joy one never tired of, and that in our century only the rich possessed it.
>
> (II, 100–9)

The enclosed atmosphere of elaborate aestheticism (redolent of

Huysmans' *A Rebours*), the theatrical image and the Nietzschean ethics are suggestive of a secret life more profound than Chiltern's wife ever suspects or discovers, a seduction with deeper implications than an offer of the means to worldly success. It is conceivable that Wilde's revisions to the passage, and the removal of circumstantial details of Mrs Cheveley's involvement with Arnheim, were intended to make the Baron a more mysterious, less clearly heterosexual figure. (See Appendix I, notes to I, 471 and II, 91–109.) The influence on a younger man of an emotionally, artistically and intellectually formidable mentor is a recurrent topic in Wilde's writings and life, and even Arnheim himself might be construed as another 'mask' of the dramatist. When Chiltern is told that the evidence of his wrongdoing has been destroyed he speaks in the language of guilt and betrayal on a Faustian level:

> I wish I had seen that one sin of my youth burning to ashes. How many men there are in modern life who would like to see their past burning to white ashes before them! (IV, 299–301)

This takes up the terms he had used in Act II when he tells Goring that 'there are terrible temptations that it requires strength, strength and courage, to yield to' (134–5) and when he rebukes his wife with having insisted on his refusing Mrs Cheveley's request:

> The sin of my youth, that I had thought was buried, rose up in front of me, hideous, horrible, with its hands at my throat. I could have killed it for ever, sent it back into its tomb, destroyed its record, burned the one witness against me. You prevented me. (II, 803–7)

In the immediate context in Act I the language seems unduly melodramatic: by the end of the play we have heard about Baron Arnheim, and such words may seem more appropriate. 'Sin' is a concept constantly under redefinition in Wilde's work, and is never used without a sense of a challenge to conventional ideas: the offence here is more to do with intellectual conviction (under Arnheim's tutelage) than the desire for a commonplace financial gain.[23] The figure of Mrs Cheveley has helped to sustain this effect.

Mrs Cheveley has had no sexual connection with Chiltern, but she is given an unmistakably erotic significance in Wilde's descriptive stage direction (I, 51 etc.): 'Lips very thin and highly-coloured, a line of scarlet on a pallid face. Venetian red hair, aquiline nose, and long throat . . . Rouge accentuates the natural paleness of her complexion . . . She looks rather like an orchid, and

---

[23] Wilde's use of the ideas of sin, guilt and atonement is discussed at length by Christopher M. Nassaar, *Into the Demon Universe: A Literary Exploration of Oscar Wilde* (New Haven, 1974).

makes great demands on one's curiosity'. The latter part of Wilde's description seems to edge away into flippancy, but the first sentences suggest a vampire, whose sensuous and decadent allure is set against the 'grave Greek beauty' of Lady Chiltern. In a stage direction in Act III (152 etc.) she is 'Lamia-like', and even more explicitly a *femme fatale*. (The costumes of the 1895 production are described in Appendix II, pp. 155–8.) Mrs Cheveley is a heterosexual symbol, acceptable in terms of the public theatre of the 1890s, for the homosexual seduction by Arnheim that constitutes Chiltern's deadly secret. The stage directions for Gertrude Chiltern in Act II reinforce this impression. When she has learned her husband's secret she 'stands like someone in a dreadful dream . . . She looks at him with strange eyes, as though she was seeing him for the first time' (760 etc.). At the end of the act her physical collapse is described sensuously:

> *Pale with anguish, bewildered, helpless, she sways like a plant in the water.*
> *Her hands, outstretched, seem to tremble in the air like blossoms in the*
> *wind . . .*   (814 etc.)

Wilde courted biographical interpretation so assiduously and dangerously that it is tempting to see this as a memory of some scene between him and his wife, Constance – especially if, as Richard Ellmann suggested, in the mid–1880s the confession of having caught syphilis at Oxford served as a pretext for breaking off sexual relations with her.[24] It seems from Wilde's comments on the play to an interviewer that he regarded its 'entire psychology' as lying in the exposition of the differences between a man's love for a woman and a woman's for a man, 'the passion that women have for making ideals', and 'the weakness of a man who dares not to show his imperfections to the thing he loves' (*The Sketch*, 9 January 1895). There is a strange pre-echo here of the poem *The Ballad of Reading Gaol*, published after Wilde's release from prison: 'For each man kills the thing he loves . . .' Betrayal, secrecy and love seem to be bound up together.

The subtext of quasi-sexual (and, more particularly, homosexual) seduction in Chiltern's fall from grace is particularly apparent when we read the stage directions added by Wilde in 1899: for the benefit of the play's readers the career of Chiltern has been transformed retrospectively into a more evidently Faustian fable than it would have seemed in its first stage production in 1895. Then Chiltern's story was perfectly capable of being read as a familiar tale of political life – as commonly represented on the

[24] Richard Ellmann, *Oscar Wilde* (London, 1987), pp. 261–2. The bleakness of the Chilterns' marriage may have some bearing on this: see *An Ideal Husband*, III, 296–307.

stage. To an audience not yet made familiar with all the details of the author's private life, the inversion of the usual terms of the 'woman question' would appear witty and well-turned rather than shocking, and the play's modernity (a valued quality in Wilde's writing) would lie in its dealing with the 'marriage question', in its presentation of fashionable society and in the more obviously Wildean figure of Lord Goring, the philosopher-dandy, who refuses to talk in such absolute terms as 'sin' and 'guilt'.

Like other, similar figures in Wilde's works, Goring offers a holiday from the serious responsibilities of speaking and feeling. There is something both daring and festive in opening the play's second act, so soon after the high moral tone has been sounded, with Goring's declaration that 'no man should have a secret from his own wife. She invariably finds it out. Women have a wonderful instinct about things. They can discover everything except the obvious' (5–8). (The implications of this in a biographical view of the work are astonishing.) Wilde makes Goring the play's *raisonneur*, the familiar stage figure of the experienced man of the world who provides the wisdom of the world and helps to resolve the difficulties of the principal couple. Such parts occur in many plays of the time, and some especially fine examples were written for Charles Wyndham by Henry Arthur Jones.[25] In this play Goring's dandyism, in the sense of detachment from conventional wisdom and a love of cleverly inverted or comically misapplied moral language, is shared by other characters, including the 'supernumeraries' who people the social life of the Chilterns. In drafts of Act III even Phipps, on whose enigmatic detachment Wilde's 1899 stage directions insist, had some dandaical lines on the demoralising effects of marriage. (See note to III, 152.) Lady Markby, who has much in common with Lady Bracknell (including a humorously absent husband) speaks in a version of the style. She seems to unite with Mrs Cheveley in debunking Gertrude Chiltern's idealism: 'I don't think man has much capacity for development. He has got as far as he can, and that is not far' is her response to Mrs Cheveley's suggestion that 'the higher education of men' is what is called for. This is very much the *lingua franca* of fashionable society in Wilde, but two important characters, both of them women, are especially significant as exponents of the style. Mabel Chiltern is one, a fashionable and witty young woman who has a few passages of Beatrice and Benedick sparring with Goring and finally is to

---

[25] The *raisonneurs* created by Jones for Charles Wyndham include Sir Richard Kato in *The Case of Rebellious Susan* (1894), Colonel Sir Christopher Deering in *The Liars* (1897) and Sir Daniel Carteret in *Mrs Dane's Defence* (1900). All these plays, especially the first two, offer interesting contrasts with Wilde's handling of the marriage question.

marry him. The other is Mrs Cheveley. It is hardly surprising that the adventuress should proclaim her cynical outlook, but here it is curiously close to that of the 'philosopher' who is to be her opponent. In terms of the plot it explains why Goring might have considered marriage to her, but in the play's balance of points of view it intriguingly allies Mrs Cheveley with Goring's serious triviality and against the earnestness of the Chilterns. It would have been perfectly possible for Goring to have spoken such lines as Mrs Cheveley's declaration that 'morality is simply the attitude we adopt towards people whom we personally dislike' (II, 720–1). By the same token, Goring's joke about the lower classes losing their relations (III, 32–3) is heartless enough to be spoken by a villainous character in a more conventional play. The usual correlation in Victorian dramaturgy between sincerity and goodness is subverted.

The detached manner and habitual witty inversion or mis-application of terms (serious/trivial, moral/immoral, etc.) is common in Wilde's work, an important component of his wit, and the common currency of his characters' talk. But in *An Ideal Husband* he insists, even more than with Cecil Graham in *Lady Windermere's Fan*, that the principal dandy should be a vitally active element in the plot. A cardinal point of dandyism, studiously repeated in Wilde's works, is the importance of doing nothing. Faust and Don Juan are too active to be dandies, who never do anything so strenuous as to make pacts with the Devil or defy God.[26] Here Chiltern the statesman, who has effectively made such a pact for the sake of success is (as has been remarked above) a reactive character, and it is Goring who takes the initiative. Wilde uses Goring's father, Lord Caversham, as a means of reinforcing the impression that Goring exemplifies the dandy's refusal to take life seriously:

LORD CAVERSHAM
    . . . Want to have a serious conversation with you, sir.

LORD GORING
    My dear father! At this hour?

LORD CAVERSHAM
    Well, sir, it is only ten o'clock. What is your objection to the hour? I think the hour is an admirable hour!

LORD GORING
    Well, the fact is, father, this is not my day for talking seriously. I am very sorry, but it is not my day.

---

[26] The distinction between the dandy and the active, defiant anti-heroes is developed by Marie-Christine Natta, *La Grandeur sans Convictions: Essai sur le Dandyisme* (Paris, 1990), chapter 3, 'Sa Majesté le Dandy'.

LORD CAVERSHAM
    What do you mean, sir?
LORD GORING
    During the season, father, I only talk seriously on the first Tuesday in
    every month, from four to seven.   (III, 72–81)

Mabel, who would not like an ideal husband – 'it sounds like something in the next world' (IV, 545–6) – is the perfect match for Goring, whose conduct in the play eventually indicates that he is far from 'heartless' (as his father pronounces him after one of their conversations). In the play's final scene he is even given the conventional theatrical reward of Mabel's hand in marriage. By the combination of professed detachment and active benevolence in Goring, the play implies that conventional understanding of 'serious' attitudes should be revised.

However, in order to reach this happy conclusion, Goring must earn some credit as a 'serious' thinker: in a scene with Gertrude Chiltern in Act IV (393–437) he has to persuade her not to stand between Chiltern and his career. In overcoming Mrs Cheveley Goring relies on a happy coincidence – the bracelet she drops – rather than any powers of argument. Indeed in their scene at the end of Act III one might be inclined to agree with her that he is using 'big words' that 'mean so little' when he denounces her blackmailing as 'vile, horrible, infamous' (506). With Gertrude Chiltern in Act IV (as in the scene in Act II, 322 etc.) argument is necessary, and he speaks in the idealistic terms that she will respect. But the context gives no clear indication that Goring consciously employs this language to deal with the 'ideal wife'. He uses the quasi-religious terms familiar from Chiltern himself: 'Why should you scourge him with rods for a sin done in his youth . . .?' (412–13). His description of the difference between the lives of men and women is entirely conventional, and has the rhetorical idiom of such texts as John Ruskin's *Sesame and Lilies* (see Appendix 1, and note to IV, 416). Wilde's 1899 stage direction at the beginning of this sequence indicates that Goring shows 'the philosopher that underlies the dandy'. It is not clear that the dramatist manages to show the one without jeopardising the effect of the other, but the contradiction is typical of Wilde's work as a whole.

In all the 'Society Comedies' Wilde tried variations on the commercial theatre's techniques of construction and characterisation. Only *The Importance of Being Earnest*, by expressly parodying these devices, stood aside from the responsibilities they entailed. With varying degrees of success he adapted familiar elements of plotting and characterisation to suit the preoccupations he had aired in his other published work. Stories of 'lost' mothers and fathers (Mrs Erlynne in *Lady Windermere's Fan*, Lord Illingworth in *A Woman of No Importance*); scenes in which characters confront each other's assumptions as a result of some crisis in the plot (the *scènes à faire* of popular French drama); striking 'pictures' to bring down the curtain at the end of each act; a cast of sophisticated and powerful personages finely dressed and moving in agreeably lavish surroundings. His relationship with conventions of the West End theatre and the actor-managers who controlled them were sometimes unhappy. George Alexander, exasperated by Wilde's intransigence over the placing of a major plot point in *Lady Windermere's Fan*, wrote privately to a critic complaining of the 'stupidity' of 'this conceited, arrogant & ungrateful man'.[27] Wilde spoke with studied nonchalance about actors and audiences. 'When a play that is a work of art is produced on stage', he told one interviewer, 'what is being tested is not the play, but the stage; when a play that is *not* a work of art is produced on the stage what is being tested is not the play but the public'.[28] Wilde's speeches as an author at the first nights of his plays, like his interviews, were provocative and dandyish in content and delivery. Such behaviour was not always taken as trivially as he insisted it should be, and Alexander was particularly incensed by comments Wilde made at a meeting of the Playgoers' Club in February 1892, to the effect that 'the present decadence of the English stage was due to the fact that the actor, the instrumentalist, the medium had become more important than the creative artist or dramatist'. One account quoted him as having described the stage as 'only a frame furnished with puppets'.[29] On the other hand, Wilde's plays were proving so successful at the box office that such annoyances would be worth bearing: in 1895 Alexander, having turned it down when it was first offered to him, was glad to acquire *The Importance of Being Earnest* from Charles Wyndham to fill the gap caused by the failure of a play by Henry James.

In dealing with the expectations of West End audiences and the authority of the actor-managers, Wilde was playing a power game. In his plays he seeks to empower the dandies, and in his statements about the theatre, as about art and life in general, he constantly disclaims any pretensions to seriousness – as commonly defined. A true dandy should always appear to do everything with ease and should not seem to need or court public favour: this attitude (an important word for Wilde) can hardly be said to be consistent with

---

[27] Joel H. Kaplan, 'A Puppet's Power: George Alexander, Clement Scott and the Replotting of *Lady Windermere's Fan*', *Theatre Notebook*, 46 (1992), 59–73.
[28] Quoted by H. Montgomery Hyde, *The Life of Oscar Wilde* (1975), p. 172.
[29] Kaplan, 'A Puppet's Power', p. 65.

Wilde's assiduous pursuit of a career as a journalist and dramatic author. This was the guise of the nonchalant amateur employed as a device at the service of professionalism – perhaps as a means of subverting and changing the rules of the professions themselves. Journalism and the West End theatre would become more playful and in consequence more genuinely serious. The marketplace would be transformed.

Perhaps the most rewarding approach to these plays, as to the writer himself, is to embrace the ambiguities and to see in them some early modernist experimentation rather than a series of failures which could only be dealt with by resort to the parodic mode of *The Importance of Being Earnest*. Like the figure called 'Oscar Wilde', they are the work of an author who enjoyed discords more than resolutions, who liked to tease his audiences with the denial of their habitual assumptions regarding character and motivation, who liked to undermine the conventional significance of formal devices; a writer for whom 'all interpretations [are] true and no interpretation final' and who consequently denied his plays a simple, unequivocal 'meaning'.[30] It is possible to argue, with Arthur Ganz, that 'behind the mechanical facades of their well-made plots the society comedies are deeply expressive of the isolation of an artist and an individual man', and to connect this with the sense of a double life enjoined on him by Wilde's homosexuality.[31] But the definition of the artist's life promulgated by Wilde was one of simultaneous revelation and disguise, 'masks' and 'intentions', seriousness and triviality. His way of challenging the notion of the writer as authoritative 'sage' was to empower the dandies, and to demote the earnestly sincere. His position as a homosexual man in a homophobic society was made all more precarious by his courting of publicity. At the time of his arrest Wilde had two plays running successfully in the West End, a world of artistic expression governed notoriously by the demands of the marketplace. He seemed to have taken one of the citadels of the enemy. He may well have felt himself to be like Chiltern, 'A personality of mark. Not popular – few personalities are. But intensely admired by the few, and deeply respected by the many'. He was also a great deal of Goring and something of Phipps, 'a mask with a manner'.

THE PLAY'S COMPOSITION AND PUBLICATION

Between June and October 1893 Wilde stayed at The Cottage,

[30] 'The Critic as Artist', *Intentions*, p. 153/*CW*, p. 1031.
[31] Arthur H. Ganz, 'The Divided Self in the Society Comedies of Oscar Wilde', *Modern Drama*, 3 (1960), 16–23.

Goring-on-Thames. In September he took rooms in St James's Place in order to settle down to work on the play he had contracted to write for the actor-manager John Hare. After a week's work, he recalled in *De Profundis*, he had 'completed in every detail, as it was ultimately performed' the first act of *An Ideal Husband* (*Letters*, p. 426). In fact many details and some major elements of the plot were not added until the play had gone through several drafts – Wilde's concern in this letter was the shaming of Lord Alfred Douglas rather than the documenting of his methods of composition. (A passage in which he complains of the distractions caused by his lover's presence will be found above, p. xiii.) According to *De Profundis*, work was resumed in December 1893 during Douglas's absence abroad. Wilde describes how he 'collected again the torn and ravelled web of [his] imagination, got [his] life back into [his] own hands, and . . . finished the three remaining acts of *An Ideal Husband*'. The first three acts were ready for Hare's inspection by mid-January, when Wilde wrote to Lewis Waller about a project for a triple-bill of short plays (*Letters*, p. 349), and the fourth was to be complete within a fortnight's time. Waller was meanwhile negotiating rights to play *Lady Windermere's Fan* and *A Woman of No Importance* in the provinces, and his interest in Wilde's work must have made it common sense to offer *An Ideal Husband* to him when Hare turned the play down. Wilde took a holiday in Paris in April 1894, and the casting of the play was being discussed (Sir Rupert Hart-Davis suggests) in July and August. Waller was to open with *An Ideal Husband* when he took the Haymarket during Herbert Beerbohm Tree's absence in America. Rehearsals took place during December – Pearson relates an anecdote concerning Wilde's late arrival at a rehearsal called on Christmas day – and the opening night was in January 1895.

Wilde's method in this, as in his other plays for commercial managements, was to make a fair copy of his manuscript in an exercise book (usually one for each act), from which a typescript would be made. This would in turn be revised and a further typescript would incorporate the alterations. The study of these documents is made difficult by a number of factors: more than one typed copy was made at each stage; sometimes Wilde returned to earlier versions in preparing his work for the printer, by-passing intermediate recensions (among them the acted text); often more than one set of revisions can be detected in a single typescript; other hands than the author's can also be distinguished. A further complication results from the typing agencies' confusing policy with regard to date-stamping: it seems likely that each 'batch' dispatched to a client was dated. Consequently, if Wilde was sent four acts in one parcel, only the first page of the whole play would be stamped;

individual acts returned one by one would each bear a date-stamp.[32] The resulting confusion, whatever its explanation, means that – with the exception of the Lord Chamberlain's copy or identifiable prompt copies – the various groups of typescripts in libraries on both sides of the Atlantic cannot be assumed to represent in themselves the state of the whole play at any given date. The unpublished drafts do not constitute a series of complete texts in successive stages of revision, but the *disjecta membra* of the play in different states. Nor have all the drafts survived or been made available – the material is rich, but it is also disparate and incomplete. In the discussion that follows, it seems prudent to give a separate account of the materials collated relating to each act. The present editor has not been able to examine the (fragmentary) early draft in the William Andrews Clark Memorial Library: the 'succession' is traced from the first complete manuscript draft.

In 1986 information was published about a typescript draft of the play's four acts now in the library of Texas Christian University. Joel H. Kaplan, who is editing the play for the forthcoming Oxford English Texts edition of Wilde's *Works*, has examined a copy of this typescript and suggests that it seems to correspond to the 'missing link' – the draft designated 'X' in the following account of the composition of Acts I to III and 'X2' in the case of Act IV. The typed copy has manuscript annotation in two hands, one of them clearly Wilde's and making alterations that bring it into line with the 1899 edition. Even if the other hand is not (as has been supposed) that of Lewis Waller, it seems probable that the typescript is the one Wilde asked the publisher Leonard Smithers to obtain from him so that he might revise it for publication. The typescript as annotated *before* Wilde's alterations corresponds in a number of particulars with that of Daniel Frohman, the American impresario.[33]

Act I

A manuscript draft (MS) of Act I was sent to a typist who produced the undated script in the Harvard Theatre Collection (HTC): this typescript adopts the revisions made by Wilde in MS. This was subjected to further revision and returned to the typist, with the instruction to send one copy to the author (at St James's Place) and

[32] A number of dramatists used privately-printed editions for rehearsal purposes. Wilde was following advice of the kind given by the anonymous author of *Playwriting: A Handbook for Would-Be Dramatic Authors, by a Dramatist* (London, n.d.) who observes that plays can be typed 'for five to ten shillings an act' by any one of the five or six firms 'in the neighbourhood of the Strand'.

[33] See Glen E. Lich, '"Anything but a Misprint": Comments on an Oscar Wilde Typescript', *Southern Christian Review*, 3 (1986), 46–54. For Wilde's request for the script see *Letters*, p. 669.

one to Hare. Another typescript in the Harvard collection (Pbk) is dated 24 January 1894 and derives from the revisions in HTC. Manuscript revisions were made in this, and some are adopted in a typescript (C) in the William Andrews Clark Memorial Library, which is dated 10 March 1894. A further typescript (BLTS), now in the British Library, based on the revised state of C, was itself altered. Among the additions is the episode in which Lord Goring acquires Mrs Cheveley's bracelet (ll. 629–55), an element of the plot which Wilde claimed had not been added until within ten days of the first performance – that is, late December 1895. The licensing copy (LC) does not include this incident and approximates to the uncorrected state of C. It must be assumed that at least one copy was typed, incorporating the revisions to C, and that this 'lost' typescript was the text performed and the basis of the working promptbook: in this account it will be designated 'X'. The changes to BLTS are not systematic enough for it to have served as the direct source of X or as a promptbook, but they include notes on groupings and business such as Wilde might have jotted down during rehearsal. Daniel Frohman was provided with a typescript evidently based on the theatre's promptbook: unlike the revised BLTS, it includes stage directions of the kind that a prompter would require (lighting cues, warnings for the curtain, detailed groupings of supernumerary actors, etc.). Frohman's copy (F) is now in New York Public Library at Lincoln Center. It includes the bracelet incident and is probably as close a guide to the performed text as we are likely to obtain in default of Waller's own promptbook or X itself. In preparing the play for publication Wilde seems to have had access both to X (or a copy of it) and to at least one of the earlier drafts, probably C or BLTS.

In the course of revision material originally drafted for Act I was transferred to later acts, many minor details were altered and one important sequence – the finding of the bracelet – was added. Of particular interest is the deletion of passages in which Baron Arnheim's relationship with Mrs Cheveley is made clearer. In the early version of Act I Mrs Cheveley owes her exclusion from good society to her having stolen money and jewels from Lady Chiltern's bedroom during a house-party at Lord Berkshire's. Although suspicion immediately fell on a servant, a confession was subsequently extracted from Mrs Cheveley; of this only Lady Chiltern and Lord Goring were aware – the culprit was allowed to withdraw to the continent.

Act II
The British Library has two manuscript versions of this act (MS1, MS2). Having drafted the first, Wilde evidently decided to revise it

before having it typed. He began the new version at the back of the exercise book containing the manuscript of Act III, giving his typist instructions in which he made the arrangement clear. The second manuscript draft resulted in a typescript (C), now in the Clark library, dated 19 February 1894. This was revised to provide copy for a further typescript (BLTS), in the British Library, dated 10 March 1894. The manuscript alterations in this result in a version nearer the undated script sent to Frohman (F) than to the licensing copy (LC), but it is likely that an intermediate typescript (X, now missing) provided the basis both of the performed text and of F itself: the changes to the BLTS typescript may have been entered (as in the corresponding script of Act I) during rehearsals, and they constitute notes *towards* a new draft rather than a fair copy suitable for a typist. As with Act I, we can suppose that X was the basis of the script used by Wilde when he prepared his play for the printer.

'*Ask him what the origin of his fortune is!*': An Ideal Husband, *II, 749–50*
(*From* The Illustrated London News, *January 1895*)

Additions to Act II included references to the bracelet (noted but not thoroughly carried out by Wilde in his revision to BLTS) and the transfer from Act I of Lady Markby's speeches on education and the habits of her husband. A longer account by her of Sir Robert's background was discarded (see note to I, 570 and Appendix I, on II, 91–109).

Act III

There is one manuscript draft (MS) of this act in the British Library, together with a typescript (BLTS) dated 16 January 1894, which derives from it. A second typescript (C, in the Clark library) is dated 20 January 1894 and adopts Wilde's revisions to BLTS. Another typescript, dated 24 January 1894, was included in the Prescott Collection sale, but has not been collated for this edition. Like its predecessors, it omits any reference to the bracelet.[34] Because the licensing copy (LC) also lacks the sequence in which the 'bracelet' plot is developed to trap Mrs Cheveley, we must assume that another script (X, now missing) furnished the performance text. Frohman's typescript (F) would have derived from this, as would the script used by Wilde to revise the play for publication. Again, it seems that he had access in this task to one of the early drafts – possibly C or BLTS – from which some details were restored in the copy sent to the printer.

The most important alterations in this act were the abbreviation of the dialogue between Lord Goring and his father, its transfer from the beginning of the act to its present position and the addition of the opening sequence with Phipps. The dialogue leading up to the discovery of Mrs Cheveley by Sir Robert was shortened and the production of the bracelet was introduced into the scene in which she is confronted by Lord Goring. The circumstances in which their engagement was broken off were originally given in greater detail. A brief soliloquy for Phipps was cut (see note to 1.152), but stage business indicated in F suggests how the character was developed by the actor – along lines reflected in the stage directions Wilde added when he published his play. The dialogue introducing the bracelet *coup* is shorter in F than in the published play: either the missing typescript (X) and the promptbook had a fuller version than was sent to Frohman, or Wilde developed the sequence as he revised it in 1898–99.

Act IV

This was the act which caused most difficulty, and which is alleged

---

[34] Lot 431, described as consisting of a title-leaf (with 'Mrs Marshall's Type-Writing Office' date stamp for 24 January 1894), and 24 leaves with 'extensive revision' (Prescott Collection catalogue, Christie's, New York, 6 February 1981).

to have caused Hare's rejection of the play. Drafts of it fall into two groups. A manuscript in the British Library (MS); a draft in typescript and manuscript acquired by the Clark library at the Prescott sale (C1, undated); a typescript in the Clark library (C), dated 6 March 1894 and clearly derived from C1; the licensing copy (LC); and Frohman's script (F), dated 13 March 1894, all give a version of the act's structure which differs radically from that in an undated British Library typescript (BLTS) and the published edition. Before summarising these differences – details of which are given in the textual notes – it should be observed that in the case of Act IV two typescripts are 'missing'. One presumably derived – as the typed pages of C1 do not – directly from MS. Another, as with the preceding acts, served as the performance text. These have been designated X1 and X2 below. The recently acquired Clark draft (C1) seems to have served as copy for the typist who prepared C: to avoid confusion, in the textual notes I have cited only the readings of C, but have included the earlier Clark draft of the proposal scene in Appendix I.

The second version of the act – represented by BLTS and the first edition – improved in a number of respects on the first. The act now begins with Lord Goring rather than with Mabel and Lady Chiltern, so that the dandy remains the centre of the audience's attention and the impetus of the plot is not impeded. The machinery by which Mabel and Lord Caversham were brought on and off stage in the original version was clumsy and repetitious: they had to be asked to go into the conservatory and made to re-emerge at the right moment. When Sir Robert Chiltern enters, reading the letter on pink paper, Wilde originally had Mabel present – obtrusively overhearing the last lines of dialogue between her sister-in-law and Lord Goring. The proposal scene has been shortened and moved nearer to the beginning of the act: in its former position near the end it held back the action and it may have seemed to Wilde (in 1898–99, after work on the publication of *The Importance of Being Earnest*) that he had already made enough use of the comic proposal. The gravity of Lady Chiltern's supposed indiscretion in seeking advice from Lord Goring (at night, unaccompanied, in a bachelor's rooms) is considerably played down, and a melodramatic speech by her (at ll. 225–7) is removed. The sequence setting out her husband's ground of refusing permission for Mabel's marriage is abbreviated. All these alterations have the cumulative effect of lightening the play's tone and accelerating its action in the final act.

Summary
The progression of the collated drafts from fair copy (MS) to print can now be summarised in diagrammatic form, incorporating the

page-proofs (PR), now in the Clark library, in which Wilde made
his final revisions. He had asked Robert Ross to read the play in
proof and to correct his uncertain use of 'shall' and 'will'. It seems
that more than one stage of proof was gone through, for Ross writes
in an edition of the play of voluminous revisions in proof and an
acrimonious correspondence about them – of which those in the
Clark library bear no trace. In the diagrams, missing copies have
been indicated as X or (in Act IV) X1 and X2. It should be borne
in mind that in each case Wilde seems to have consulted a pre-
production draft of the act when preparing copy for the printer.[35]

ACT I

                                    LC
MS—HTC—Pbk—C—BLTS—
                                'X' —F
                                    PR — 1st Ed.

ACT II

                                    LC
MS1 — MS2 — C — BLTS —
                                'X' —F
                                    PR — 1st Ed.

ACT III

                                    LC
MS — BLTS — [?Prescott copy] — C —
                                'X' —F
                                    PR — 1st Ed.

---

[35] Ross's introduction is of some interest. In apologising for his excisions and
alterations (mostly on account of changing fashions, the need to avoid obscure
references and the fact that no 'acting edition' had been published) he recalls the
circumstances of the first publication:

In very different plays, *Salomé* and *The Importance of Being Earnest*, Wilde had almost
unconsciously adopted the 'new technique' [i.e., of writing dialogue]. I remember
Wilde himself expressing his regret that some of the dialogue was already a trifle
old-fashioned when he was correcting the proofs of *An Ideal Husband* . . . Indeed,
he contemplated re-writing the play, but I foresaw that his health would not have
permitted him to carry out this intention. The publisher, moreover, was becoming
impatient for copy, and Wilde's constant additions and alterations in the proofs were
a source of acrimonious correspondence.

(*An Ideal Husband by Oscar Wilde. A new acting version produced by Sir
George Alexander at the St James's Theatre* [1914], p. 6.)

ACT IV

```
                                LC — F(?)
MS — 'X1' — Prescott copy — C —
                                'X2' — BLTS — PR — 1st Ed.
```

The drafts of *An Ideal Husband* show Wilde's attention to detail and his willingness to adapt his work to the demands of performance. The play as it stands in the British Library manuscripts has more melodrama in certain episodes – notably in the final act – and Wilde's control of the Mabel/Goring sub-plot is less assured. Without the bracelet the thwarting of Mrs Cheveley is much less striking – its addition enables Wilde to give this turn in the plot a physical embodiment more interesting than the exchange of letters. Perhaps we are meant to see that Mrs Cheveley's past clasps her as – in his dream – Sir Robert Chiltern's attached itself to him.

There were few changes in the names of the characters, and only two alternative titles appear in the drafts: in MS Act IV is entitled *'Mrs Cheveley'* and in HTC the typed title *'An Ideal Husband'* has been changed in manuscript to *'The Foolish Journalist'* (possibly so as to conceal the play's title until the appropriate time for public announcements).

In revising *An Ideal Husband* for the press, Wilde added a number of passages – those referred to in the textual notes as first appearing in PR – and cut some others: there seem to have been more additions than omissions. He elaborated the stage directions, adding adverbs and adjectives to the bald entrances and exits of the drafts and providing elaborate descriptions of the principal characters. In the case of Lord Goring further material was added at page-proof (see notes to I, 198 and III, 1). It is tempting to interpret these as Wilde's commentary – in 1898–99 – on his prelapsarian self. In the direction that Goring shows 'the philosopher that underlies the dandy' (IV, 401) Wilde evidently hopes that his character will achieve a result he himself aimed for. Although he had misgivings concerning the propriety of bothering his readers with the colour of a character's hair and other physical details, Wilde was joining in the movement towards the effective presentation of plays for the reading public – Shaw, Pinero and Jones made similar efforts. The directions in F suggest that most of his additions in this respect were true to the effects achieved in performance.

A NOTE ON THE TEXT AND
ANNOTATION

The text printed in this volume follows that of the first edition, published by Leonard Smithers in 1899 and limited to 1000 copies. Smithers' edition was printed from copy prepared by Wilde and from proofs revised by him (PR). In the absence of a promptbook it is not possible to positively establish a version of the play as performed in the first production, but the typescript supplied to Daniel Frohman (F) seems to derive directly from the acted text. Readings noted as making their first appearance in the proofs (PR) were the product of Wilde's revisions when he was working on copy for Smithers' printer in 1899: the typescript used for this purpose may be that now at Texas Christian University.

In the manuscript and in most of the subsequent typescript drafts Wilde made numerous alterations in pencil and a variety of inks. It is not possible to confidently identify successive stages of revision within each document: in the manuscripts, for example, Wilde began in ink, continued in pencil and revised in both mediums, often leaving gaps to be filled in later. In references to the manuscripts (MS) I have generally cited the *final* state of the draft. In the case of typescripts (BLTS, C, LC, F) I have distinguished where necessary between the typed version and its revised state.

The footnotes to the present edition give an account of Wilde's revisions to the play up to the first performance and in preparation for publication. Critical annotation of the text has generally been restricted to indicating Wilde's use of material from his other works and to explaining contemporary references or nuances of meaning which a contemporary audience would have readily caught. The punctuation and spelling of a few words (principally 'to-night', 'sha'n't', 'one's-self' and 'now-a-days') have been changed to accord with modern practice. Some minor errors in the 1899 edition have been corrected.[36]

---

[36] The following emendations have been made to the first edition: 'I, 1 'Hartlocks'' for 'Hartlocks'; I, 4 'why I go.' for 'why I go'; I, 52 'almost?' for 'almost'; I, 491 'ruined,' for 'ruined'; II, 28 '...' for '....'; II, 481 'remember' for 'remember,'; II, 650 'I think,' for 'I think'; II, 777 'to me.' for 'to me'; III, 1 'Adam' for 'Adams' in s.d.; III, 50 'Berkshires'' for 'Berkshires'; III, 225 addition to s.d.; IV, 37 *Times*'' for '*Times*';IV, 61 'Parliament.' for 'Parliament?'; IV, 273 'mine?' for 'mine!'; IV, 635 'Her' for 'He'.

FURTHER READING

Bibliography

Ian Fletcher and John Stokes, 'Oscar Wilde' in *Anglo-Irish Literature, A Review of Research,* ed. R. J. Finneran (New York, 1976).

'Stuart Mason' (C. S. Millard), *Bibliography of Oscar Wilde* (London, 1908; reissued 1967).

E. H. Mikhail *Oscar Wilde: An Annotated Bibliography of Criticism* (London, 1987).

Ian Small, *Oscar Wilde Revalued: An Essay on New Materials and Methods of Research* (Greensboro, N.C., 1993).

John Stokes, *Oscar Wilde* (London, 1978).

Biography

Richard Ellman, Oscar Wilde (London, 1987).

H. Montgomery Hyde, *The Trials of Oscar Wilde* (rev. edition, London, 1973).

– *Oscar Wilde* (London, 1975).

E. H. Mikhail, ed., *Oscar Wilde: Interviews and Recollections* (London, 2 vols., 1979).

Richard Pine, *Oscar Wilde* (Dublin, 1983).

Collections of Criticism

Karl Beckson, ed., *Oscar Wilde: The Critical Heritage* (London, 1970).

Richard Ellmann, ed., *Oscar Wilde: A Collection of Critical Essays* (Englewood Cliffs, New Jersey, 1969).

William Tydeman, ed., *Wilde: Comedies: A Casebook* (London, 1982).

Criticism

Karl Beckson, *London in the 1890s. A Cultural History* (New York and London, 1992).

Alan Bird, *The Plays of Oscar Wilde* (London, 1977).

Richard Dellamora, 'Oscar Wilde, Social Purity, and *An Ideal Husband*', *Modern Drama*, Vol. 37, No. 1 (1994), pp. 120-38

Jonathan Dollimore, 'Different Desires: Subjectivity and Transgression in Wilde and Gide', *Textual Practice*, I, 1 (1987), 48–67.

Richard Ellmann, 'Romantic Pantomime in Oscar Wilde', *Partisan Review*, 30 (1963), 342–55.

Sos Eltis, *Revising Wilde. Society and Subversion in the Plays of Oscar Wilde* (Oxford, 1996).

Reginia Gagnier, *Idylls of the Marketplace: Oscar Wilde and the Victorian Public* (London, 1987).

Arthur H. Ganz, 'The Divided Self in the Society Comedies of Oscar Wilde', *Modern Drama*, 3 (1960), 16–23.

Ian Gregor, 'Comedy and Oscar Wilde', *Sewanee Review*, 74 (1966), 501–21.

Joel Kaplan and Sheila Stowell, 'The Dandy and the dowager: Oscar Wilde and Audience Resistance', *New Theatre Quarterly*, Vol. 15 (1999), pp.318–31

Joel Kaplan and Sheila Stowell, *Theatre and Fashion. Oscar Wilde to the Suffragettes* (Cambridge, 1994).

Norbert Kohl, *Oscar Wilde, The Works of a Conformist Rebel* (Cambridge, 1988).

Jerusha McCormack, 'Masks Without Faces: The Personalities of Oscar Wilde', *English Literature in Transition*, 22 (1979), 253–69.

Christopher M. Nassaar, *Into the Demon Universe: A Literary Exploration of Oscar Wilde* (New Haven, Conn., 1974).

Kerry Powell, *Oscar Wilde and the Theatre of the 1890s* (Cambridge, 1990).

Peter Raby, *Oscar Wilde* (Cambridge, 1988).

– ed. *The Cambridge Companion to Oscar Wilde* (Cambridge, 1997).

Gary Schmidgall, *The Stranger Wilde. Interpreting Oscar* (London, 1994).

Rodney Shewan, *Oscar Wilde: Art and Egotism* (London, 1977).

Alan Sinfield, *The Wilde Century. Effeminacy, Oscar Wilde and the Queer Movement* (London, 1994).

Katharine Worth, *Oscar Wilde* (London, 1983).

OVERHEARD FRAGMENT OF A DIALOGUE

Lord Illingworth. My dear GORING, I assure you that a well-tied tie is the first serious step in life.

Lord Goring. My dear ILLINGWORTH, five well-made button-holes a day are far more essential. They please women, and women rule society.

Lord Illingworth. I understood you considered women of no importance?

Lord Goring. My dear GEORGE, a man's life revolves on curves of intellect. It is on the hard lines of the emotions that a woman's life progresses. Both revolve in cycles of masterpieces. They should revolve on bi-cycles; built, if possible, for two. But I am keeping you?

Lord Illingworth. I wish you were. Nowadays it is only the poor who are kept at the expense of the rich.

Lord Goring. Yes. It is perfectly comic, the number of young men going about the world nowadays who adopt perfect profiles as a useful profession.

Lord Illingworth. Surely that must be the next world? How about the Chiltern Thousands?

Lord Goring. Don't GEORGE. Have you seen WINDERMERE lately? Dear WINDERMERE! I should like to be exactly unlike WINDERMERE.

"Full of good things!"

Lord Illingworth. Poor WINDERMERE! He spends his mornings in doing what is possible, and his evenings in saving what is probable. By the way, do you really understand all I say?

Lord Goring. Yes, when I don't listen attentively.

Lord Illingworth. Reach me the matches, like a good boy—thanks. Now—define these cigarettes—as tobacco.

Lord Goring. My dear GEORGE, they are atrocious. And they leave me unsatisfied.

Lord Illingworth. You are a promising disciple of mine. The only use of a disciple is that at the moment of one's triumph he stands behind one's chair and shouts that after all he is immortal.

Lord Goring. You are quite right. It is as well, too, to remember from time to time that nothing that is worth knowing can be learnt.

Lord Illingworth. Certainly, and ugliness is the root of all industry.

Lord Goring. GEORGE, your conversation is delightful, but your views are terribly unsound. You are always saying insincere things.

Lord Illingworth. If one tells the truth, one is sure sooner or later to be found out.

Lord Goring. Perhaps. The sky is like a hard hollow sapphire. It is too late to sleep. I shall go down to Covent Garden and look at the roses. Good-night, GEORGE! I have had such a pleasant evening!

Ada Leverson's parody of Wilde's comedies in Punch, *12 January 1895: Wilde was delighted by the joke, and wrote 'You are more than all criticisms' (Letters, pp. 380-81).*

AN IDEAL HUSBAND

Oscar Wilde in 1985 (from The Sketch, *9 January 1895)*

AN IDEAL HUSBAND

TO
FRANK HARRIS
A SLIGHT TRIBUTE TO
HIS POWER AND DISTINCTION
AS AN ARTIST
HIS CHIVALRY AND NOBILITY
AS A FRIEND

Dedication Frank Harris (1856-1931), journalist and man of letters; loyal friend and vivid biographer of Wilde. His most notable publication is the sexually explicit and tantalisingly unreliable autobiography, *My Life and Loves* (5 vols., 1923-7; one vol., 1963).

THE PERSONS OF THE PLAY

[Haymarket Theatre, 3 January 1895]

THE EARL OF CAVERSHAM, K.G.	*Mr Alfred Bishop*
VISCOUNT GORING, *his son*	*Mr Charles H. Hawtrey*
SIR ROBERT CHILTERN, *Bart.,*	*Mr Lewis Waller*
Under-Secretary for Foreign Affairs	
VICOMTE DE NANJAC, *Attaché at*	*Mr Cosmo Stuart*
the French Embassy in London	
MR MONTFORD	*Mr Harry Stanford*
MASON, *Butler to Sir Robert Chiltern*	*Mr H. Deane*
PHIPPS, *Lord Goring's Servant*	*Mr C.H. Brookfield*
JAMES	*Mr Charles Mayrick*
HAROLD *Footmen*	*Mr Goodheart*
LADY CHILTERN	*Miss Julia Neilson*
LADY MARKBY	*Miss Fanny Brough*
THE COUNTESS OF BASILDON	*Miss Vane Featherston*
MRS MARCHMONT	*Miss Helen Forsyth*
MISS MABEL CHILTERN, *Sir Robert*	*Miss Maude Millet*
Chiltern's Sister	
MRS CHEVELEY	*Miss Florence West*

Persons of the Play
As in his other plays, Wilde employed place-names for some of characters and ensured that titles did not correspond to those of any living person. Of particular interest here is *Goring*, where Wilde began work on *Husband*. E.H. Mikhail suggests that *de Nanjac* has been taken from the name of a character in Dumas *fils'* play *Le Demi-Monde* (1885, see footnote 14, p. xvii above). Other names in the present list appear elsewhere in Wilde, notably *Markby* (the firm of solicitors who represent Jack in *Earnest*), *Montford* (original name of Algernon Moncrieff in the same play) and *Mason* (used for a servant in drafts of *Woman*). In the first drafts of the play *Mabel* is referred to as Violet: the name *Mabel* also appears in the early drafts of *Woman*.

Actors' Names
Charles *Hawtrey* (1858-1923): a fine light comedian 'with a quiet humorous style of his own', he had a 'very pale face, accentuated by jet black hair' and a black moustache (*The Dramatic Peerage*, 1892).
Lewis *Waller* (1860-1915): a strikingly handsome actor, excelling in 'costume' plays of a romantic, heroic kind – less well suited to contemporary comedy, but appropriate to the serious role he played in *Husband*. According to *The Times* he played it 'in his manliest and most robust style'. This was his first step in management.
Charles *Brookfield* (1860-1912): a generous choice for the role, since he had written a satirical playlet against Wilde (*The Poet and the Puppets*, 1892) and made no secret

THE SCENES OF THE PLAY

Act I   *The Octagon Room in Sir Robert Chiltern's House in Grosvenor Square.*
Act II   *Morning-room in Sir Robert Chiltern's House.*
Act III   *The Library of Lord Goring's House in Curzon Street.*
Act IV   *Same as Act II.*

Time – The Present
Place – London

The Action of the Play is completed within twenty-four hours.

of his antipathy. He collected evidence to support Queensberry's case in the libel action.

Julia *Neilson* (1868-1957): a statuesque, graceful actress whose first success had been as Cynisca in a production of Gilbert's *Pygmalion and Galatea*.

Fanny *Brough* (1854-1914): daughter of the dramatist Robert Brough and niece of the comic actor Lionel Brough. *The Dramatic Peerage* praises her 'quaint humour, intelligent brightness, and quickness of repartee' but notes that she suffers from first-night nerves. This may explain her poor reception in the part (*The Theatre* was surprised that a comedian of her reputation should give 'so ineffective a sketch').

Act I

Scene – The Octagon room at SIR ROBERT CHILTERN'S *house in
Grosvenor Square.
The room is brilliantly lighted and full of guests.
At the top of the staircase stands* LADY CHILTERN, *a
woman of grave Greek beauty, about twenty-seven
years of age. She receives the guests as they come up.
Over the well of the staircase hangs a great chandelier
with wax lights, which illumine a large eighteenth-
century French tapestry – representing the Triumph
of Love, from a design by Boucher – that is stretched
on the staircase wall. On the right is the entrance
to the music-room. The sound of a string quartette is
faintly heard. The entrance on the left leads to
other reception-rooms.* MRS MARCHMONT *and* LADY
BASILDON, *two very pretty women, are seated together
on a Louis Seize sofa. They are types of exquisite
fragility. Their affectation of manner has a delicate
charm. Watteau would have loved to paint them.*

MRS MARCHMONT
    Going on to the Hartlocks' tonight, Margaret?

LADY BASILDON
    I suppose so. Are you?

MRS MARCHMONT
    Yes. Horribly tedious parties they give, don't they?

LADY BASILDON
    Horribly tedious! Never know why I go. Never know why I
    go anywhere.   5

MRS MARCHMONT
    I come here to be educated.

---

1 s.d. first appears in full in PR. Earlier drafts indicate the setting as the Chilterns'
drawing-room, brilliantly lit and full of guests. F gives details of the movements of
the non-speaking actors (40 in all) and specifies '*Music in Music Room (classical
quartette) to open*' and '*flowers in scene*'. *Grosvenor Square* had many titled residents
in 1895, including Lord Randolph Churchill. The paintings by *Boucher* (1703-70)
and *Watteau* (1684-1721) reflect fashionable interest in these French painters of
pastoral, mythological and delicately erotic subjects. In Pater's *Imaginary Portraits*
(1887) the exquisite fragility' and 'delicate charm' of Watteau's figures had been
emphasized. Wilde specified *Louis Seize* furniture in drafts of *LWF* and a discarded
passage in *Husband* credited Baron Arnhelm with the tastes reflected here (cf.
Appendix 1).

LADY BASILDON
  Ah! I hate being educated!

MRS MARCHMONT
  So do I. It puts one almost on a level with the commercial
  classes, doesn't it? But dear Gertrude Chiltern is always telling
  me that I should have some serious purpose in life. So I come   10
  here to try to find one.

LADY BASILDON (*Looking round through her lorgnette*)
  I don't see anybody here tonight whom one could possibly call
  a serious purpose. The man who took me in to dinner talked
  to me about his wife the whole time.

MRS MARCHMONT
  How very trivial of him!   15

LADY BASILDON
  Terribly trivial! What did your man talk about?

MRS MARCHMONT
  About myself.

LADY BASILDON (*Languidly*)
  And were you interested?

MRS MARCHMONT (*Shaking her head*)
  Not in the smallest degree.

LADY BASILDON
  What martyrs we are, dear Margaret!   20

MRS MARCHMONT (*Rising*)
  And how well it becomes us, Olivia!

8 *commercial* (lower LC, BLTS, C). The sentence does not appear in MS. Wilde added
  it to HTC, then added and deleted another line: 'I think education [?was] made for
  the lower classes. They appreciate it so much. We don't'. Cf. Lady Bracknell on
  education: 'Fortunately in England, at any rate, education produces no effect
  whatsoever. If it did, it would prove a serious danger to the upper classes, and
  probably lead to acts of violence in Grosvenor Square' (*Earnest*, I, 498-502).
15 *trivial* an important word for Wilde, who could not decide on the appropriate balance
  between this and the line following. In BLTS 'trivial' is substituted here for 'rude'
  in the typescript (and HTC, MS), with a corresponding change in the next line. C
  has 'very trivial . . . very rude'. In Pbk 'rude . . . trivial' has been changed to 'trivial
  . . . rude'.

They rise and go towards the music-room. The VICOMTE DE
NANJAC, *a young attaché known for his neckties and his
Anglomania, approaches with a low bow, and enters into
conversation*

MASON (*Announcing guests from the top of the staircase*)
Mr and Lady Jane Barford. Lord Caversham.
Enter LORD CAVERSHAM, *an old gentleman of seventy, wearing
the riband and star of the Garter. A fine Whig type. Rather like
a portrait by Lawrence*

LORD CAVERSHAM
Good evening, Lady Chiltern! Has my good-for-nothing
young son been here?

LADY CHILTERN (*Smiling*)
I don't think Lord Goring has arrived yet.   25

MABEL CHILTERN (*Coming up to* LORD CAVERSHAM)
Why do you call Lord Goring good-for-nothing?
MABEL CHILTERN *is a perfect example of the English type of
prettiness, the apple-blossom type. She has all the fragrance and
freedom of a flower. There is ripple after ripple of sunlight in her
hair, and the little mouth, with its parted lips, is expectant, like
the mouth of a child. She has the fascinating tyranny of youth, and
the astonishing courage of innocence. To sane people she is not
reminiscent of any work of art. But she is really like a Tanagra
statuette, and would be rather annoyed if she were told so*

LORD CAVERSHAM
Because he leads such an idle life.

21, 22 s.d. descriptions of de Nanjac and Lord C first appear in PR. On neckties, Cf.
     Woman, III, 61–6 ('A well-tied necktie is the first serious step in life'). Lord C recalls
     the character of Lord Fermor in *Dorian Gray*, Chapter III: 'In politics he was a Tory,
     except when the Tories were in office, during which period he roundly abused them
     for being a pack of Radicals ... Only England could have produced him, and he
     always said that the country was going to the dogs. His principles were out of date,
     but there was a good deal to be said for his prejudices' (*DG* p. 31/ *CW* p. 38). Wilde
     makes Lord C a *Whig* (the landed, aristocratic staple of early 19th-century Liberalism)
     so that his intimacy with the Liberal administration will be credible. Sir Thomas
     Lawrence (1769-1830) was the most notable British portraitist of his generation.
26 s.d. again, a descriptive s.d. that first appears in PR. Both Sybil Vane in *Dorian Gray*
     (*DG*, p 75/*CW*, p. 67) and Sybil Merton in *Lord Arthur Savile's Crime* (*CSF*, p. 32/
     CW, pp. 177–8) are compared to the small statuettes of terracotta found in tombs in
     the late 4th and 3rd centuries B.C. at *Tanagra* in Greece. Miss Merton's lips are also
     'slightly parted' and she emanates 'all the tender purity of girlhood'. The insistence
     on the *tyranny of youth* recalls Gwendolen's regret in *Earnest* that 'the old-fashioned
     respect for the young is fast dying out'(I,703–4). Wilde's use of *sane* implies a casual
     taunt for critics who found his work 'unhealthy'.

MABEL CHILTERN

How can you say such a thing? Why, he rides in the Row at
ten o'clock in the morning, goes to the Opera three times a
week, changes his clothes at least five times a day, and dines   30
out every night of the season. You don't call that leading an
idle life, do you?

LORD CAVERSHAM (*Looking at her with a kindly twinkle in his
eyes*)
You are a very charming young lady!

MABEL CHILTERN

How sweet of you to say that, Lord Caversham! Do come to
us more often. You know we are always at home on   35
Wednesdays, and you look so well with your star!

LORD CAVERSHAM

Never go anywhere now. Sick of London Society. Shouldn't
mind being introduced to my own tailor; he always votes on
the right side. But object strongly to being sent down to
dinner with my wife's milliner. Never could stand Lady   40
Caversham's bonnets.

MABEL CHILTERN

Oh, I love London Society! I think it has immensely
improved. It is entirely composed now of beautiful idiots and
brilliant lunatics. Just what Society should be.

LORD CAVERSHAM

Hum! Which is Goring? Beautiful idiot, or the other thing?   45

28 *in the Row* i.e. Rotten Row, in Hyde Park. Details of the daily routine vary from draft
to draft. F follows LC and earlier versions in reading 'twice a day' for *ten in the morning*
(1st ed, PR). In PR *changes . . . a day* first appears (with 'six' altered in manuscript
to *five*). Before PR we are informed that Lord Goring dines out every night 'of his
life' and F adds 'twice on Sundays'.
33–6 *You are . . . your star!* MS has a longer version of the conversation, in which Lord
C observes that his wife 'has grown rather short sighted in the last few years. I don't
think she quite sees my good qualities' to which Mabel retorts, 'How strange! for they
are all on the surface are they not?'. She claims that to be considered 'dangerous' is
the dream of her life when Lord C suggests that she will be a danger to Goring. After
additions and revisions through HTC, Pbk and C, the passage was dropped, and does
not appear in LC.
36 *your star* i.e. the insignia of the Order of the Garter. In *Lord Arthur Savile's Crime*
'Six Cabinet Ministers had come on [to the reception] from the Speaker's Levée in
their stars and ribands' (*CSF*, p. 19/*CW*, p. 168).
37–41 *Sick . . . bonnets* elaborated in the course of revision from a simple line in MS:
'Hate London Society. The thing has gone to the dogs, a lot of demmed nobodies
talking about nothing' (cf. note 1. 22, s.d., above). In F only Lord C remarks that
'all tailors are volunteers'. HTC has an addition – 'It has got so mixed' – also found
in the Pbk typescript but deleted there. Cf. below, II, 546–9.
42–3 *immensely improved* in MS and HTC it has 'become quite ideal'.

MABEL CHILTERN (*Gravely*)
I have been obliged for the present to put Lord Goring into
a class quite by himself. But he is developing charmingly!

LORD CAVERSHAM
Into what?

MABEL CHILTERN (*With a little curtsey*)
I hope to let you know very soon, Lord Caversham!

MASON (*Announcing guests*)
Lady Markby. Mrs Cheveley.   50
Enter LADY MARKBY *and* MRS CHEVELEY. LADY MARKBY *is a*
pleasant, kindly, popular woman, with gray hair à la marquise
and good lace. MRS CHEVELEY, *who accompanies her, is tall and*
rather slight. Lips very thin and highly-coloured, a line of scarlet
on a pallid face. Venetian red hair, aquiline nose, and long throat.
Rouge accentuates the natural paleness of her complexion.
Gray-green eyes that move restlessly. She is in heliotrope, with
diamonds. She looks rather like an orchid, and makes great
demands on one's curiosity. In all her movements she is extremely
graceful. A work of art, on the whole, but showing the influence
of too many schools

LADY MARKBY
Good evening, dear Gertrude! So kind of you to let me bring
my friend, Mrs Cheveley. Two such charming women should
know each other!

LADY CHILTERN (*Advances towards* MRS CHEVELEY *with a sweet*
smile. Then suddenly stops, and bows rather distantly)
I think Mrs Cheveley and I have met before. I did not know
she had married a second time.   55

LADY MARKBY (*Genially*)
Ah, nowadays people marry as often as they can, don't they?
It is most fashionable. (*To* DUCHESS OF MARYBOROUGH) Dear
Duchess, and how is the Duke? Brain still weak, I suppose?

50 s.d. *Lady Markby is a pleasant . . . too many schools* first appears in PR. Lady M's hair
    is dressed in a popular style derived from the period of Louis XV. The description
    of Mrs C. is consistent with the later description by Lord G (II, 238–40) and with
    the accounts of contemporary reviewers. William Archer described her as 'tawny-
    haired, red-cheeked, white-shouldered'; to *The Times* she was 'an overdressed
    adventuress of cosmopolitan experience.' For a description of her dress, see Appendix
    II.
56 *nowadays . . . as they can* a recurrent joke in Wilde, who enjoyed speaking flippantly
    of such topics of solemn contemporary debate as divorce law reform. Cf. *Earnest*, I,
    707: 'I may marry someone else, and marry often'.

Well, that is only to be expected, is it not? His good father
was just the same. There is nothing like race, is there?   60

MRS CHEVELEY (*Playing with her fan*)
But have we really met before, Lady Chiltern? I can't
remember where. I have been out of England for so long.

LADY CHILTERN
We were at school together, Mrs Cheveley.

MRS CHEVELEY (*Superciliously*)
Indeed? I have forgotten all about my schooldays. I have a
vague impression that they were detestable.   65

LADY CHILTERN (*Coldly*)
I am not surprised!

MRS CHEVELEY (*In her sweetest manner*)
Do you know, I am quite looking forward to meeting your
clever husband, Lady Chiltern. Since he has been at the
Foreign Office, he has been so much talked of in Vienna.
They actually succeed in spelling his name right in the   70
newspapers. That in itself is fame, on the continent.

LADY CHILTERN
I hardly think there will be much in common between you and
my husband, Mrs Cheveley!   *Moves away*

59–60 *His good father ... is there?* first appears in PR. It is difficult not to read this
1898-99 addition in the light of Wilde's experience of the Douglas family. At this point
F notes '*music off*' (i.e. off-stage) to motivate the departure of most of the guests to
the music-room: later in the same script one extra is deputed to '*tell crowd to
disperse*'.
65 *detestable* in MS and HTC this is followed by Lady M recalling that she had 'no
schooldays' herself and that in her time 'it was not considered the thing for young
people to know too much'. This material (originally from drafts of *Woman* – see note
to *Woman*, II, 219-21) was later revised and transferred to Act II (584 etc.). It was
deleted from the HTC typescript of Act I.
68–9 *Since ... Vienna* in MS, HTC, Pbk Chiltern has 'had charge of the Foreign Office',
which does not leave enough scope for promotion in the final act. In BLTS this is
changed (in manuscript) to 'has been undersecretary for Foreign Affairs'. The present
reading first appears in PR.
70–1 *They actually ... continent* these two sentences first appear in PR, and the final three
words were added in manuscript to the proof.
72–3 *I hardly..Mrs Cheveley!* MS and HTC include a reference to Mrs C's schoolgirl
misdemeanours in an exchange deleted from HTC:
　　MRS CHEVELEY
　　　　Oh! we can always talk of finance. I am deeply interested in finance.
　　LADY CHILTERN
　　　　So I remember.   (*Turns away*)

VICOMTE DE NANJAC
    Ah! chère Madame, quelle surprise! I have not seen you since
    Berlin!   75

MRS CHEVELEY
    Not since Berlin, Vicomte. Five years ago!

VICOMTE DE NANJAC
    And you are younger and more beautiful than ever. How do
    you manage it?

MRS CHEVELEY
    By making it a rule only to talk to perfectly charming people
    like yourself.   80

VICOMTE DE NANJAC
    Ah! you flatter me. You butter me, as they say here.

MRS CHEVELEY
    Do they say that here? How dreadful of them!

VICOMTE DE NANJAC
    Yes, they have a wonderful language. It should be more
    widely known.
        SIR ROBERT CHILTERN *enters. A man of forty, but looking
        somewhat younger. Clean-shaven, with finely-cut features, dark-
        haired and dark-eyed. A personality of mark. Not popular – few
        personalities are. But intensely admired by the few, and deeply
        respected by the many. The note of his manner is that of perfect
        distinction, with a slight touch of pride. One feels that he is
        conscious of the success he has made in life. A nervous
        temperament, with a tired look. The firmly-chiselled mouth and
        chin contrast strikingly with the romantic expression in the deep-set
        eyes. The variance is suggestive of an almost complete separation*

74–6 *Ah! chère ... Vicomte* the passage first appears in this form in an addition to
    Pbk.
79–80 *By making ... like yourself* further evidence of her un-British outlook is given in
    MS and IITC. 'And so are you, Baron. You know you have something that these
    Englishmen haven't got, a style, an air, something. You have, really. No one would
    ever mistake you for an Englishman.' This would scarcely be a compliment to an
    Anglophile, and may have been dropped for the sake of consistency.
81 *Ah! ... here* in HTC and one of the revisions in MS this is followed by Lady M's
    speech on curates (transferred to II, 635 etc.).
83–4 *Yes ... known* first appears in PR.
84 s.d. *A man ... his head* first appears in PR. The idealised picture of Sir Robert owes
    more to Wilde's private imagery than to the actor's appearance (Waller, who first
    played the part, was famous for his more robust, conventional good looks). The hands
    recall the 'cool, white, flower-like hands' of Lord Henry Wotton (*DG* p. 21 / *CW* p.
    31) and the 'white lily hands' attributed to Willie Hughes in 'The Picture of Mr W.H.'
    (*CSF*, p. 159/*CW*, p. 1169). Sir Anthony *Vandyck*, a Flemish painter, (1599–1641)
    worked in London from 1631 and executed many portraits of Charles I's court.

of passion and intellect, as though thought and emotion were each
isolated in its own sphere through some violence of will-power.
There is nervousness in the nostrils, and in the pale, thin, pointed
hands. It would be inaccurate to call him picturesque. Picturesque-
ness cannot survive the House of Commons. But Vandyck would
have liked to have painted his head

SIR ROBERT CHILTERN
Good evening, Lady Markby! I hope you have brought Sir   85
John with you?

LADY MARKBY
Oh! I have brought a much more charming person than Sir
John. Sir John's temper since he has taken seriously to politics
has become quite unbearable. Really, now that the House of
Commons is trying to become useful, it does a great deal of   90
harm.

SIR ROBERT CHILTERN
I hope not, Lady Markby. At any rate we do our best to waste
the public time, don't we? But who is this charming person
you have been kind enough to bring to us?

LADY MARKBY
Her name is Mrs Cheveley! One of the Dorsetshire Cheveleys,   95
I suppose. But I really don't know. Families are so mixed
nowadays. Indeed, as a rule, everybody turns out to be
somebody else.

SIR ROBERT CHILTERN
Mrs Cheveley? I seem to know the name.

LADY MARKBY
She has just arrived from Vienna.   100

SIR ROBERT CHILTERN
Ah! yes. I think I know whom you mean.

---

85 *Good evening* F indicates that he shakes her hand, the customary greeting between
   close friends.
87–98 *Oh! . . . somebody else* at this point MS and HTC include Lady M's account of the
   effect of Parliament on her husband (transferred to II, 595 etc.). The first two
   speeches are added to Pbk and carried into C; the first two sentences of the third
   speech also appear in addition to Pbk, but the final sentence does not appear until
   PR.
99–107 *Mrs Cheveley? . . . see her* F, LC, BLTS, C and Pbk have a simpler form of this,
   omitting the reference to the chef. In MS and HTC Lady M observes: 'Oh yes, she
   is here in white satin and gold, but Markby, whose brutality of Language is notorious,
   tells me to my face that it does not suit me' (del. from HTC). Later the colour of
   Mrs C's gown became 'green', then, finally 'heliotrope' (i.e. a shade of purple).

LADY MARKBY

Oh! she goes everywhere there, and has such pleasant scandals about all her friends. I really must go to Vienna next winter. I hope there is a good chef at the Embassy.

SIR ROBERT CHILTERN

If there is not, the Ambassador will certainly have to be recalled. Pray point out Mrs Cheveley to me. I should like to see her.   105

LADY MARKBY

Let me introduce you. (*To* MRS CHEVELEY) My dear, Sir Robert Chiltern is dying to know you!

SIR ROBERT CHILTERN (*Bowing*)

Everyone is dying to know the brilliant Mrs Cheveley. Our attachés at Vienna write to us about nothing else.   110

MRS CHEVELEY

Thank you, Sir Robert. An acquaintance that begins with a compliment is sure to develop into a real friendship. It starts in the right manner. And I find that I know Lady Chiltern already.   115

SIR ROBERT CHILTERN

Really?

MRS CHEVELEY

Yes. She has just reminded me that we were at school together. I remember it perfectly now. She always got the good conduct prize. I have a distinct recollection of Lady Chiltern always getting the good conduct prize!   120

SIR ROBERT CHILTERN (*Smiling*)

And what prizes did you get, Mrs Cheveley?

MRS CHEVELEY

My prizes came a little later on in life. I don't think any of them were for good conduct. I forget!

SIR ROBERT CHILTERN

I am sure they were for something charming!

MRS CHEVELEY

I don't know that women are always rewarded for being charming. I think they are usually punished for it! Certainly, more women grow old nowadays through the faithfulness of their admirers than through anything else! At least that is the only way I can account for the terribly haggard look of most of your pretty women in London!   130

SIR ROBERT CHILTERN
What an appalling philosophy that sounds! To attempt to
classify you, Mrs Cheveley, would be an impertinence. But
may I ask, at heart, are you an optimist or a pessimist? Those
seem to be the only two fashionable religions left to us
nowadays.   135

MRS CHEVELEY
Oh, I'm neither. Optimism begins in a broad grin, and
Pessimism ends with blue spectacles. Besides, they are both
of them merely poses.

SIR ROBERT CHILTERN
You prefer to be natural?

MRS CHEVELEY
Sometimes. But it is such a very difficult pose to keep up.   140

SIR ROBERT CHILTERN
What would those modern psychological novelists, of whom
we hear so much, say to such a theory as that?

MRS CHEVELEY
Ah! the strength of women comes from the fact that
psychology cannot explain us. Men can be analyzed, women
. . . merely adored.   145

SIR ROBERT CHILTERN
You think science cannot grapple with the problem of
women?

MRS CHEVELEY
Science can never grapple with the irrational. That is why it
has no future before it, in this world.

---

131 *appalling* first appears in PR (terrible LC, C, BLTS; modern Pbk, HTC, MS). F
   omits the line and picks up again with l.141 ('What would . . . '). After the first
   sentence ('What . . . sounds!') the MS cuts to l.153 ('Do sit down . . . ').
131–3 *To attempt . . . I ask* first appears in PR.
133 *an optimist or a pessimist* Cf. Act II, 375–6. Pessimism, associated in particular with
   the German philosopher Schopenhauer, was considered part of the decadent
   sensibility. Cf. 'The Decay of Lying': 'Schopenhauer has analysed the pessimism
   that characterises modern thought, but Hamlet invented it. The world has become
   sad because a puppet was once melancholy' (*Intentions*, p. 35/*CW*, p. 983).
   Those . . . nowadays first appears in PR.
137 *blue spectacles* worn to protect the eyes from strong light: perhaps, in this context,
   the pessimistic equivalent of rose-tinted spectacles.
140 *Sometimes* altered from 'Yes' in manuscript changes to PR. In Pbk Wilde deleted
   another sentence: 'Ah, being natural is the most artificial pose of all.'
141 *modern psychological novelists* The term was used loosely by critics hostile to the
   modern movements, but Wilde may be thinking of Paul Bourget, whose novels and
   psychological studies he knew and whom he had met in Paris.

SIR ROBERT CHILTERN
And women represent the irrational.   150

MRS CHEVELEY
Well-dressed women do.

SIR ROBERT CHILTERN (*With a polite bow*)
I fear I could hardly agree with you there. But do sit down.
And now tell me, what makes you leave your brilliant Vienna
for our gloomy London – or perhaps the question is
indiscreet?   155

MRS CHEVELEY
Questions are never indiscreet. Answers sometimes are.

SIR ROBERT CHILTERN
Well, at any rate, may I know if it is politics or pleasure?

MRS CHEVELEY
Politics are my only pleasure. You see nowadays it is not
fashionable to flirt till one is forty, or to be romantic till one
is forty-five, so we poor women who are under thirty, or say   160
we are, have nothing open to us but politics or philanthropy.
And philanthropy seems to me to have become simply the
refuge of people who wish to annoy their fellow-creatures. I
prefer politics. I think they are more . . . becoming!

SIR ROBERT CHILTERN
A political life is a noble career!   165

MRS CHEVELEY
Sometimes. And sometimes it is a clever game, Sir Robert.
And sometimes it is a great nuisance.

SIR ROBERT CHILTERN
Which do you find it?

154–7 *or perhaps. .if it is* first appears in this form in PR, and (in different phrasing) in
    F.
158–64 *Politics . . . becoming!* details in this speech were altered in successive drafts.
    Including the change in ages from 40 and 45 to 50 and 65 respectively. In MS
    'pessimism' is the alternative to politics (l. 161) and the sentence following ('And
    . . . creatures') is absent. In PR, C, BLTS 'wish to annoy' is 'absolutely detest' and
    in Pbk this reading has been inserted to replace 'hate' in the typescript. MS follows
    this speech with further evidence of dandyism in Mrs C:
        SIR ROBERT
        Everything becomes you, Mrs Cheveley.
        MRS CHEVELEY
        Oh! not this month's bonnets. You must not see me in this month's bonnets.
        I look a fright in them. But a political life gives one colour, I think.
    On philanthropy, Cf. *Woman.* I, 257–62 and *Dorian Gray*: 'Philanthropic people
    lose all sense of humanity. It is their distinguishing characteristic' (*DG*, p. 35/ *CW*,
    p. 40).

MRS CHEVELEY
   I? A combination of all three.   *Drops her fan*

SIR ROBER CHILTERN (*Picks up fan*)
   Allow me!   170

MRS CHEVELEY
   Thanks.

SIR ROBERT CHILTERN
   But you have not told me yet what makes you honour London
   so suddenly. Our season is almost over.

MRS CHEVELEY
   Oh! I don't care about the London season! It is too
   matrimonial. People are either hunting for husbands, or   175
   hiding from them. I wanted to meet you. It is quite true. You
   know what a woman's curiosity is. Almost as great as a man's!
   I wanted immensely to meet you, and . . . to ask you to do
   something for me.

SIR ROBERT CHILTERN
   I hope it is not a little thing, Mrs Cheveley. I find that little   180
   things are so very difficult to do.

MRS CHEVELEY (*After a moment's reflection*)
   No, I don't think it is quite a little thing.

SIR ROBERT CHILTERN
   I am so glad. Do tell me what it is.

169 *I? . . . three* in MS and HTC Mrs. C claims to love the 'gambling element in politics',
    and says that she 'would rather play with people than with cards.' The conversation
    also turns to her relationship with one Count Horwitz in Vienna:
       SIR ROBERT
          They say you are his Egeria.
       MRS CHEVELEY
          I assure you that is only for five o'clock tea that he comes to my political
          cave!
    (The reference is to the nymph Egeria, who instructed the Roman king Numa
    Pompilius in the foundations of his city's laws.)
174-7 *Oh!. . . . .a man's* om. MS and F. In LC, BLTS, C and Pbk the second and third
    sentences are replaced by 'It is only meant for the overdressed and the
    undereducated', echoing an epigram in *Dorian Gray* (*DG*, p. 182/*CW*, p. 138),
    Earnest (II, 396) and 'Phrases and Philosophies for the Use of the Young' (*CW*, p.
    1205). It does not appear to have been added to *Earnest* until after the licensing copy
    of that play was prepared (January 1895). Cf. Act II, 544–5 (and footnote) below.
182 *No I don't . . . thing* in C and one of the alterations to Pbk Mrs C's reasons for not
    telling him her request include the fact that 'There are either too many people, or
    too few in the room' because ' . . . to be without an audience is like being without
    a looking-glass. One can't understand oneself'.

MRS CHEVELEY
Later on. (*Rises*) And now may I walk through your beautiful
house? I hear your pictures are charming. Poor Baron   185
Arnheim – you remember the Baron? – used to tell me you
had some wonderful Corots.

SIR ROBERT CHILTERN (*With an almost imperceptible start*)
Did you know Baron Arnheim well?

MRS CHEVELEY (*Smiling*)
Intimately. Did you?

SIR ROBERT CHILTERN
At one time.   190

MRS CHEVELEY
Wonderful man, wasn't he?

SIR ROBERT CHILTERN (*After a pause*)
He was very remarkable, in many ways.

MRS CHEVELEY
I often think it such a pity he never wrote his memoirs. They
would have been most interesting.

SIR ROBERT CHILTERN
Yes: he knew men and cities well, like the old Greek.   195

MRS CHEVELEY
Without the dreadful disadvantage of having a Penelope
waiting at home for him.

MASON
Lord Goring.
Enter LORD GORING. *Thirty-four, but always says he is younger.*

186–7 *used to tell me you had some* (told me you have two. I think he gave them to you,
did he not? HTC, MS; told me you have two LC, C, Pbk). The MS and HTC version
makes Arnheim's artistic seduction of Sir Robert more specific. *Jean-Baptiste Corot*
(1796-1815), French landscape painter, liked to paint in the open air, and was noted
for his twilight scenes. Cf. 'The Critic as Artist': 'It is twilight always for the dancing
nymphs whom Corot set free among the silver poplars of France . . . ' (*Intentions*,
p. 139/*CW*, p. 1026).
188–97 *Did you know . . . at home for him* in MS and HTC these speeches are different,
and the mysterious suddenness of Arnheim's death is remarked on. In BLTS 'At
one time' is replaced by 'For a few years of my life, when I was very young'. Wilde
may have had in mind the suicide of Baron Jaques Reinach, the German Jewish
banker involved in the Panama Canal scandal. Cf. note to ll.399–400 below.
193–7 *I often think . . . at home for him* first appears in PR. The *old Greek* is Odysseus,
described in Book I of Homer's *Odyssey*: 'He saw the cities of many men, and knew
their mind'. *Penelope*, his wife, waited for him patiently in Ithaca, never giving up
hope that he would return from Troy and warding off the attentions of a host of
suitors. Mrs C is making a not-so-veiled attack on marriage
198 s.d. *Thirty-four . . . vantage* added in manuscript to PR. On lying about one's age
cf. *Woman*, I, 427–8 and *Earnest*, III, 249–51.

A well-bred, expressionless face. He is clever, but would not like
to be thought so. A flawless dandy, he would be annoyed if he were
considered romantic. He plays with life, and is on perfectly good
terms with the world. He is fond of being misunderstood. It gives
him a post of vantage

SIR ROBERT CHILTERN
Good evening, my dear Arthur! Mrs Cheveley, allow me to
introduce to you Lord Goring, the idlest man in London.　　200

MRS CHEVELEY
I have met Lord Goring before.

LORD GORING (*Bowing*)
I did not think you would remember me, Mrs Cheveley.

MRS CHEVELEY
My memory is under admirable control. And are you still a
bachelor?

LORD GORING
I . . . believe so.　　205

MRS CHEVELEY
How very romantic!

LORD GORING
Oh! I am not at all romantic. I am not old enough. I leave
romance to my seniors.

SIR ROBERT CHILTERN
Lord Goring is the result of Boodle's Club, Mrs Cheveley.

MRS CHEVELEY
He reflects every credit on the institution.　　210

LORD GORING
May I ask are you staying in London long?

MRS CHEVELEY
That depends partly on the weather, partly on the cooking,
and partly on Sir Robert.

200 *the idlest man in London* om. F, LC, BLTS. Wilde is restoring part of the line from
    MS: 'one of my friends and the idlest man in London'. The typescript of Pbk added
    'which is saying a good deal for him, as there is so much competition'. A manuscript
    alteration prolongs the joke with 'for that at present, amongst elder sons.' The fullest
    version then appears in C. Cf. Lady Bracknell in *Earnest*, reassured by Jack's
    admission that he smokes: 'A man should have an occupation of some kind. There
    are far too many idle men in London as it is' (I, 487-9).
203–10 *And are you . . . institution* first appears in PR. *Boodle's*, in St James's Street, is
    one of the oldest clubs in London.
212 *partly on the cooking* first appears in PR.

SIR ROBERT CHILTERN
You are not going to plunge us into a European war, I
hope?   215

MRS CHEVELEY
There is no danger, at present!
She nods to LORD GORING, *with a look of amusement in her eyes,
and goes out with* SIR ROBERT CHILTERN. LORD GORING *saunters
over to* MABEL CHILTERN

MABEL CHILTERN
You are very late!

LORD GORING
Have you missed me?

MABEL CHILTERN
Awfully!

LORD GORING
Then I am sorry I did not stay away longer. I like being   220
missed.

MABEL CHILTERN
How very selfish of you!

LORD GORING
I am very selfish.

MABEL CHILTERN
You are always telling me of your bad qualities, Lord
Goring.   225

LORD GORING
I have only told you half of them as yet, Miss Mabel!

MABEL CHILTERN
Are the others very bad?

LORD GORING
Quite dreadful! When I think of them at night I go to sleep
at once.

MABEL CHILTERN
Well, I delight in your bad qualities. I wouldn't have you part   230
with one of them.

216 s.d. PR's elaboration of a simple *exeunt* in earlier versions. In F, Goring is watching
    Sir Robert and Mrs C. Mabel Chiltern touches him on the arm to get his
    attention.
230 *I delight in your bad qualities* Wilde may have recalled Benedick's question in *Much
    Ado About Nothing* V, ii: 'And I pray thee now tell me, for which of my bad parts
    didst thou first fall in love with me?'

LORD GORING
How very nice of you! But then you are always nice. By the
way, I want to ask you a question, Miss Mabel. Who brought
Mrs Cheveley here? That woman in heliotrope, who has just
gone out of the room with your brother?   235

MABEL CHILTERN
Oh, I think Lady Markby brought her. Why do you ask?

LORD GORING
I hadn't seen her for years, that is all.

MABEL CHILTERN
What an absurd reason!

LORD GORING
All reasons are absurd.

MABEL CHILTERN
What sort of woman is she?   240

LORD GORING
Oh! a genius in the daytime and a beauty at night!

MABEL CHILTERN
I dislike her already.

LORD GORING
That shows your admirable good taste.

VICOMTE DE NANJAC (*Approaching*)
Ah, the English young lady is the dragon of good taste, is she
not? Quite the dragon of good taste.   245

LORD GORING
So the newspapers are always telling us.

VICOMTE DE NANJAC
I read all your English newspapers. I find them so amusing.

238–9 *What ... absurd* om. MS, added to HTC.
241 *Oh!* MS and HTC add 'a very interesting type' and Pbk 'a very characteristic modern
    type'. The phrase was deleted from HTC.
244–5 *Ah, ... taste* added to HTC typescript.
246 *newspapers* F and an alteration to BLTS specify 'evening newspapers'. Cf. *Woman*,
    II, 376–7 and *Lord Arthur Savile's Crime* (CSF, p. 34/*CW*, p. 179).
247–50 *I read all ... I should like to* om. LC. In MS this reads 'Ah! your English
    newspapers how gay they always are! Their gaiety is quite a ... a serious thing is
    it not?' (Wilde's dots) to which Sir Robert replies: 'It is no laughing matter I assure
    you'. After this de Nanjac leaves with Miss C and the equivalent of l. 257 follows
    ('Well, Goring, dissipating as usual!').

LORD GORING
Then, my dear Nanjac, you must certainly read between the lines.

VICOMTE DE NANJAC
I should like to, but my professor objects. (*To* MABEL   250
CHILTERN) May I have the pleasure of escorting you to the music-room, Mademoiselle?

MABEL CHILTERN (*Looking very disappointed.*)
Delighted, Vicomte, quite delighted! (*Turning to* LORD
GORING) Aren't you coming to the music-room?

LORD GORING
Not if there is any music going on, Miss Mabel.   255

MABEL CHILTERN (*Severely*)
The music is in German. You would not understand it.
                                     Goes out with the VICOMTE DE NANJAC
                        LORD CAVERSHAM *comes up to his son*

LORD CAVERSHAM
Well, sir! what are you doing here? Wasting your life as usual!
You should be in bed, sir. You keep too late hours! I heard
of you the other night at Lady Rufford's dancing till four
o'clock in the morning!   260

LORD GORING
Only a quarter to four, father.

LORD CAVERSHAM
Can't make out how you stand London Society. The thing has
gone to the dogs, a lot of damned nobodies talking about
nothing.

LORD GORING
I love talking about nothing, father. It is the only thing I know   265
anything about.

250 *but my professor objects* added in manuscript to PR.
256 *The music is in German* Cf. 'The Critic as Artist' where one Baroness Bernstein is
    said to have talked about music 'as if it were actually written in the German language.
    Now whatever music sounds like, I am glad to say that it does not sound in the
    smallest degree like German' (*Intentions*, p. 103/*CW*, p. 1610–11).
259 *Lady Rufford's* (Lady Radley's MS). The name is also used in *LWF*.
262–/1 *Can't make out . . . Lady Basildon* this is omitted in MS and HTC, which use the
    first speech earlier, at the equivalent of 1. 37.

LORD CAVERSHAM
You seem to me to be living entirely for pleasure.

LORD GORING
What else is there to live for, father? Nothing ages like happiness.

LORD CAVERSHAM
You are heartless, sir, very heartless!   270

LORD GORING
I hope not, father. Good evening, Lady Basildon!

LADY BASILDON (*Arching two pretty eyebrows*)
Are you here? I had no idea you ever came to political parties!

LORD GORING
I adore political parties. They are the only place left to us where people don't talk politics.   275

LADY BASILDON
I delight in talking politics. I talk them all day long. But I can't bear listening to them. I don't know how the unfortunate men in the House stand these long debates.

LORD GORING
By never listening.

LADY BASILDON
Really?   280

LORD GORING (*In his most serious manner*)
Of course. You see, it is a very dangerous thing to listen. If one listens one may be convinced; and a man who allows himself to be convinced by an argument is a thoroughly unreasonable person.

LADY BASILDON
Ah! that accounts for so much in men that I have never   285

267–9 *You seem ... happiness* first appears in additions to HTC typescript: taken up by BLTS and F but absent in Pbk and LC. In F it is followed by the following exchange:

    LORD CAVERSHAM
      As far as I can make out you seem to care for no one but yourself.
    LORD GORING
      To be very fond of oneself is the beginning of a life-long romance.

The second speech appears, slightly altered, in 'Phrases and Philosophies for the Use of the Young' (*CW*, p. 1206). Cf. references to living for pleasure in *Earnest*, including Lady Bracknell's description of the widowed Lady Harbury 'who seems ... to be living entirely for pleasure now' (I, 319-20).

281–4 *If one listens ... person* Cf. *Earnest*, III, 383-4: 'I dislike arguments of any kind. They are always vulgar, and often convincing'.

understood, and so much in women that their husbands never appreciate in them!

MRS MARCHMONT (*With a sigh*)
Our husbands never appreciate anything in us. We have to go to others for that!

LADY BASILDON (*Emphatically*)
Yes, always to others, have we not?   290

LORD GORING (*Smiling*)
And those are the views of the two ladies who are known to have the most admirable husbands in London.

MRS MARCHMONT
That is exactly what we can't stand. My Reginald is quite hopelessly faultless. He is really unendurably so, at times! There is not the smallest element of excitement in knowing   295
him.

LORD GORING
How terrible! Really, the thing should be more widely known!

LADY BASILDON
Basildon is quite as bad; he is as domestic as if he was a bachelor.   300

MRS MARCHMONT (*Pressing* LADY BASILDON's *hand*)
My poor Olivia! We have married perfect husbands, and we are well punished for it.

LORD GORING
I should have thought it was the husbands who were punished.

MRS MARCHMONT (*Drawing herself up*)
Oh, dear no! They are as happy as possible! And as for   305
trusting us, it is tragic how much they trust us.

295–6 *There . . . knowing him* this version of the speech first appears in PR. F, LC and BLTS read 'He has got all the seven deadly virtues in their most exaggerated British form,' an elaboration on earlier texts. HTC contains an additional line (subsequently deleted) in manuscript: 'If I allowed him he would have tea with me at five every afternoon'. There is a reference to the seven deadly sins in *Woman* (I, 302–4).

299–300 *a bachelor* in MS and HTC she continues: 'He hasn't a single weakness. He won't even quarrel. I do nothing but yawn when I am with him' (carried into PbA, where the second sentence is deleted). Cf. *Earnest*, II, 584–7: 'The home seems to me to be the proper sphere for the man'.

LADY BASILDON
    Perfectly tragic!

LORD GORING
    Or comic, Lady Basildon?

LADY BASILDON
    Certainly not comic, Lord Goring. How unkind of you to
    suggest such a thing!   310

MRS MARCHMONT
    I am afraid Lord Goring is in the camp of the enemy, as usual.
    I saw him talking to that Mrs Cheveley when he came in.

LORD GORING
    Handsome woman, Mrs Cheveley!

LADY BASILDON (*Stiffly*)
    Please don't praise other women in our presence. You might
    wait for us to do that!   315

LORD GORING
    I did wait.

MRS MARCHMONT
    Well, we are not going to praise her. I hear she went to the
    Opera on Monday night, and told Tommy Rufford at supper
    that, as far as she could see, London Society was entirely made
    up of dowdies and dandies.   320

LORD GORING
    She is quite right, too. The men are all dowdies and the
    women are all dandies, aren't they?

MRS MARCHMONT (*After a pause*)
    Oh! do you really think that is what Mrs Cheveley meant?

LORD GORING
    Of course. And a very sensible remark for Mrs Cheveley to
    make, too.   325
          Enter MABEL CHILTERN. *She joins the group*

307–8 *tragic* . . . *comic* Wilde's work abounds in pseudo-definitions of tragedy and
    comedy (e.g. *Woman*, I, 474–9 III, 159–163 and IV, 454–5) and deliberate
    misapplications of the terms.
319–20 *as far as she could see* . . . *dandies* Cf. *Woman*, III 275–6. MS, HTC, Pbk and C
    have a different comparison, of which Pbk gives the fullest version: 'she had never
    seen so many dowdies and dandies in the whole course of her life! said that it
    reminded her of a badly-arranged conservatory full of nothing but wallflowers and
    orchids!'.
321–5 *She is* . . . *to make, too* see Appendix I.
325 s.d. F and LC place this entrance earlier, after 1.320 ('dowdies and dandies').

MABEL CHILTERN
Why are you talking about Mrs Cheveley? Everybody is
talking about Mrs Cheveley! Lord Goring says – what did you
say, Lord Goring, about Mrs Cheveley? Oh! I remember, that
she was a genius in the daytime and a beauty at night.

LADY BASILDON
What a horrid combination! So very unnatural!   330

MRS MARCHMONT (*In her most dreamy manner*)
I like looking at geniuses, and listening to beautiful people.

LORD GORING
Ah! that is morbid of you, Mrs Marchmont!

MRS MARCHMONT (*Brightening to a look of real pleasure*)
I am so glad to hear you say that. Marchmont and I have been
married for seven years, and he has never once told me that
I was morbid. Men are so painfully unobservant!   335

LADY BASILDON (*Turning to her*)
I have always said, dear Margaret, that you were the most
morbid person in London.

MRS MARCHMONT
Ah! but you are always sympathetic, Olivia!

MABEL CHILTERN
Is it morbid to have a desire for food? I have a great desire for
food. Lord Goring, will you give me some supper?   340

LORD GORING
With pleasure, Miss Mabel. (*Moves away with her*)

MABEL CHILTERN
How horrid you have been! You have never talked to me the
whole evening!

LORD GORING
How could I? You went away with the child-diplomatist.

MABEL CHILTERN
You might have followed us. Pursuit would have been only   345
polite. I don't think I like you at all this evening!

---

330 *What . . . unnatural!* first appears in Pbk.
332 *morbid* Cf. Introduction, p. xx.
339–40 *I have a great desire for food* MS adds 'I am positively starving'.
344 *The child-diplomatist* first appears in PR, replacing the cruder phrase of earlier
   versions: 'that dreadful little Frenchman'.
345–6 *Pursuit would have been only polite* added in manuscript to HTC typescript.

LORD GORING
I like you immensely.

MABEL CHILTERN
Well, I wish you'd show it in a more marked way!

They go downstairs

MRS MARCHMONT
Olivia, I have a curious feeling of absolute faintness. I think
I should like some supper very much. I know I should like   350
some supper.

LADY BASILDON
I am positively dying for supper, Margaret!

MRS MARCHMONT
Men are so horribly selfish, they never think of these
things.

LADY BASILDON
Men are grossly material, grossly material!   355
The VICOMTE DE NANJAC *enters from the music-room with some
other guests. After having carefully examined all the people
present, he approaches* LADY BASILDON

VICOMTE DE NANJAC
May I have the honour of taking you down to supper,
Comtesse?

LADY BASILDON (*Coldly*)
I never take supper, thank you, Vicomte. (*The* VICOMTE *is
about to retire.* LADY BASILDON, *seeing this, rises at once and takes
his arm*) But I will come down with you with pleasure.

---

348 *Well . . . way!* F has the s.d. 'stop music' to motivate an influx of guests from the
music-room.
356 *supper* 'At an evening party or a ball the supper . . . forms an important element . . .
which closely resembles a wedding breakfast' (*Etiquette of Good Society*, ed. Lady
Colin Campbell, 1895). The appropriate form for taking a lady in to supper after
dancing with her also applied (with modifications) to the equivalent situation at an
evening party: 'The gentleman asks his partner whether she will take any refresh-
ment, and if she replies in the affirmative he escorts her to the room and procures her
an ice, offers to hold a cup for her, and when the music for the next dance begins, he
conducts her to her chaperon, when she disengages herself from his arm, they bow to
one another, and he leaves her'.
358 s.d. like others at ll. 363 and 368, this s.d. first appears in PR.

VICOMTE DE NANJAC
  I am so fond of eating! I am very English in all my tastes.   360

LADY BASILDON
  You look quite English, Vicomte, quite English.
  They pass out. MR MONTFORD, *a perfectly groomed young dandy,*
  approaches MRS MARCHMONT

MR MONTFORD
  Like some supper, Mrs Marchmont?

MRS MARCHMONT (*Languidly*)
  Thank you, Mr Montford, I never touch supper. (*Rises hastily*
  and takes his arm) But I will sit beside you, and watch you.

MR MONTFORD
  I don't know that I like being watched when I am eating!   365

MRS MARCHMONT
  Then I will watch someone else.

MR MONTFORD
  I don't know that I should like that either.

MRS MARCHMONT (*Severely*)
  Pray, Mr Montford, do not make these painful scenes of
  jealousy in public!
  They go downstairs with the other guests, passing SIR ROBERT
  CHILTERN *and* MRS CHEVELEY, *who now enter*

---

360 *I am so fond ... tastes* MS and HTC read: 'I always eat a great deal in England. I
  do it on purpose. It is an occupation. In eating, as you say, I always take the cake.'
  Lady Basildon replies: 'Oh! but I don't say that, Vicomte!' The lines are deleted
  from Pbk and do not appear in C, which locates ll. 81-2 ('Ah! you butter me ...
  ') at this point. Cf. the earlier references to the chef at Vienna and 'cooking' in
  London (ll. 104, 212). In the drafts of *Earnest* Algernon's debt of £762 14s 2d is
  for meals at the Savoy, and Miss Prism observes that 'There can be little good in
  any young man who eats so much, and so often' (*Earnest* Appendix I, p. 108).
  Although the eating of cucumber sandwiches and muffins plays a significant comic
  role in *Earnest* Wilde was (he later claimed) fighting a serious, losing battle against
  the extravagant tastes of Lord Alfred Douglas, for which he was usually expected
  to pay the bill.
366 *Then ... else* F has the s.d. 'check sunlight', indicating that the lights are to be
  lowered ('check' being the equivalent of the verb 'dim'). The 'sunlight' was usually
  the large chandelier that served as principal source of light in the auditorium: it is
  possible that until this point the house lights have not been dimmed. Although
  Henry Irving at the Lyceum had adopted the practice of darkening the auditorium
  during performances, it was not yet a matter of course in every theatre.
369 s.d. F and LC locate the entrance earlier, after l.362.

SIR ROBERT CHILTERN
And are you going to any of our country houses before you   370
leave England, Mrs Cheveley?

MRS CHEVELEY
Oh, no! I can't stand your English house-parties. In England
people actually try to be brilliant at breakfast. That is so
dreadful of them! Only dull people are brilliant at breakfast.
And then the family skeleton is always reading family prayers.   375
My stay in England really depends on you, Sir Robert. (*Sits
down on the sofa*)

SIR ROBERT CHILTERN (*Taking a seat beside her*)
Seriously?

MRS CHEVELEY
Quite seriously. I want to talk to you about a great political
and financial scheme, about this Argentine Canal Company,
in fact.   380

SIR ROBERT CHILTERN
What a tedious, practical subject for you to talk about, Mrs
Cheveley!

MRS CHEVELEY
Oh, I like tedious, practical subjects. What I don't like are
tedious, practical people. There is a wide difference. Besides,
you are interested, I know, in International Canal schemes.   385
You were Lord Radley's secretary, weren't you, when the
Government bought the Suez Canal shares?

SIR ROBERT CHILTERN
Yes. But the Suez Canal was a very great and splendid
undertaking. It gave us our direct route to India. It had
imperial value. It was necessary that we should have control.   390

370–6 *And are you going* . . . (Sits down on sofa) this passage first appears thus in PR and,
  in slightly different form, in F. In MS Sir Robert is anxious to reach the House of
  Commons before an important division. This is deleted in HTC, where Wilde has
  added a version of the lines about country house-parties, which is absent from Pbk,
  the typescript of BLTS and LC. It reappears in manuscript alterations to BLTS,
  and is taken up in F.
373 *actually* manuscript substitution for 'always' in PR.
381–4 *What . . . Besides* added to BLTS typescript and adopted in F; om. LC, Pbk, C,
  MS.
386 *Lord Radley's* the name had been used as that of Dorian Gray's guardian: in MS and
  HTC we are told that Sir Robert had been Lord C's secretary at the time.
388 *Yes* F precedes this with the s.d. '*look*'. The purchase of Suez shares took place in
  1875, on Disraeli's initiative.
388–92 *Yes . . . swindle* a number of details were added in the course of revision. *It gave
  . . . India* first appears in C, *It had . . . control* in PR. The swindle is *commonplace*
  in Pbk and *Stock Exchange* appears in C.

This Argentine scheme is a commonplace Stock Exchange swindle.

MRS CHEVELEY
A speculation, Sir Robert! A brilliant, daring speculation.

SIR ROBERT CHILTERN
Believe me, Mrs Cheveley, it is a swindle. Let us call things by their proper names. It makes matters simpler. We have all   395
the information about it at the Foreign Office. In fact, I sent out a special Commission to inquire into the matter privately, and they report that the works are hardly begun, and as for the money already suscribed, no one seems to know what has become of it. The whole thing is a second Panama, and with   400
not a quarter of the chance of success that miserable affair ever had. I hope you have not invested in it. I am sure you are far too clever to have done that.

MRS CHEVELEY
I have invested very largely in it.

SIR ROBERT CHILTERN
Who could have advised you to do such a foolish thing?   405

MRS CHEVELEY
Your old friend – and mine.

SIR ROBERT CHILTERN
Who?

MRS CHEVELEY
Baron Arnheim.

SIR ROBERT CHILTERN (*Frowning*)
Ah! yes. I remember hearing, at the time of his death, that he had been mixed up in the whole affair.   410

398–400 *and as for . . . The whole thing* first appears in PR ('It' LC, etc.) After the *Panama Canal* project foundered in 1889, with massive debts and unaccounted-for expenditures, a national scandal in France resulted in legal action against the speculators, who were revealed to have involved senators and deputies in the corruption. A series of trials took place in Paris in 1892-3 but one of the principal backers of the scheme, Baron Jaques Reinach, took his life on the day he was to face the court. The Canal was later completed after a new directorate had been set up. In MS and HTC there are additional details of Mrs C's scheme, including the fact that it is in the hands (as Sir Robert tells her) 'of three rather shady bankers, one in Paris, one in Berlin and one . . . one in Vienna' (Wilde's dots). The passage was deleted from HTC.
404 *I have . . . in it* in versions before PR she adds 'and I hope to invest still more!'.
405–19 *Who could have . . . England, and* om. F and LC, where Sir Robert replies 'I am sorry to hear it Lady [sic] Cheveley, as I am going . . . ' and continues with l.420. In F he brings a chair over from the fireplace and sits down.

MRS CHEVELEY
It was his last romance. His last but one, to do him justice.

SIR ROBERT CHILTERN (*Rising*)
But you have not seen my Corots yet. They are in the
music-room. Corots seem to go with music, don't they? May
I show them to you?

MRS CHEVELEY (*Shaking her head*)
I am not in a mood tonight for silver twilights, or rose-pink   415
dawns. I want to talk business. (*Motions to him with her fan
to sit down again beside her*)

SIR ROBERT CHILTERN
I fear I have no advice to give you, Mrs Cheveley, except to
interest yourself in something less dangerous. The success of
the Canal depends, of course, on the attitude of England, and
I am going to lay the report of the Commissioners before the   420
House tomorrow night.

MRS CHEVELEY
That you must not do. In your own interests, Sir Robert, to
say nothing of mine, you must not do that.

SIR ROBERT CHILTERN (*Looking at her in wonder*)
In my own interests? My dear Mrs Cheveley, what do you
mean? (*Sits down beside her*)   425

MRS CHEVELEY
Sir Robert, I will be quite frank with you. I want you to
withdraw the report that you had intended to lay before the
House, on the ground that you have reasons to believe that
the Commissioners have been prejudiced or misinformed, or
something. Then I want you to say a few words to the effect   430
that the Government is going to reconsider the question, and
that you have reason to believe that the Canal, if completed,

411 *His last but one, to do him justice* added in MS to PR, perhaps implying that Mrs C
     had been his final romance.
415-6 *or rose-pink dawns* added to PR. *Rose-pink* has connotations of both deceit and
     theatrical make-up (cf. the examples from Carlyle, Meredith and Dickens in
     OED).
417-21 *I fear ... tomorrow night* in MS and HTC Sir Robert declares his intention to
     warn the Argentine Republic of the Syndicate's machinations.
417-8 *except . . . dangerous* added to PR.
422-3 *to say nothing of mine* first appears in PR.
421 *House* LC and earlier versions read 'Cabinet' (cf. note to ll. 68-9, above). In MS
     and HTC more details of the plan are given: Mrs C reminds Sir Robert that news
     of the government's support will send up the value of the stock, enabling the
     Syndicate to sell at a profit 'and leave the wretched poor investors in the lurch'. This
     was deleted from HTC. BLTS has two versions of similar material, with 'Cut???'
     beside them.

will be of great international value. You know the sort of
things ministers say in cases of this kind. A few ordinary
platitudes will do. In modern life nothing produces such an   435
effect as a good platitude. It makes the whole world kin. Will
you do that for me?

SIR ROBERT CHILTERN
Mrs Cheveley, you cannot be serious in making me such a
proposition!

MRS CHEVELEY
I am quite serious.   440

SIR ROBERT CHILTERN (*Coldly*)
Pray allow me to believe that you are not!

MRS CHEVELEY (*Speaking with great deliberation and emphasis*)
Ah! but I am. And, if you do what I ask you, I . . . will pay
you very handsomely!

SIR ROBERT CHILTERN
Pay me!

MRS CHEVELEY
Yes.   445

SIR ROBERT CHILTERN
I am afraid I don't quite understand what you mean.

MRS CHEVELEY (*Leaning back on the sofa and looking at him*)
How very disappointing! And I have come all the way from
Vienna in order that you should thoroughly understand me.

SIR ROBERT CHILTERN
I fear I don't.

MRS CHEVELEY (*In her most nonchalant manner*)
My dear Sir Robert, you are a man of the world, and you have   450
your price, I suppose. Everybody has nowadays. The
drawback is that most people are so dreadfully expensive. I
know I am. I hope you will be more reasonable in your
terms.

434–7 *A few ordinary platitudes . . . for me?* first appears in alterations to Pbk. The allusion
is to Shakespeare's *Troilus and Cressida* (III, iii, 171 etc.): 'One touch of nature
makes the whole world kin' – the 'touch' being a disposition to praise 'newborn
gauds/ Though they are made and moulded of things past/ And give to dust that
is a little gilt/ More laud than gilt o'e'r-dusted.' Wilde may be thinking of the
phrase's own status as an 'ordinary platitude' rather than the irony of its original
context.
446–50 *I am afraid . . . of the world, and* added to HTC. The s.d. in this sequence first
appear in PR, although F indicates '*fan business*' at 1.458.

SIR ROBERT CHILTERN (*Rises indignantly*)
    If you will allow me, I will call your carriage for you. You have   455
    lived so long abroad, Mrs Cheveley, that you seem to be
    unable to realize that you are talking to an English gentle-
    man.

MRS CHEVELEY (*Detains him by touching his arm with her fan, and
    keeping it there while she is talking*)
    I realize that I am talking to a man who laid the foundation
    of his fortune by selling to a Stock Exchange speculator a   460
    Cabinet secret.

SIR ROBERT CHILTERN (*Biting his lip*)
    What do you mean?

MRS CHEVELEY (*Rising and facing him*)
    I mean that I know the real origin of your wealth and your
    career, and I have got your letter, too.

SIR ROBERT CHILTERN
    What letter?   465

MRS CHEVELEY (*Contemptuously*)
    The letter you wrote to Baron Arnheim, when you were Lord
    Radley's secretary, telling the Baron to buy Suez Canal shares
    – a letter written three days before the Government an-
    nounced its own purchase.

SIR ROBERT CHILTERN (*Hoarsely*)
    It is not true.   470

MRS CHEVELEY
    You thought that letter had been destroyed. How foolish of
    you! It is in my possession.

SIR ROBERT CHILTERN
    The affair to which you allude was no more than a speculation.
    The House of Commons had not yet passed the bill; it might
    have been rejected.   475

MRS CHEVELEY
    It was a swindle, Sir Robert. Let us call things by their proper
    names. It makes everything simpler. And now I am going to
    sell you that letter, and the price I ask for it is your public
    support of the Argentine scheme. You made your own fortune

---

471–2 *You thought . . . possession* in successive drafts of the lines leading up to this speech,
    Wilde tidied up the business of introducing the letter into the play: the earliest
    versions of ll. 466–9 include interesting details of Mrs C's relationship with
    Arnheim, and the means by which she obtained the incriminating evidence. Cf.
    Appendix I.

out of one canal. You must help me and my friends to make   480
our fortunes out of another!

SIR ROBERT CHILTERN
It is infamous, what you propose – infamous!

MRS CHEVELEY
Oh, no! This is the game of life as we all have to play it, Sir
Robert, sooner or later!

SIR ROBERT CHILTERN
I cannot do what you ask me.   485

MRS CHEVELEY
You mean you cannot help doing it. You know you are
standing on the edge of a precipice. And it is not for you to
make terms. It is for you to accept them. Supposing you refuse
–

SIR ROBERT CHILTERN
What then?   490

MRS CHEVELEY
My dear Sir Robert, what then? You are ruined, that is all!
Remember to what a point your Puritanism in England has
brought you. In old days nobody pretended to be a bit better
than his neighbours. In fact, to be a bit better than one's
neighbour was considered excessively vulgar and middle-   495
class. Nowadays, with our modern mania for morality,
everyone has to pose as a paragon of purity, incorruptibility,
and all the other seven deadly virtues – and what is the result?
You all go over like ninepins – one after the other. Not a year
passes in England without somebody disappearing. Scandals   500
used to lend charm, or at least interest, to a man – now they
crush him. And yours is a very nasty scandal. You couldn't
survive it. If it were known that as a young man, secretary to
a great and important minister, you sold a Cabinet secret for
a large sum of money, and that that was the origin of your   505

491–521 *My dear . . . this scheme* the principal alterations to this speech consisted in the
removal of two passages from MS and HTC which served to amplify Sir Robert C's
'splendid position' and the ironies of his prospective degradation. Both passages
reached the Pbk typescript but were deleted there. In BLTS a variation on the
material dealing with scandal was marked for cutting: on the page opposite Wilde
noted 'Tartuffe and Caliban hounding you down together'. For the text of these
omissions, see Appendix I. In F there is considerable re-arrangement: the speech
is slightly shorter and less rhetorically mannered. Among the *scandals* of which the
speech may have reminded its first audience would have been the divorce
proceedings which in 1885 precipitated the fall of Sir Charles Dilke (1843-1911),
a brilliant statesman, once thought a potential leader of the Liberal Party.

wealth and career, you would be hounded out of public life, you would disappear completely. And after all, Sir Robert, why should you sacrifice your entire future rather than deal diplomatically with your enemy? For the moment I am your enemy. I admit it ! And I am much stronger than you are. The 510
big battalions are on my side. You have a splendid position, but it is your splendid position that makes you so vulnerable. You can't defend it! And I am in attack. Of course I have not talked morality to you. You must admit in fairness that I have spared you that. Years ago you did a clever, unscrupulous 515
thing; it turned out a great success. You owe to it your fortune and position. And now you have got to pay for it. Sooner or later we all have to pay for what we do. You have to pay now. Before I leave you tonight, you have got to promise me to suppress your report, and to speak in the House in favour of 520
this scheme.

SIR ROBERT CHILTERN
What you ask is impossible.

MRS CHEVELEY
You must make it possible. You are going to make it possible. Sir Robert, you know what your English newspapers are like. Suppose that when I leave this house I drive down to some 525
newspaper office, and give them this scandal and the proofs of it! Think of their loathsome joy, of the delight they would have in dragging you down, of the mud and mire they would plunge you in. Think of the hypocrite with his greasy smile penning his leading article, and arranging the foulness of the 530
public placard.

SIR ROBERT CHILTERN
Stop! You want me to withdraw the report and to make a short speech stating that I believe there are possibilities in the scheme?

MRS CHEVELEY (*Sitting down on the sofa*)
Those are my terms.   535

SIR ROBERT CHILTERN (*In a low voice*)
I will give you any sum of money you want.

MRS CHEVELEY
Even you are not rich enough, Sir Robert, to buy back your

---

527 *loathsome* (terrible F).
529 *greasy* (oily F). In BLTS Wilde tried 'cunning' but did not adopt it subsequently.
535 *Those are my terms* MS and HTC have a shorter version of the sequence following, in which ll. 536–59 are omitted ('*I will give you . . . on the subject*'). These lines were added to Pbk and adopted in the C typescript.

past. No man is.

SIR ROBERT CHILTERN
I will not do what you ask me. I will not.

MRS CHEVELEY
You have to. If you don't . . .   *Rises from the sofa*   540

SIR ROBERT CHILTERN (*Bewildered and unnerved*)
Wait a moment! What did you propose? You said that you
would give me back my letter, didn't you?

MRS CHEVELEY
Yes. That is agreed. I will be in the Ladies' Gallery tomorrow
night at half-past eleven. If by that time – and you will have
had heaps of opportunity—you have made an announcement
to the House in the terms I wish, I shall hand you back your
letter with the prettiest thanks, and the best, or at any rate the
most suitable, compliment I can think of. I intend to play
quite fairly with you. One should always play fairly . . . when
one has the winning cards. The Baron taught me that . . .   550
amongst other things.

SIR ROBERT CHILTERN
You must let me have time to consider your proposal.

MRS CHEVELEY
No; you must settle now!

SIR ROBERT CHILTERN
Give me a week – three days!

MRS CHEVELEY
Impossible! I have got to telegraph to Vienna tonight.   555

SIR ROBERT CHILTERN
My God! what brought you into my life?

MRS CHEVELEY
Circumstances.   *Moves towards the door*

SIR ROBERT CHILTERN
Don't go. I consent. The report shall be withdrawn. I will
arrange for a question to be put to me on the subject.

543–51 *I will be . . . amongst other things* first appears in PR. A separate *Ladies' Gallery*,
    with a grille in front of it, was provided above the Press Gallery in the House of
    Commons.
556–7 *My God! . . . Circumstances* first appears in PR.
558–9 *I will . . . subject* first appears in PR. Wilde is specifying the appropriate
    parliamentary procedure: a question from his own side of the house will be set up
    to facilitate his making a statement.

MRS CHEVELEY
  Thank you. I knew we should come to an amicable agreement.   560
  I understood your nature from the first. I analyzed you,
  though you did not adore me. And now you can get my
  carriage for me, Sir Robert. I see the people coming up from
  supper, and Englishmen always get romantic after a meal, and
  that bores me dreadfully.   565

                         Exit SIR ROBERT CHILTERN
       Enter GUESTS, LADY CHILTERN, LADY MARKBY, LORD
          CAVERSHAM, LADY BASILDON, MRS MARCHMONT,
                VICOMTE DE NANJAC, MR MONTFORD

LADY MARKBY
  Well, dear Mrs Cheveley, I hope you have enjoyed yourself.
  Sir Robert is very entertaining, is he not?

MRS CHEVELEY
  Most entertaining! I have enjoyed my talk with him immensely.

LADY MARKBY
  He has had a very interesting and brilliant career. And he has   570
  married a most admirable wife. Lady Chiltern is a woman of
  the very highest principles, I am glad to say. I am a little too
  old now, myself, to trouble about setting a good example, but
  I always admire people who do. And Lady Chiltern has a very
  ennobling effect on life, though her dinner-parties are rather   575
  dull sometimes. But one can't have everything, can one? And
  now I must go, dear. Shall I call for you tomorrow?

MRS CHEVELEY
  Thanks.

LADY MARKBY
  We might drive in the Park at five. Everything looks so fresh
  in the Park now!   580

561–2 *I understood . . . adore me* first appears in additions to Pbk. The second sentence
    is omitted in F. The opposition *analyse/adore* is a characteristic Wildean contrast of
    pseudo-scientific detachment (as in Lord G's 'psychological experiments') and its
    most extreme contrary: Cf. ll. 131–2, above ('To attempt to classify you, Mrs
    Cheveley would be an impertinence').
563–5 *I see . . . dreadfully* first appears in PR, where 'Englishmen' has been altered in
    manuscript from 'English people' and 'dreadfully' has been added.
570 *He has had . . . career* in MS and HTC Lady Markby gives further details of his
    background: see Appendix I. The passage is deleted from HTC and does not
    reappear. In alterations to Pbk (and in C) *career* is followed by 'And his philanthropy,
    of course, is very well known'. F provides s.d. for Lady C to be busy upstage,
    shaking hands with departing guests during this conversation.
576–7 *And now . . . dear* MS and HTC include here the passage concerning Blue Books
    subsequently transferred to III, 618, etc. The lines are deleted in HTC.
579 *the Park* i.e. Hyde Park (cf. note to l. 28, above).

MRS CHEVELEY
Except the people!

LADY MARKBY
Perhaps the people are a little jaded. I have often observed that
the Season as it goes on produces a kind of softening of the
brain. However, I think anything is better than high
intellectual pressure. That is the most unbecoming thing   585
there is. It makes the noses of the young girls so particularly
large. And there is nothing so difficult to marry as a large nose,
men don't like them. Good-night dear! (*To* LADY CHILTERN)
Good-night, Gertrude!

Goes out on LORD CAVERSHAM'S *arm*

MRS CHEVELEY
What a charming house you have, Lady Chiltern! I have spent   590
a delightful evening. It has been so interesting getting to know
your husband.

LADY CHILTERN
Why did you wish to meet my husband, Mrs Cheveley?

MRS CHEVELEY
Oh, I will tell you. I wanted to interest him in this Argentine
Canal scheme, of which I dare say you have heard. And I   595
found him most susceptible, – susceptible to reason, I mean.
A rare thing in a man. I converted him in ten minutes. He is
going to make a speech in the House tomorrow night in favour
of the idea. We must go to the Ladies' Gallery and hear him!
It will be a great occasion!   600

LADY CHILTERN
There must be some mistake. That scheme could never have
my husband's support.

MRS CHEVELEY
Oh, I assure you it's all settled, I don't regret my tedious

---

587 *so difficult to marry* i.e. dispose of in marriage, the preoccupation of mothers during
the Season. The claim that intellectual development made women ugly was
commonplace in anti-feminist propaganda and humour. An idiosyncratic specimen
occurs in the MS of *Earnest* 'She is one of those dull, intellectual girls one meets
all over the place. Girls who have got large minds and large feet' (I, 667-8, note).
Cf. ll. 635–6, below, where Mabel complains that pearls make one look 'so plain,
so good and so intellectual'. The play on physical plainness and moral worth occurs
a number of times in *LWF*.

593–602 *Why did you wish . . . support* MS and HTC have a longer version of this dialogue,
marked for deletion in the PUk typescript.

603–8 *I don't regret . . . myself* the full version, with the insulting reference to a secret
held in common with Sir Robert, does not appear until PR.

journey from Vienna now. It has been a great success. But,
of course, for the next twenty-four hours the whole thing is   605
a dead secret.

LADY CHILTERN (*Gently*)
A secret? Between whom?

MRS CHEVELEY (*With a flash of amusement in her eyes*)
Between your husband and myself.

SIR ROBERT CHILTERN (*Entering*)
Your carriage is here, Mrs Cheveley!

MRS CHEVELEY
Thanks! Good evening, Lady Chiltern! Good-night, Lord   610
Goring! I am at Claridge's. Don't you think you might leave
a card?

LORD GORING
If you wish it, Mrs Cheveley!

MRS CHEVELEY
Oh, don't be so solemn about it, or I shall be obliged to leave
a card on you. In England I suppose that would be hardly   615
considered *en règle*. Abroad, we are more civilized. Will you
see me down, Sir Robert? Now that we have both the same
interests at heart we shall be great friends, I hope!
            Sails out on SIR ROBERT CHILTERN's *arm*
LADY CHILTERN *goes to the top of the staircase and looks down
at them as they descend. Her expression is troubled. After a little
time she is joined by some of the guests, and passes with them into
another reception-room*

MABEL CHILTERN
What a horrid woman!

LORD GORING
You should go to bed, Miss Mabel.   620

MABEL CHILTERN
Lord Goring!

611 *Claridge's* fashionable hotel in Brook Street, Mayfair.
615–6 *In England . . . civilized* first appears in alterations to BLTS, in a slightly different
    form: 'I suppose in England that would be considered most improper. In Vienna
    we are more civilized'. As printed, the line does not appear until PR. Mrs C is, of
    course, correct in assuming that it is contrary to etiquette for a lady to leave her card
    on a gentleman without first having received the courtesy from him.
618 s.d. *Sails* altered in manuscript from 'Goes' in PR. In LC, etc., the s.d. is simply
    '*Exit*' without any of the detail supplied for the first time in PR.

LORD GORING
My father told me to go to bed an hour ago. I don't see why
I shouldn't give you the same advice. I always pass on good
advice. It is the only thing to do with it. It is never of any use
to oneself.   625

MABEL CHILTERN
Lord Goring, you are always ordering me out of the room. I
think it most courageous of you. Especially as I am not going
to bed for hours. (*Goes over to the sofa*) You can come and sit
down if you like, and talk about anything in the world, except
the Royal Academy, Mrs Cheveley, or novels in Scotch   630
dialect. They are not improving subjects. (*Catches sight of
something that is lying on the sofa half-hidden by the cushion*)
What is this? Someone has dropped a diamond brooch! Quite
beautiful, isn't it? (*Shows it to him*) I wish it was mine, but
Gertrude won't let me wear anything but pearls, and I am
thoroughly sick of pearls. They make one look so plain, so   635
good and so intellectual. I wonder whom the brooch belongs
to.

LORD GORING
I wonder who dropped it.

MABEL CHILTERN
It is a beautiful brooch.

LORD GORING
It is a handsome bracelet.   640

MABEL CHILTERN
It isn't a bracelet. It's a brooch.

LORD GORING
It can be used as a bracelet.
Takes it from her, and pulling out a green letter-case, puts the

624–5 *It is never . . . oneself* first appears in PR. F (following manuscript alterations to
     BLTS) reads 'I am not a bit selfish about it'
627 *courageous* (rude LC. BLTS, C; foolish F and alterations to BLTS).
627–55 *Especially . . . goodnight* this sequence, including the discovery of the brooch,
     does not appear in LC or earlier versions, except for some additions to BLTS. F
     gives a version slightly different to that printed in PR and 1st Ed.
630 *The Royal Academy* the Royal Academy of Arts, with its annual exhibitions of work
     by members, had come to represent the 'establishment'. *Novels in Scotch dialect*:
     in the MS draft of the dictation scene in *Earnest* (II, 439 etc.), Cecily tells Algernon
     not to cough because she does not know how to spell a cough, although it is done
     'by realistic novelists who write in horrid dialect'.
642 s.d. *with . . . sangfroid* added to PR. The s.d. at 11. 646, 647, 654 were added in
     the same way: Wilde evidently did not feel the necessity of guiding the reader's
     visualization of the scene until he saw it in print.

ornament carefully in it, and replaces the whole thing in his breast-pocket with the most perfect sangfroid

MABEL CHILTERN
What are you doing?

LORD GORING
Miss Mabel, I am going to make a rather strange request to you. 645

MABEL CHILTERN (*Eagerly*)
Oh, pray do! I have been waiting for it all the evening.

LORD GORING (*Is a little taken aback, but recovers himself*)
Don't mention to anybody that I have taken charge of this brooch. Should anyone write and claim it, let me know at once.

MABEL CHILTERN
That is a strange request. 650

LORD GORING
Well, you see I gave this brooch to somebody once, years ago.

MABEL CHILTERN
You did?

LORD GORING
Yes.

    LADY CHILTERN *enters alone. The other guests have gone*

MABEL CHILTERN
Then I shall certainly bid you good-night. Good-night, 655 Gertrude! *Exit*

LADY CHILTERN
Good-night, dear! (*to* LORD GORING) You saw whom Lady Markby brought here tonight.

LORD GORING
Yes. It was an unpleasant surprise. What did she come here for? 660

LADY CHILTERN
Apparently to try and lure Robert to uphold some fraudulent scheme in which she is interested. The Argentine Canal, in fact.

LORD GORING
She has mistaken her man, hasn't she?

LADY CHILTERN
She is incapable of understanding an upright nature like my   665
husband's!

LORD GORING
Yes. I should fancy she came to grief if she tried to get Robert
into her toils. It is extraordinary what astounding mistakes
clever women make.

LADY CHILTERN
I don't call women of that kind clever. I call them stupid!   670

LORD GORING
Same thing often. Good-night, Lady Chiltern!

LADY CHILTERN
Good-night!

        Enter SIR ROBERT CHILTERN

SIR ROBERT CHILTERN
My dear Arthur, you are not going? Do stop a little!

LORD GORING
Afraid I can't, thanks. I have promised to look in at the
Hartlocks'. I believe they have got a mauve Hungarian band   675
that plays mauve Hungarian music. See you soon. Good-
bye!   *Exit*

SIR ROBERT CHILTERN
How beautiful you look tonight, Gertrude!

LADY CHILTERN
Robert, it is not true, is it? You are not going to lend your
support to this Argentine speculation? You couldn't!   680

SIR ROBERT CHILTERN (*Starting*)
Who told you I intended to do so?

LADY CHILTERN
That woman who has just gone out, Mrs Cheveley, as she calls
herself now. She seemed to taunt me with it. Robert, I know
this woman. You don't. We were at school together. She was
untruthful, dishonest, an evil influence on everyone whose   685

675–6 *I believe . . . music* first appears in PR. *Hungarian* (usually, gypsy) bands enjoyed
a vogue at the time. The notion of *mauve* music is a comic application of the
contention that the terms of one sense should be used to describe the sensations of
another. For a serious use of it, cf. 'The Critic as Artist', Part I: 'Let me play
to you some mad scarlet thing by Dvořák' (*Intentions*, p. 115/CW, p. 1015).

678 *How beautiful you look* in LC and earlier versions the opening gambit is weaker:
'Perfectly lovely the flowers . . . ' (F and alterations to BLTS have a variant on the
line as printed).

trust or friendship she could win. I hated, I despised her. She
stole things, she was a thief. She was sent away for being a
thief. Why do you let her influence you?

SIR ROBERT CHILTERN
Gertrude, what you tell me may be true, but it happened many
years ago. It is best forgotten! Mrs Cheveley may have   690
changed since then. No one should be entirely judged by their
past.

LADY CHILTERN (*Sadly*)
One's past is what one is. It is the only way by which people
should be judged.

SIR ROBERT CHILTERN
That is a hard saying, Gertrude!   695

LADY CHILTERN
It is a true saying, Robert. And what did she mean by boasting
that she had got you to lend your support, your name to a
thing I have heard you describe as the most dishonest and
fraudulent scheme there has ever been in political life?

SIR ROBERT CHILTERN (*Biting his lip*)
I was mistaken ·in the view I took. We all may make   700
mistakes.

LADY CHILTERN
But you told me yesterday that you had received the report
from the Commission, and that it entirely condemned the
whole thing.

SIR ROBERT CHILTERN (*Walking up and down*)
I have reasons now to believe that the Commission was   705
prejudiced, or, at any rate, misinformed. Besides, Gertrude,
public and private life are different things. They have
different laws, and move on different lines.

LADY CHILTERN
They should both represent man at his highest. I see no
difference between them.   710

686–7 *She stole things* MS and HTC include more details of the crime. Mrs C, when a
young girl, was present at a house party when money and jewels were stolen from
Lady C's room. A servant was blamed and dismissed on account of it, but Lady C
later extracted a confession (in writing) from Mrs C. In early versions of the play
Wilde used this 'confession' as the means by which Lord G defeated Mrs C's
blackmail of Sir Robert. The passage was deleted from HTC typescript.
693–4 *One's past ... judged* first appears in PR.
706–14 *Besides ... Yes!* this sequence, with its important distinctions between public
and private life, ideals and 'practical politics', does not appear until C.

SIR ROBERT CHILTERN (*Stopping*)
In the present case, on a matter of practical politics, I have
changed my mind. That is all.

LADY CHILTERN
All!

SIR ROBERT CHILTERN (*Sternly*)
Yes!

LADY CHILTERN
Robert! Oh! it is horrible that I should have to ask you such   715
a question – Robert, are you telling me the whole truth?

SIR ROBERT CHILTERN
Why do you ask me such a question?

LADY CHILTERN (*After a pause*)
Why do you not answer it?

SIR ROBERT CHILTERN (*Sitting down*)
Gertrude, truth is a very complex thing, and politics is a very
complex business. There are wheels within wheels. One may   720
be under certain obligations to people that one must pay.
Sooner or later in political life one has to compromise.
Everyone does.

LADY CHILTERN
Compromise? Robert, why do you talk so differently tonight
from the way I have always heard you talk? Why are you   725
changed?

SIR ROBERT CHILTERN
I am not changed. But circumstances alter things.

LADY CHILTERN
Circumstances should never alter principles!

SIR ROBERT CHILTERN
But if I told you –

LADY CHILTERN
What?   730

SIR ROBERT CHILTERN
That it was necessary, vitally necessary.

719–20 *a very complex business* the phrase was established after some difficulty. MS and
HTC read 'a very difficult complex business' changed in alterations to HTC to 'a
very vague complex business.'

LADY CHILTERN
  It can never be necessary to do what is not honourable. Or if
  it be necessary, then what is it that I have loved! But it is not,
  Robert; tell me it is not. Why should it be? What gain would
  you get? Money? We have no need of that! And money that   735
  comes from a tainted source is a degradation. Power? But
  power is nothing in itself. It is power to do good that is fine
  – that, and that only. What is it, then? Robert, tell me why
  you are going to do this dishonourable thing!

SIR ROBERT CHILTERN
  Gertrude, you have no right to use that word. I told you it was   740
  a question of rational compromise. It is no more than that.

LADY CHILTERN
  Robert, that is all very well for other men, for men who treat
  life simply as a sordid speculation; but not for you, Robert,
  not for you. You are different. All your life you have stood
  apart from others. You have never let the world soil you. To   745
  the world, as to myself, you have been an ideal always. Oh!
  be that ideal still. That great inheritance throw not away – that
  tower of ivory do not destroy. Robert, men can love what is
  beneath them – things unworthy, stained, dishonoured. We
  women worship when we love; and when we lose our worship,   750
  we lose everything. Oh! don't kill my love for you, don't kill
  that!

SIR ROBERT CHILTERN
  Gertrude!

LADY CHILTERN
  I know that there are men with horrible secrets in their lives
  – men who have done some shameful thing, and who in some   755
  critical moment have to pay for it, by doing some other act
  of shame – oh! don't tell me you are such as they are! Robert,
  is there in your life any secret dishonour or disgrace? Tell me,
  tell me at once, that –

733 *what is it that I have loved!* LC and earlier versions have 'What a thing have I loved!',
       recalling perhaps the exclamation of the painter Hallward when he learns the secret
       of Dorian Gray's double life (*DG*, p. 157/*CW*, p. 122): 'Christ! what a thing I must
       have worshipped!'
736 *degradation* MS, HTC and Pbk add 'I know you too well to think that one can't love
       a man for ten years as I have loved you, without knowing him well' (del. from
       Pbk).
738 *What is it then?* F indicates a pause after this.
747–8 *That great ... destroy* like Mrs Arbuthnot and Hester Worsley, Lady C falls at
       moments of crisis into a 'scriptural' mode of speech. F om. this sentence, perhaps
       reflecting stage practice. The final speeches of the scene underwent only minor
       revisions between MS and publication.

SIR ROBERT CHILTERN
    That what?   760

LADY CHILTERN (*Speaking very slowly*)
    That our lives may drift apart.

SIR ROBERT CHILTERN
    Drift apart?

LADY CHILTERN
    That they may be entirely separate. It would be better for us
    both.

SIR ROBERT CHILTERN
    Gertrude, there is nothing in my past life that you might not   765
    know.

LADY CHILTERN
    I was sure of it, Robert, I was sure of it. But why did you say
    those dreadful things, things so unlike your real self? Don't
    let us ever talk about the subject again. You will write, won't
    you, to Mrs Cheveley, and tell her that you cannot support   770
    this scandalous scheme of hers? If you have given her any
    promise you must take it back, that is all!

SIR ROBERT CHILTERN
    Must I write and tell her that?

LADY CHILTERN
    Surely, Robert! What else is there to do?

SIR ROBERT CHILTERN
    I might see her personally. It would be better.   775

LADY CHILTERN
    You must never see her again, Robert. She is not a woman you
    should ever speak to. She is not worthy to talk to a man like
    you. No; you must write to her at once, now, this moment,
    and let your letter show her that your decision is quite
    irrevocable!   780

SIR ROBERT CHILTERN
    Write this moment!

761 *drift apart* in MS, HTC and Pbk she speaks more frankly of 'leaving' him. The
    alterations to Pbk that result in this vaguer threat may be designed to protect Lady
    C from the imputation of a reprehensible public breach with her husband. F, which
    om 11 759 64 ('that . . . us both'), is even less specific.
780 *irrevocable* F cuts to 1. 784 ('She must know'), removing the additional
    prevarication.

LADY CHILTERN
  Yes.

SIR ROBERT CHILTERN
  But it is so late. It is close on twelve.

LADY CHILTERN
  That makes no matter. She must know at once that she has
  been mistaken in you – and that you are not a man to do   785
  anything base or underhand or dishonourable. Write here,
  Robert. Write that you decline to support this scheme of hers,
  as you hold it to be a dishonest scheme. Yes – write the word
  dishonest. She knows what that word means. (SIR ROBERT
  CHILTERN *sits down and writes a letter. His wife takes it up and
  reads it*) Yes; that will do. (*Rings bell*) And now the envelope.   790
  (*He writes the envelope slowly. Enter* MASON) Have this letter
  sent at once to Claridge's Hotel. There is no answer. (*Exit*
  MASON. LADY CHILTERN *kneels down beside her husband and puts
  her arms round him*) Robert, love gives one a sort of instinct
  to things. I feel tonight that I have saved you from something
  that might have been a danger to you, from something that   795
  might have made men honour you less than they do. I don't
  think you realize sufficiently, Robert, that you have brought
  into the political life of our time a nobler atmosphere, a finer
  attitude towards life, a freer air of purer aims and higher ideals
  – I know it, and for that I love you, Robert.   800

SIR ROBERT CHILTERN
  Oh, love me always, Gertrude, love me always!

LADY CHILTERN
  I will love you always, because you will always be worthy of
  love. We needs must love the highest when we see it!
                    Kisses him and rises and goes out
  SIR ROBERT CHILTERN *walks up and down for a moment; then sits
  down and buries his face in his hands. The* SERVANT *enters and
  begins putting out the lights.* SIR ROBERT CHILTERN *looks up*

787–9 *Write that you decline ... means* first appears in C.
799 *a freer ... ideals* om. F.
803 *We needs ... when we see it!* om. F. Cf. the lament of the guilty Queen in Tennyson's
    'Guinevere' (*Idylls of the King*, 1854):
        It was my duty to have loved the highest:
        It surely was my profit had I known:
        It would have been my pleasure had I seen.
        We needs must love the highest when we see it.
        Not Lancelot, nor another.
    In these lines 'the highest' is King Arthur, described earlier in terms not
    inappropriate to Sir Robert Chiltern: he is 'cold,/High, self-contain'd, and
    passionless' and has the 'pure severity of perfect light'.

SIR ROBERT CHILTERN
> Put out the lights, Mason, put out the lights!
>> *The* SERVANT *puts out the lights. The room becomes
>> almost dark. The only light there is comes from the
>> great chandelier that hangs over the staircase and
>> illumines the tapestry of the Triumph of Love*

ACT-DROP

Act II

Scene – Morning-room at SIR ROBERT CHILTERN's *house.*
*LORD GORING, dressed in the height of fashion, is
lounging in an armchair.* SIR ROBERT CHILTERN *is
standing in front of the fireplace. He is evidently
in a state of great mental excitement and distress. As
the scene progresses he paces nervously up and down
the room*

LORD GORING
> My dear Robert, it's a very awkward business, very awkward
> indeed. You should have told your wife the whole thing.
> Secrets from other people's wives are a necessary luxury in
> modern life. So, at least, I am always told at the club by people
> who are bald enough to know better. But no man should have   5
> a secret from his own wife. She invariably finds it out. Women
> have a wonderful instinct about things. They can discover
> everything except the obvious.

SIR ROBERT CHILTERN
> Arthur, I couldn't tell my wife. When could I have told her?
> Not   last   night.   It   would   have   made   a   life-long   10

---

804 *Put out . . . the lights!* perhaps reminiscent of Othello's 'Put out the light, and then put out the light' as he prepares to kill Desdemona (*Othello*, V, ii).

804 s.d. *The only . . . 'Triumph of Love'* first appears in PR. F indicates 'lights down at back'.

1 s.d. the full version of the s.d. first appears in PR: earlier texts simply indicate the location and the discovery of the characters.

4–5 *So . . . know better* first appears in PR. Another play on the notion of 'the tyranny of youth'. In BLTS the preceding sentence is deleted.

6–8 *Women . . . obvious* first appears in MS2.

10–14 *It would have made . . . quite impossible* om. MS1, which has 'She would have left me' and the following exchange:
> LORD GORING
> Left you?
> SIR ROBERT
> Yes.

separation between us, and I would have lost the love of the one woman in the world I worship, of the only woman who has ever stirred love within me. Last night it would have been quite impossible. She would have turned from me in horror ... in horror and in contempt. 15

LORD GORING
Is Lady Chiltern as perfect as all that?

SIR ROBERT CHILTERN
Yes; my wife is as perfect as all that.

LORD GORING (*Taking off his left-hand glove*)
What a pity! I beg your pardon, my dear fellow, I didn't quite mean that. But if what you tell me is true, I should like to have a serious talk about life with Lady Chiltern. 20

SIR ROBERT CHILTERN
It would be quite useless.

LORD GORING
May I try?

SIR ROBERT CHILTERN
Yes; but nothing could make her alter her views.

LORD GORING
Well, at the worst it would simply be a psychological experiment. 25

SIR ROBERT CHILTERN
All such experiments are terribly dangerous.

LORD GORING
Everything is dangerous, my dear fellow. If it wasn't so, life wouldn't be worth living ... Well, I am bound to say that I think you should have told her years ago.

LORD GORING
  Are you serious?
In MS2 the last line is 'Are you serious when you talk of a lifelong separation?' The passage was given an approximation of its present form in the typescript of C. Cf. the similar changes noted at the end of Act I (ll. 761 etc.).
14–15 *She ... contempt* the first part of the sentence first appears in F, following an alteration to BLTS; the second in PR.
16–29 *Is Lady Chiltern ... years ago* om. MS1, MS2. A version of these lines first appears in C.
24–6 *Well, ... dangerous* Wilde added to C a version of the exchange found in F, LC and BLTS: 'It would be quite a psychological experiment – Those experiments don't succeed with women'.
27–8 *Everything ... living* first appears in PR.

SIR ROBERT CHILTERN

When? When we were engaged? Do you think she would have　30
married me if she had known that the origin of my fortune is
such as it is, the basis of my career such as it is, and that I had
done a thing that I suppose most men would call shameful and
dishonourable?

LORD GORING (*Slowly*)

Yes; most men would call it ugly names. There is no doubt　35
of that.

SIR ROBERT CHILTERN (*Bitterly*)

Men who every day do something of the same kind
themselves. Men who, each one of them, have worse secrets
in their own lives.

LORD GORING

That is the reason they are so pleased to find out other people's　40
secrets. It distracts public attention from their own.

SIR ROBERT CHILTERN

And, after all, whom did I wrong by what I did? No one.

LORD GORING (*Looking at him steadily*)

Except yourself, Robert.

SIR ROBERT CHILTERN (*After a pause*)

Of course I had private information about a certain transaction contemplated by the Government of the day, and I acted　45
on it. Private information is practically the source of every
large modern fortune.

LORD GORING (*Tapping his boot with his cane*)

And public scandal invariably the result.

SIR ROBERT CHILTERN (*Pacing up and down the room*)

Arthur, do you think that what I did nearly eighteen years ago
should be brought up against me now? Do you think it fair　50
that a man's whole career should be ruined for a fault done

---

37 *of the same kind* (infinitely worse C, MS2, MS1). The published phrase is added to
　C.
38 *themselves* after this all versions before PR add an interjection by Lord G: 'That is
　why they know about it so well'. Lines 40–1 ('That is . . . their own') were added in
　MS2.
43 s.d. this and most of the other s.d. in this scene first appear in PR. In F there are
　notes for the placing of the characters on stage.
49 *nearly eighteen* (om. F). This fixes the time of the action as early 1893 (the Suez
　transaction took place in November 1875).
50-2 *Do you . . . almost* (om. F).

in one's boyhood almost? I was twenty-two at the time, and
I had the double misfortune of being well-born and poor, two
unforgivable things nowadays. Is it fair that the folly, the sin
of one's youth, if men choose to call it a sin, should wreck a   55
life like mine, should place me in the pillory, should shatter
all that I have worked for, all that I have built up? Is it fair,
Arthur?

LORD GORING
Life is never fair, Robert. And perhaps it is a good thing for
most of us that it is not.   60

SIR ROBERT CHILTERN
Every man of ambition has to fight his century with its own
weapons. What this century worships is wealth. The God of
this century is wealth. To succeed one must have wealth. At
all costs one must have wealth.

LORD GORING
You underrate yourself, Robert. Believe me, without wealth   65
you could have succeeded just as well.

SIR ROBERT CHILTERN
When I was old, perhaps. When I had lost my passion for
power, or could not use it. When I was tired, worn out,
disappointed. I wanted my success when I was young. Youth
is the time for success. I couldn't wait.   70

LORD GORING
Well, you certainly have had your success while you are still
young. No one in our day has had such a brilliant success.
Under-Secretary for Foreign Affairs at the age of forty – that's
good enough for anyone, I should think.

SIR ROBERT CHILTERN
And if it is all taken away from me now? If I lose everything   75
over a horrible scandal? If I am hounded from public life?

LORD GORING
Robert, how could you have sold yourself for money?

52–8 *I was twenty-two . . . Arthur?* first appears in MS2. The omission of Lady M's speech
      (in MS1 of Act I) on Chiltern's background makes this addition useful.
59–60 *And perhaps . . . not* first appears in MS2.
62–4 *The God . . . wealth* first appears in MS2.
67–90 *When I was old . . . the whole thing* first appears in MS2.
73–4 *Under-Secretary . . . I should think* first appears in PR. MS2, BLTS add 'My
      father is always holding you up to me as a model' (del. in C).
75–6 *over a horrible scandal* (om. LC, C, MS1, MS2). Added to BLTS typescript.

SIR ROBERT CHILTERN (*Excitedly*)
I did not sell myself for money. I bought success at a great
price. That is all.

LORD GORING (*Gravely*)
Yes; you certainly paid a great price for it. But what first made   80
you think of doing such a thing?

SIR ROBERT CHILTERN
Baron Arnheim.

LORD GORING
Damned scoundrel!

SIR ROBERT CHILTERN
No; he was a man of a most subtle and refined intellect. A man
of culture, charm, and distinction. One of the most intellec-   85
tual men I ever met.

LORD GORING
Ah! I prefer a gentlemanly fool any day. There is more to be
said for stupidity than people imagine. Personally I have a
great admiration for stupidity. It is a sort of fellow-feeling, I
suppose. But how did he do it? Tell me the whole thing.   90

SIR ROBERT CHILTERN (*Throws himself into an armchair by the
writing-table*)
One night after dinner at Lord Radley's the Baron began
talking about success in modern life as something that one
could reduce to an absolutely definite science. With that
wonderfully fascinating quiet voice of his he expounded to us
the most terrible of all philosophies, the philosophy of power,   95
preached to us the most marvellous of all gospels, the gospel
of gold. I think he saw the effect he had produced on me, for
some days afterwards he wrote and asked me to come and see
him. He was living then in Park Lane, in the house Lord
Woolcomb has now. I remember so well how, with a strange   100
smile on his pale curved lips, he led me through his wonderful
picture gallery, showed me his tapestries, his enamels, his
jewels, his carved ivories, made me wonder at the strange
loveliness of the luxury in which he lived; and then told me
that luxury was nothing but a background, a painted scene in   105
a play, and that power, power over other men, power over the

84–5 *A man of culture, charm and distinction* first appears in PR.
87 *a gentlemanly* first appears in PR (an honest LC etc.). *There . . . I suppose* first appears
    in PR: in C and MS2 the first sentence of the speech is followed by 'I am a little out
    of date.' (del. from C, om. BLTS). F om. the first four sentences of the speech
    altogether.
91–109 *One night after dinner . . . possessed it* see Appendix I.

world was the one thing worth having, the one supreme
pleasure worth knowing, the one joy one never tired of, and
that in our century only the rich possessed it.

LORD GORING (*With great deliberation*)
A thoroughly shallow creed.   110

SIR ROBERT CHILTERN (*Rising*)
I didn't think so then. I don't think so now. Wealth has given
me enormous power. It gave me at the very outset of my life
freedom, and freedom is everything. You have never been
poor, and never known what ambition is. You cannot
understand what a wonderful chance the Baron gave me. Such   115
a chance as few men get.

LORD GORING
Fortunately for them, if one is to judge by results. But tell me
definitely, how did the Baron finally persuade you to – well,
to do what you did?

SIR ROBERT CHILTERN
When I was going away he said to me that if I ever could give   120
him any private information of real value he would make me
a very rich man. I was dazed at the prospect he held out to
me, and my ambition and my desire for power were at that
time boundless. Six weeks later certain private documents
passed through my hands.   125

LORD GORING (*Keeping his eyes steadily fixed on the carpet*)
State documents?

SIR ROBERT CHILTERN
Yes.
LORD GORING *sighs, then passes his hand across his forehead and
looks up*

LORD GORING
I had no idea that you, of all men in the world, could have been
so weak, Robert, as to yield to such a temptation as Baron
Arnheim held out to you.   130

SIR ROBERT CHILTERN
Weak? Oh, I am sick of hearing that phrase. Sick of using it

126–33 *State ... I tell you* LC om. this and the two speeches following, and leads into
l. 133 with 'I know that people always say that to yield to temptation is weak and
shows weakness. I don't think so. I think ... '. The same arrangement is found in
C and BLTS. In F Chiltern's speech at 120–5 ('When ... hands') is followed by 'I
sat down the same afternoon ... ' and ll. 128–38 ('I had no idea ... terrible courage')
are transposed to follow l. 153 ('our prayers'). The final version does not emerge
until PR.

about others. Weak? Do you really think, Arthur, that it is
weakness that yields to temptation? I tell you that there are
terrible temptations that it requires strength, strength and
courage, to yield to. To stake all one's life on a single moment,   135
to risk everything on one throw, whether the stake be power
or pleasure, I care not – there is no weakness in that. There
is a horrible, a terrible courage. I had that courage. I sat down
the same afternoon and wrote Baron Arnheim the letter this
woman now holds. He made three-quarters of a million over   140
the transaction.

LORD GORING
And you?

SIR ROBERT CHILTERN
I received from the Baron £110,000.

LORD GORING
You were worth more, Robert.

SIR ROBERT CHILTERN
No; that money gave me exactly what I wanted, power over   145
others. I went into the House immediately. The Baron
advised me in finance from time to time. Before five years I
had almost trebled my fortune. Since then everything that I
have touched has turned out a success. In all things connected
with money I have had a luck so extraordinary that sometimes   150
it has made me almost afraid. I remember having read
somewhere, in some strange book, that when the gods wish
to punish us they answer our prayers.

140 *three-quarters of a million* 1st ed, PR (a quarter of a million LC etc.).
143 *£110,000* 1st ed., PR (£85,000 LC, BLTS, C; £35,000 MS2; £50,000 MS1). Reviews
    of the first production specify C's profit as £85,000: the omission of the line in F
    suggests that it does not constitute a faithful transcript of the play as performed in
    London.
145–6 *power over others* 1st ed., PR (om. F; freedom of action LC; freedom of action,
    security of position and power over others BLTS, C, MS2). The first two reasons
    are deleted from BLTS.
146 *I went into ... immediately* in LC, BLTS, C and MS2 Chiltern claims 'I went into
    Parliament at once. I made a name there. I held the position I was entitled to'. The
    final four words were deleted from BLTS. In F the amended BLTS version is
    followed ('a' for 'the' in the final sentence) and in PR only the first sentence appears,
    with 'Parliament' changed in manuscript to 'the House'. Here, as in ll. 145–6,
    Chiltern's character is made slightly less unsympathetic and self-assertive by the
    alterations.
147–53 *Before ... prayers* first appears in MS2 (with 'good fortune' for 'luck'). MS1
    reads: 'In two years I had doubled the £50,000. I have security at my bank now for
    a quarter of a million.' The notion of a 'strange book' and its influence turns up
    frequently in Wilde, notably in *Dorian Gray*. Yeats records in *The Trembling of the
    Veil* that Wilde spoke of Pater's *Studies in the History of the Renaissance* as 'My golden
    book, I never travel anywhere without it' (*Autobiographies*, 1955, p. 130).

LORD GORING
But tell me, Robert, did you never suffer any regret for what
you had done?   155

SIR ROBERT CHILTERN
No. I felt that I had fought the century with its own weapons,
and won.

LORD GORING (*Sadly*)
You thought you had won?

SIR ROBERT CHILTERN
I thought so. (*After a long pause*) Arthur, do you despise me
for what I have told you?   160

LORD GORING (*With deep feeling in his voice*)
I am very sorry for you, Robert, very sorry indeed.

SIR ROBERT CHILTERN
I don't say that I suffered any remorse. I didn't. Not remorse
in the ordinary, rather silly sense of the word. But I have paid
conscience money many times. I had a wild hope that I might
disarm destiny. The sum Baron Arnheim gave me I have   165
distributed twice over in public charities since then.

LORD GORING (*Looking up*)
In public charities? Dear me! what a lot of harm you must
have done, Robert!

SIR ROBERT CHILTERN
Oh, don't say that, Arthur; don't talk like that.

LORD GORING
Never mind what I say, Robert. I am always saying what I   170
shouldn't say. In fact, I usually say what I really think. A great
mistake nowadays. It makes one so liable to be misunderstood. As regards this dreadful business, I will help you in
whatever way I can. Of course you know that.

SIR ROBERT CHILTERN
Thank you, Arthur, thank you. But what is to be done? What   175
can be done?

LORD GORING (*Leaning back with his hands in his pockets*)
Well, the English can't stand a man who is always saying he

162–74 *I don't say . . . you know that* first appears in MS2. *Not remorse* first appears in
    PR. The repetition emphasizes a characteristically Wildean refusal to accept an
    'ordinary, rather silly sense' of a word.
177 *Well . . . in* MS2 and C this word is followed by a passage marked for deletion in
    C and not subsequently relocated. Cf. Appendix I.

is in the right, but they are very fond of a man who admits
that he has been in the wrong. It is one of the best things in
them. However, in your case, Robert, a confession would not   180
do. The money, if you will allow me to say so, is . . . awkward.
Besides, if you did make a clean breast of the whole affair, you
would never be able to talk morality again. And in England
a man who can't talk morality twice a week to a large, popular,
immoral audience is quite over as a serious politician. There   185
would be nothing left for him as a profession except Botany
or the Church. A confession would be of no use. It would ruin
you.

SIR ROBERT CHILTERN
It would ruin me. Arthur, the only thing for me to do now
is to fight the thing out.   190

LORD GORING (*Rising from his chair*)
I was waiting for you to say that, Robert. It is the only thing
to do now. And you must begin by telling your wife the whole
story.

SIR ROBERT CHILTERN
That I will not do.

LORD GORING
Robert, believe me, you are wrong.   195

SIR ROBERT CHILTERN
I couldn't do it. It would kill her love for me. And now about
this woman, this Mrs Cheveley. How can I defend myself
against her? You knew her before, Arthur, apparently.

LORD GORING
Yes.

SIR ROBERT CHILTERN
Did you know her well?   200

179–80 *It is . . . in them* first appears in PR.
184–5 *a large, popular, immoral audience* the third adjective first appears in F, where the
second is omitted.
185–7 *There . . . Church* the sentence first appears in MS2, with 'bimetallism' for
'botany', which first appears in an alteration to C and is adopted in LC. On
bimetallism, cf. *Woman*, III, 206.
187–8 *It would ruin you* first appears in MS2.
189 *It would ruin me* first appears in MS2, which omits a line from MS1: 'It would be
of no use and it would rob me of my wife's love. If she thought I was guilty of
something like that she would never forgive me'.
194 *That I will not do* see Appendix I.

LORD GORING (*Arranging his necktie*)
So little that I got engaged to be married to her once, when
I was staying at the Tenbys'. The affair lasted for three days
... nearly.

SIR ROBERT CHILTERN
Why was it broken off?

LORD GORING (*Airily*)
Oh, I forget. At least, it makes no matter. By the way, have   205
you tried her with money? She used to be confoundedly fond
of money.

SIR ROBERT CHILTERN
I offered her any sum she wanted. She refused.

LORD GORING
Then the marvellous gospel of gold breaks down sometimes.
The rich can't do everything, after all.   210

SIR ROBERT CHILTERN
Not everything. I suppose you are right. Arthur, I feel that
public disgrace is in store for me. I feel certain of it. I never
knew what terror was before. I know it now. It is as if a hand
of ice were laid upon one's heart. It is as if one's heart were
beating itself to death in some empty hollow.   215

LORD GORING (*Striking the table*)
Robert, you must fight her. You must fight her.

SIR ROBERT CHILTERN
But how?

LORD GORING
I can't tell you how, at present. I have not the smallest idea.
But everyone has some weak point. There is some flaw in each
one of us. (*Strolls over to the fireplace and looks at himself in the*   220
glass) My father tells me that even I have faults. Perhaps I
have. I don't know.

SIR ROBERT CHILTERN
In defending myself against Mrs Cheveley, I have a right to
use any weapon I can find, have I not?

212–3 *I feel ... I know it now* first appears in alterations to C. The 9 lines following,
from 'It is as if ... ' to 'Perhaps I have' were added to BLTS and appear in F but
are absent in LC. In LC and BLTS Mason arrives with a letter and announces that
Lord Berkshire is waiting for an answer. In MS2 Chiltern has already received the
'curious letter' intimating that Lord Berkshire wishes to tell him about 'a certain
person whom he saw here last night of whose character he feels sure that my wife
and I know nothing.'
221–2 *Perhaps I have* added in manuscript to PR.

LORD GORING (*Still looking in the glass*)

In your place I don't think I should have the smallest scruple   225
in doing so. She is thoroughly well able to take care of
herself.

SIR ROBERT CHILTERN (*Sits down at the table and takes a pen in his
hand*)

Well, I shall send a cipher telegram to the Embassy at Vienna,
to inquire if there is anything known against her. There may
be some secret scandal she might be afraid of.   230

LORD GORING (*Settling his buttonhole*)

Oh, I should fancy Mrs Cheveley is one of those very modern
women of our time who find a new scandal as becoming as a
new bonnet, and air them both in the Park every afternoon
at five-thirty. I am sure she adores scandals, and that the
sorrow of her life at present is that she can't manage to have   235
enough of them.

SIR ROBERT CHILTERN (*Writing*)

Why do you say that?

LORD GORING (*Turning round*)

Well, she wore far too much rouge last night, and not quite
enough clothes. That is always a sign of despair in a
woman.   240

SIR ROBERT CHILTERN (*Striking a bell*)

But it is worth while my wiring to Vienna, is it not?

LORD GORING

It is always worth while asking a question, though it is not

---

225 *in your place* F reads: 'In the case of a woman who dyes her hair, sex is a challenge,
    not a defence. Personally I admire women who dye their hair. They look so well
    at a distance'. This is followed by 'I don't think she should have . . . ' (l. 225).
226 *in doing so* MS2, C add 'she is a bad lot, and clever as they make them, too' (del.
    in C).
228–30 *Well . . . afraid of* first appears, in substance, in F: see note to ll.212–3, above.
231 *very modern* (astounding C, MS2) changed in revision of C.
238 *Well, she wore . . .* (She is not as handsome as she used to be, but she wore . . . C,
    MS2). The beginning of the speech was changed in a manuscript alteration to C.
241 *wiring to Vienna* LC and earlier versions have 'seeing Lord Berkshire'.
242–3 *It is always . . . answering one* first appears in a slightly different form in F,
    following MS revision to BLTS. At this point LC, BLTS and revised state of C have
    the following:
        LORD GORING
            Certainly, show me his letter.
        SIR ROBERT
            Here! (*Hands letter.*)

always worth while answering one.
Enter MASON

SIR ROBERT CHILTERN
Is Mr Trafford in his room?

MASON
Yes, Sir Robert.   245

SIR ROBERT CHILTERN (*Puts what he has written into an envelope,
which he then carefully closes*)
Tell him to have this sent off in cipher at once. There must
not be a moment's delay.

MASON
Yes, Sir Robert.

SIR ROBERT CHILTERN
Oh! just give that back to me again.
Writes something on the envelope. MASON *then
goes out with the letter*

SIR ROBERT CHILTERN
She must have had some curious hold over Baron Arnheim.   250
I wonder what it was.

LORD GORING (*Smiling*)
I wonder.

SIR ROBERT CHILTERN
I will fight her to the death, as long as my wife knows
nothing.

LORD GORING (*Strongly*)
Oh, fight in any case – in any case.   255

SIR ROBERT CHILTERN (*With a gesture of despair*)
If my wife found out, there would be little left to fight for.
Well, as soon as I hear from Vienna, I shall let you know the
result. It is a chance, just a chance, but I believe in it. And

LORD GORING
It certainly is a very curious communication. (*Hands back letter.*)
They then proceed with l. 253 ('I will fight her to the death'). In F l. 243 is followed
by l. 274 ('Good afternoon, Lord Goring') and then l. 318 ('You are not going,
Robert?'). The sequence as printed first appears in PR.
257–73 *Well, as soon as . . . my wife's voice* om. MS1. These lines first appear in MS2.
In PR the references to telegraphing Vienna replace allusions to Lord Berkshire's
communication; ll. 266–9 ('I should not fancy . . . presence of mind') first appear
in PR. In LC and earlier versions 'a slightly décolleté one' reads 'one from Paris':
the notion of a low-cut reputation seems to have come to Wilde as he prepared copy
for Smithers' printer.

as I fought the age with its own weapons, I will fight her with
her weapons. It is only fair, and she looks like a woman with   260
a past, doesn't she?

LORD GORING
Most pretty women do. But there is a fashion in pasts just as
there is a fashion in frocks. Perhaps Mrs Cheveley's past is
merely a slightly *décolleté* one, and they are excessively
popular nowadays. Besides, my dear Robert, I should not   265
build too high hopes on frightening Mrs Cheveley. I should
not fancy Mrs Cheveley is a woman who would be easily
frightened. She has survived all her creditors, and she shows
wonderful presence of mind.

SIR ROBERT CHILTERN
Oh! I live on hopes now. I clutch at every chance. I feel like   270
a man on a ship that is sinking. The water is round my feet,
and the very air is bitter with storm. Hush! I hear my wife's
voice.
                Enter LADY CHILTERN *in walking dress*

LADY CHILTERN
Good afternoon, Lord Goring!

LORD GORING
Good afternoon, Lady Chiltern! Have you been in the   275
Park?

LADY CHILTERN
No: I have just come from the Woman's Liberal Association,
where, by the way, Robert, your name was received with loud
applause, and now I have come in to have my tea. (*To* LORD
GORING) You will wait and have some tea, won't you?   280

LORD GORING
I'll wait for a short time, thanks.

LADY CHILTERN
I will be back in a moment. I am only going to take my hat
off.

271–2 *The water . . . Hush!* (Stop! LC, BLTS, C, MS2). The elaboration first appears
      in PR.
277–9 *No . . . and now* (Yes, and LC etc.). The *Woman's Liberal Association* (now
      Women's Liberal Federation) founded in 1886; opposed Gladstone in 1892 by
      supporting the campaign for women's suffrage.
282–3 *I am only going . . . off* LC and earlier versions omit this and the following six
      speeches. MS1 continues with l, 318 ('Are you going, Robert?'); MS2 with ll.317–9
      ('Thanks . . . Robert'), 296–8 ('You . . . me') and a version of 304–7 ('Ah! I get rid
      of it as soon as possible. Bad habit, by the way. Makes one very unpopular. But it
      keeps one in good condition'). A number of other transpositions and alterations are
      made in C and BLTS.

LORD GORING (*In his most earnest manner*)
>Oh! please don't. It is so pretty. One of the prettiest hats I ever
>saw. I hope the Woman's Liberal Association received it with   285
>loud applause.

LADY CHILTERN (*With a smile*)
>We have much more important work to do than to look at each
>other's bonnets, Lord Goring.

LORD GORING
>Really? What sort of work?

LADY CHILTERN
>Oh! dull, useful, delightful things, Factory Acts, Female   290
>Inspectors, the Eight Hours' Bill, the Parliamentary Fran-
>chise. . . . Everything, in fact, that you would find thoroughly
>uninteresting.

LORD GORING
>And never bonnets?

LADY CHILTERN (*With mock indignation*)
>Never bonnets, never!   295
>LADY CHILTERN *goes out through the door leading to her boudoir*

SIR ROBERT CHILTERN (*Takes* LORD GORING'S *hand*)
>You have been a good friend to me, Arthur, a thoroughly good
>friend.

LORD GORING
>I don't know that I have been able to do much for you, Robert,
>as yet. In fact, I have not been able to do anything for you,
>as far as I can see. I am thoroughly disappointed with   300
>myself.

SIR ROBERT CHILTERN
>You have enabled me to tell you the truth. That is something.
>The truth has always stifled me.

LORD GORING
>Ah! the truth is a thing I get rid of as soon as possible! Bad

290 *dull, useful, delightful things* the list includes matters on which the Liberal party had
    pledged itself to introduce legislation in its 1892 election manifesto (the 'Newcastle
    Programme'): the limiting of working hours, the introduction of female inspectors
    to monitor the application of the Factory Acts, and the reform of the franchise.
296–7 *a thoroughly good friend* first appears in PR, together with the s.d. at the beginning
    of the speech.
298–316 *I don't know . . . Curzon Street* much expanded in PR from the shorter versions
    of the scene in F, LC etc. The most notable addition is in ll. 308–9: 'to live the truth.
    Ah! that is the great thing in life, to live the truth'. *Curzon Street,* a respectable
    Mayfair address, is also Mrs Erlynne's home in *LWF.*

habit, by the way. Makes one very unpopular at the club ...   305
with the older members. They call it being conceited. Perhaps
it is.

SIR ROBERT CHILTERN

I would to God that I had been able to tell the truth ... to live
the truth. Ah! that is the great thing in life, to live the truth.   310
(*Sighs, and goes towards the door*) I'll see you soon again,
Arthur, shan't I?

LORD GORING

Certainly. Whenever you like. I'm going to look in at the
Bachelors' Ball tonight, unless I find something better to do.
But I'll come round tomorrow morning. If you should want
me tonight by any chance, send round a note to Curzon   315
Street.

SIR ROBERT CHILTERN

Thank you.
As he reaches the door, LADY CHILTERN *enters from her boudoir*

LADY CHILTERN

You are not going, Robert?

SIR ROBERT CHILTERN

I have some letters to write, dear.

LADY CHILTERN (*Going to him*)

You work too hard, Robert. You seem never to think of   320
yourself, and you are looking so tired.

SIR ROBERT CHILTERN

It is nothing, dear, nothing.

He kisses her and goes out

LADY CHILTERN (*To* LORD GORING)

Do sit down. I am so glad you have called. I want to talk to
you about ... well, not about bonnets, or the Woman's
Liberal Association. You take far too much interest in the first   325
subject, and not nearly enough in the second.

---

313 *The Bachelors' Ball* the London 'season' included 'private' dances, given by the
parents of marriageable girls, and 'public' festivities, organized by associations of
like-minded acquaintances: the Bachelors' Ball was among the latter.
318 *You ... Robert?* F and MS1 resume at this point (see note to ll. 282–3, above).
323–6 *I want ... second* first appears in PR. In F, C, MS2 and MS1 the introduction
is different: 'Do sit down. I am so glad to have an opportunity of a moment's talk
in private'. This is deleted from C and does not appear in BLTS or LC. The revisions
to BLTS include the addition of s.d., which may reflect its being used during
rehearsals.

LORD GORING
You want to talk to me about Mrs Cheveley?

LADY CHILTERN
Yes. You have guessed it. After you left last night I found out
that what she had said was really true. Of course I made
Robert write her a letter at once, withdrawing his promise.   330

LORD GORING
So he gave me to understand.

LADY CHILTERN
To have kept it would have been the first stain on a career that
has been stainless always. Robert must be above reproach. He
is not like other men. He cannot afford to do what other men
do. (*She looks at* LORD GORING, *who remains silent*) Don't you   335
agree with me? You are Robert's greatest friend. You are our
greatest friend, Lord Goring. No one, except myself, knows
Robert better than you do. He has no secrets from me, and
I don't think he has any from you.

LORD GORING
He certainly has no secrets from me. At least I don't think   340
so.

LADY CHILTERN
Then am I not right in my estimate of him? I know I am right.
But speak to me frankly.

LORD GORING (*Looking straight at her*)
Quite frankly?

LADY CHILTERN
Surely. You have nothing to conceal, have you?   345

LORD GORING
Nothing. But, my dear Lady Chiltern, I think, if you will
allow me to say so, that in practical life –

LADY CHILTERN (*Smiling*)
Of which you know so little, Lord Goring –

LORD GORING
Of which I know nothing by experience, though I know
something by observation. I think that in practical life there   350
is something about success, actual success, that is a little
unscrupulous, something about ambition that is unscrupulous always. Once a man has set his heart and soul on getting
to a certain point, if he has to climb the crag, he climbs the

328 *You have guessed it* first appears in PR.

crag; if he has to walk in the mire –   355

LADY CHILTERN
  Well?

LORD GORING
  He walks in the mire. Of course I am only talking generally
  about life.

LADY CHILTERN (*Gravely*)
  I hope so. Why do you look at me so strangely, Lord
  Goring?   360

LORD GORING
  Lady Chiltern, I have sometimes thought that . . . perhaps you
  are a little hard in some of your views on life. I think that . . .
  often you don't make sufficient allowances. In every nature
  there are elements of weakness, or worse than weakness.
  Supposing, for instance, that – that any public man, my   365
  father, or Lord Merton, or Robert, say, had, years ago,
  written some foolish letter to some one . . .

LADY CHILTERN
  What do you mean by a foolish letter?

LORD GORING
  A letter gravely compromising one's position. I am only
  putting an imaginary case.   370

LADY CHILTERN
  Robert is as incapable of doing a foolish thing as he is of doing
  a wrong thing.

LORD GORING (*After a long pause*)
  Nobody is incapable of doing a foolish thing. Nobody is
  incapable of doing a wrong thing.

LADY CHILTERN
  Are you a Pessimist? What will the other dandies say? They   375

361–7 *Lady Chiltern . . . to some one* in MS1 this is blunter: 'Lady Chiltern, supposing
  that Robert had, years ago . . . '. Later revisions make it less downright, and the
  full array of qualifying phrases ('sometimes . . . perhaps . . . a little . . . some') does
  not appear until PR.
375–6 *Are you a pessimist? . . . mourning* in F this line and the reply are as follows:
          LADY CHILTERN
            Surely you are not going to join the Pessimists?
          LORD GORING
            Oh, no. I can't stand the Pessimists. I don't like the way they wear their
            hair.
  This joke (which develops an idea in MS revisions to BLTS) was reported in *The
  Times'* review of the first performance. In MS1 the speech is 'You teach as a pessimist

will all have to go into mourning.

LORD GORING (*Rising*)
No, Lady Chiltern, I am not a Pessimist. Indeed I am not sure
that I quite know what Pessimism really means. All I do know
is that life cannot be understood without much charity, cannot
be lived without much charity. It is love, and not German   380
philosophy, that is the true explanation of this world,
whatever may be the explanation of the next. And if you are
ever in trouble, Lady Chiltern, trust me absolutely, and I will
help you in every way I can. If you ever want me, come to me
for my assistance, and you shall have it. Come at once to   385
me.

LADY CHILTERN (*Looking at him in surprise*)
Lord Goring, you are talking quite seriously. I don't think I
ever heard you talk seriously.before.

LORD GORING (*Laughing*)
You must excuse me, Lady Chiltern. It won't occur again, if
I can help it.   390

LADY CHILTERN
But I like you to be serious.
      Enter MABEL CHILTERN, *in the most ravishing frock*

MABEL CHILTERN
Dear Gertrude, don't say such a dreadful thing to Lord
Goring. Seriousness would be very unbecoming to him. Good
afternoon, Lord Goring! Pray be as trivial as you can.

LORD GORING
I should like to, Miss Mabel, but I am afraid I am . . . a little   395
out of practice this morning; and besides, I have to be going
now.

MABEL CHILTERN
Just when I have come in! What dreadful manners you have!
I am sure you were very badly brought up.

LORD GORING
I was.   400

today; that is not like you' which was carried (with 'talk' for 'teach') into MS2, C,
BLTS and LC. In MS1 this is followed by two blank leaves and a note indicating
an entrance for Mabel (the manuscript picks up again at l. 495). A number of details
in Lord G's reply first appear in PR: 'I am not sure . . . means' (377–8); 'Cannot
be lived . . . charity' (379–80) and 'German' (380). LC and BLTS read 'as well as
the next' at l. 382. On *Pessimism*, cf. I, 133, above.
391 s.d. *Enter* . . . *frock* first appears in PR, developing the simple s.d. in earlier texts.
For a description of the 'frock', see Appendix II.

MABEL CHILTERN
I wish I had brought you up!

LORD GORING
I am so sorry you didn't.

MABEL CHILTERN
It is too late now, I suppose?

LORD GORING (*Smiling*)
I am not so sure.

MABEL CHILTERN
Will you ride tomorrow morning?   405

LORD GORING
Yes, at ten.

MABEL CHILTERN
Don't forget.

LORD GORING
Of course I shan't. By the way, Lady Chiltern, there is no list
of your guests in *The Morning Post* of today. It has apparently
been crowded out by the County Council, or the Lambeth   410
Conference, or something equally boring. Could you let me
have a list? I have a particular reason for asking you.

LADY CHILTERN
I am sure Mr Trafford will be able to give you one.

LORD GORING
Thanks, so much.

MABEL CHILTERN
Tommy is the most useful person in London.   415

LORD GORING (*Turning to her*)
And who is the most ornamental?

408–18 *By the way . . . to guess it* the sequence does not appear before F, and the sentence
referring to the County Council and the Lambeth Conference first appears in PR.
The Morning Post was a leading society newspaper, especially noted for its
'fashionable intelligence': 'It was not only serviceable in the way of extending the
circulation . . . in aristocratic and fashionable circles, but "during the season" it
brought in a large amount of money in the shape of payments for the paragraphs
sent to its columns giving a list of the names of those that were present at dinner
parties, evening parties, or by whatever other name these gatherings of the West
End society were brought together' (James Grant, *The Newspaper Press: Its Origin,
Progress – and Present Position*, 1871). The *London County Council* was formed in
1889 to gather together the functions of local government in the Capital previously
discharged by parish 'vestries'. The *Lambeth Conference* of Anglican bishops is held
annually at Lambeth Palace, London residence of the Archbishop of Canterbury.

MABEL CHILTERN (*Triumphantly*)
I am.

LORD GORING
How clever of you to guess it! (*Takes up his hat and cane*)
Good-bye, Lady Chiltern! You will remember what I said to
you, won't you?   420

LADY CHILTERN
Yes; but I don't know why you said it to me.

LORD GORING
I hardly know myself. Good-bye, Miss Mabel!

MABEL CHILTERN (*With a little moue of disappointment*)
I wish you were not going. I have had four wonderful
adventures this morning; four and a half, in fact. You might
stop and listen to some of them.   425

LORD GORING
How very selfish of you to have four and a half! There won't
be any left for me.

MABEL CHILTERN
I don't want you to have any. They would not be good for
you.

LORD GORING
That is the first unkind thing you have ever said to me. How   430
charmingly you said it! Ten tomorrow.

MABEL CHILTERN
Sharp.

LORD GORING
Quite sharp. But don't bring Mr Trafford.

MABEL CHILTERN (*With a little toss of the head*)
Of course I shan't bring Tommy Trafford. Tommy Trafford
is in great disgrace.   435

LORD GORING
I am delighted to hear it.

                                        Bows and goes out

---

423 *four* F and earlier versions read 'seven' and om. 'four-and-a-half' in the line
    following; *wonderful* is added in manuscript to C.
428–9 *They would not be good for you* F indicates '*bus. with hand*', but does not specify
    its nature. As Lord G is taking his leave of her, it would be natural for him to shake
    hands with Mabel: she may detain him by not releasing his hand.
431 *ten* versions before PR read 'half-past ten'.

MABEL CHILTERN

Gertrude, I wish you would speak to Tommy Trafford.

LADY CHILTERN

What has poor Mr Trafford done this time? Robert says he
is the best secretary he has ever had.

MABEL CHILTERN

Well, Tommy has proposed to me again. Tommy really does   440
nothing but propose to me. He proposed to me last night in
the music-room, when I was quite unprotected, as there was
an elaborate trio going on. I didn't dare to make the smallest
repartee, I need hardly tell you. If I had, it would have
stopped the music at once. Musical people are so absurdly   445
unreasonable. They always want one to be perfectly dumb at
the very moment when one is longing to be absolutely deaf.
Then he proposed to me in broad daylight this morning, in
front of that dreadful statue of Achilles. Really, the things that
go on in front of that work of art are quite appalling. The   450
police should interfere. At luncheon I saw by the glare in his
eye that he was going to propose again, and I just managed
to check him in time by assuring him that I was a bimetallist.
Fortunately I don't know what bimetallism means. And I
don't believe anybody else does either. But the observation   455
crushed Tommy for ten minutes. He looked quite shocked.
And then Tommy is so annoying in the way he proposes. If
he proposed at the top of his voice, I should not mind so much.
That might produce some effect on the public. But he does
it in a horrid confidential way. When Tommy wants to be   460
romantic he talks to one just like a doctor. I am very fond of
Tommy, but his methods of proposing are quite out of date.

438–9 *Robert ... had* first appears in BLTS: om. in LC. In view of the comic light in
    which he appears in the next speech, Wilde may have wished to establish Trafford's
    suitability for the trust placed in him by Sir Robert C.
440–66 *Well, Tommy ... some attention* this speech (which might be compared with the
    'proposal' in Act I of *Earnest*) was revised considerably after its introduction in MS2.
    The 'elaborate trio' is a duet in MS2; 'bimetallist' and 'bimetallism' are revised from
    'socialist' and 'socialism' in manuscript alterations to C, where 'public' is substituted
    for 'people who heard him'. In LC and earlier versions 'quite out of date' is replaced
    by 'disgraceful'. In F (only) Mabel had checked Tommy by assuring him that she
    thought 'the first duty of woman was to look pretty, and that what the second duty
    was, no-one had yet discovered' (cf. 'Phrases and Philosophies for the Use of the
    Young': 'The first duty in life is to be as artificial as possible. What the second duty
    is no one has yet discovered' – *CW*, p. 1205). At this he 'looked so pleased' that she
    'felt sure he must be shocked'. The naked, heroic statue of *Achilles* in Hyde Park
    was erected in 1822, inscribed by 'the women of England' to the Duke of Wellington
    'and his brave companions in Arms'. On *bimetallism*, cf. *Woman*, III, 206. F has an s.d.
    '(*on arm of sofa*)' after the last word of the speech: in BLTS '(*sits on arm of Lady C's
    chair*)' is added to 'I know, dear' at l. 473.

I wish, Gertrude, you would speak to him, and tell him that
once a week is quite often enough to propose to anyone, and
that it should always be done in a manner that attracts some   465
attention.

LADY CHILTERN
Dear Mabel, don't talk like that. Besides, Robert thinks very
highly of Mr Trafford. He believes he has a brilliant future
before him.

MABEL CHILTERN
Oh! I wouldn't marry a man with a future before him for   470
anything under the sun.

LADY CHILTERN
Mabel!

MABEL CHILTERN
I know, dear. You married a man with a future, didn't you?
But then Robert was a genius, and you have a noble,
self-sacrificing character. You can stand geniuses. I have no   475
character at all, and Robert is the only genius I could ever
bear. As a rule, I think they are quite impossible. Geniuses
talk so much, don't they? Such a bad habit! And they are
always thinking about themselves, when I want them to be
thinking about me. I must go round now and rehearse at Lady   480
Basildon's. You remember we are having *tableaux*, don't you?
The Triumph of something, I don't know what! I hope it will
be triumph of me. Only triumph I am really interested in at
present. (*Kisses* LADY CHILTERN *and goes out; then comes
running back*) Oh, Gertrude, do you know who is coming to   485
see you? That dreadful Mrs Cheveley, in a most lovely gown.
Did you ask her?

---

475 *self-sacrificing* first appears in PR. *geniuses* a favourite term with Wilde, especially
when applied to himself. Chiltern is, like his creator, a brilliant man whose qualities
isolate him and make him prey to envious scandal, likely to be idolised and destroyed
by the public.

481 tableaux *tableaux vivants*, in which performers (usually amateur) gave a costumed
representation of some familiar painting or historical scene, were a popular pastime
and were often staged for charitable fund-raising events. Mabel's interest in
self-display is comically indecorous. Cf. Mrs Eliza Lynn Linton's denunciation of
the 'Wild Women' whose 'advanced' behaviour seemed to threaten society.
According to her, the 'Wild Woman' appears on the public stage 'and executes
dances which one would not like one's daughter to see, still less perform. She herself
knows no shame in showing her skill – and her legs' (*Nineteenth Century*, October
1891).

486 *That dreadful . . . gown* the last five words first appear in PR; *dreadful* is omitted in
LC, and the whole sentence in F.

LADY CHILTERN (*Rising*)
Mrs Cheveley! Coming to see me? Impossible!

MABEL CHILTERN
I assure you she is coming upstairs, as large as life and not
nearly so natural.   490

LADY CHILTERN
You need not wait, Mabel. Remember, Lady Basildon is
expecting you.

MABEL CHILTERN
Oh! I must shake hands with Lady Markby. She is delightful.
I love being scolded by her.
                           Enter MASON

MASON
Lady Markby. Mrs Cheveley.   495
            Enter LADY MARKBY *and* MRS CHEVELEY

LADY CHILTERN (*Advancing to meet them*)
Dear Lady Markby, how nice of you to come and see me!
(*Shakes hands with her, and bows somewhat distantly to* MRS
CHEVELEY) Won't you sit down, Mrs Cheveley?

MRS CHEVELEY
Thanks. Isn't that Miss Chiltern? I should like so much to
know her.

LADY CHILTERN
Mabel, Mrs Cheveley wishes to know you.   500
                    MABEL CHILTERN *gives a little nod*

MRS CHEVELEY (*Sitting down*)
I thought your frock so charming last night, Miss Chiltern.
So simple and ... suitable.

MABEL CHILTERN
Really? I must tell my dressmaker. It will be such a surprise
to her. Good-bye, Lady Markby!

---

488 *Coming? ... me* in LC and earlier versions her reaction is 'Impossible! No! I am glad
she has come. I shall be able to tell her what I think of her, and prevent her ever
entering my house again.' (C adds 'now' after 'tell her'.) Before PR the entry of the
new guests is followed by a shorter exchange between Mabel and Lady M:
      LADY MARKBY
          Good afternoon, Mabel.
      MABEL
          Good afternoon, Lady Markby. I am just off ...
MS1 moves from the entrance to 1. 527.

LADY MARKBY
  Going already?   505

MABEL CHILTERN
  I am so sorry but I am obliged to. I am just off to rehearsal.
  I have got to stand on my head in some *tableaux*.

LADY MARKBY
  On your head, child? Oh! I hope not. I believe it is most
  unhealthy.
                    Takes a seat on the sofa next LADY CHILTERN

MABEL CHILTERN
  But it is for an excellent charity: in aid of the Undeserving,   510
  the only people I am really interested in. I am the secretary,
  and Tommy Trafford is treasurer.

MRS CHEVELEY
  And what is Lord Goring?

MABEL CHILTERN
  Oh! Lord Goring is president.

MRS CHEVELEY
  The post should suit him admirably, unless he has deterior-   515
  ated since I knew him first.

LADY MARKBY (*Reflecting*)
  You are remarkably modern, Mabel. A little too modern,
  perhaps. Nothing is so dangerous as being too modern. One
  is apt to grow old-fashioned quite suddenly. I have known
  many instances of it.   520

MABEL CHILTERN
  What a dreadful prospect!

LADY MARKBY
  Ah! my dear, you need not be nervous. You will always be as
  pretty as possible. That is the best fashion there is, and the
  only fashion that England succeeds in setting.

510 *the Undeserving* in F the charity is 'the Grosvenor Square Mission' and its object 'to
     try and bring a little happiness into the homes of the Upper Classes'. Cf. Canon
     Chasuble's sermon on the Manna in the Wilderness, preached as a charity sermon
     for 'the Society for the Prevention of Discontent among the Upper Orders' (*Earnest*,
     II, 249-50). The distinction between the 'deserving' and 'undeserving' poor was
     important in Victorian philanthropy.
511–6 *I am the secretary ... first* first appears in PR.
518–20 *Nothing ... instances of it* (Nothing ages one so rapidly as being too modern F,
     LC, BLTS, C, MS2).
521 *What a dreadful prospect ... and myself* first appears in PR.

MABEL CHILTERN (*With a curtsey*)
Thank you so much, Lady Markby, for England ... and   525
myself.   *Goes out*

LADY MARKBY (*Turning to* LADY CHILTERN)
Dear Gertrude, we just called to know if Mrs Cheveley's
diamond brooch has been found.

LADY CHILTERN
Here?

MRS CHEVELEY
Yes. I missed it when I got back to Claridge's, and I thought   530
I might possibly have dropped it here.

LADY CHILTERN
I have heard nothing about it. But I will send for the butler
and ask.   *Touches the bell*

MRS CHEVELEY
Oh, pray don't trouble, Lady Chiltern. I daresay I lost it at
the Opera, before we came on here.   535

LADY MARKBY
Ah yes, I suppose it must have been at the Opera. The fact
is, we all scramble and jostle so much nowadays that I wonder
we have anything at all left on us at the end of an evening. I
know myself that, when I am coming back from the Drawing
Room, I always feel as if I hadn't a shred on me, except a small   540
shred of decent reputation, just enough to prevent the lower
classes making painful observations through the windows of
the carriage. The fact is that our Society is terribly overpopu-
lated. Really, some one should arrange a proper scheme of
assisted emigration. It would do a great deal of good.   545

528 *brooch* first appears in F: LC and earlier texts read 'star' throughout.
538–45 *I know myself ... of good* om. MS1, which follows 'evening' with ll. 532–5 ('But
    I will send ... came on here') and l. 553 ('What sort of a star ... '). The passage
    first appears in MS2, where Lady M's shred of reputation is, she says, 'just enough
    to cover me and prevent the lower classes making painful observations'. In
    manuscript revisions to C 'cover me and' is deleted and 'through the windows of
    the carriage' added.
539–40 *the Drawing Room* the formal presentation of ladies to the Queen and her court
    took place at a 'Drawing-Room'; 'Her Majesty is graciously accessible to all persons
    of rank and title, provided they bear a good character in society ... ' (*Etiquette of
    Good Society*, p. 204). Lady M would have been 'presenting' *débutantes* to the
    court.
544–5 *assisted emigration* frequently advocated as a radical means of reforming the
    'criminal classes' and practised by a number of charitable organizations as an aid to
    the respectable as well as the 'fallen'. (Cf. *Woman*, III, 245.) Such schemes were not
    usually proposed as a way of improving fashionable society in Lady M's sense of the

MRS CHEVELEY
I quite agree with you, Lady Markby. It is nearly six years since I have been in London for the season, and I must say Society has become dreadfully mixed. One sees the oddest people everywhere.

LADY MARKBY
That is quite true, dear. But one needn't know them. I'm sure   550
I don't know half the people who come to my house. Indeed, from all I hear, I shouldn't like to.
                    Enter MASON

LADY CHILTERN
What sort of a brooch was it that you lost, Mrs Cheveley?

MRS CHEVELEY
A diamond snake-brooch with a ruby, a rather large ruby.

LADY MARKBY
I thought you said there was a sapphire on the head, dear?   555

MRS CHEVELEY (*Smiling*)
No, Lady Markby – a ruby.

LADY MARKBY (*Nodding her head*)
And very becoming, I am quite sure.

LADY CHILTERN
Has a ruby and diamond brooch been found in any of the rooms this morning, Mason?

MASON
No, my lady.   560

MRS CHEVELEY
It really is of no consequence, Lady Chiltern. I am so sorry to have put you to any inconvenience.

---

word. F follows l. 545 with a variation on the *overdressed/educated* joke (cf. note to I, 174) and Mrs C observes: 'The overdressed should certainly be sent to the colonies, there is great demand for them there. The over-educated should certainly be kept in London, they are very much wanted.' Wilde is taking up material deleted from *Woman*, where the contrast between clothing (and nakedness) and civilization is used. It should be noted that dress for a 'Drawing Room' was especially elaborate, including a long, broad train attached to the costume and a head-dress of feathers, lace or tulle.

554 *A diamond snake-brooch with a ruby* first appears in PR. F has 'a diamond snake brooch with ruby eyes' and earlier versions specify 'a rather large eight-pointed star'. Wilde corrected the BLTS typescript to 'brooch' in some lines, but did not carry this revision through systematically. In earlier versions the jewel served only as a pretext for Mrs C's visit to Lady C.

LADY CHILTERN (*Coldly*)
Oh, it has been no inconvenience. That will do, Mason. You
can bring tea.

Exit MASON

LADY MARKBY
Well, I must say it is most annoying to lose anything. I   565
remember once at Bath, years ago, losing in the Pump Room
an exceedingly handsome cameo bracelet that Sir John had
given me. I don't think he has ever given me anything since,
I am sorry to say. He has sadly degenerated. Really, this
horrid House of Commons quite ruins our husbands for us.   570
I think the Lower House by far the greatest blow to a happy
married life that there has been since that terrible thing called
the Higher Education of Women was invented.

LADY CHILTERN
Ah! it is heresy to say that in this house, Lady Markby. Robert
is a great champion of the Higher Education of Women, and   575
so, I am afraid, am I.

MRS CHEVELEY
The higher education of men is what I should like to see. Men
need it so sadly.

LADY MARKBY
They do, dear. But I am afraid such a scheme would be quite
unpractical. I don't think man has much capacity for   580
development. He has got as far as he can, and that is not far,
is it? With regard to women, well, dear Gertrude, you belong
to the younger generation, and I am sure it is all right if you
approve of it. In my time, of course, we were taught not to
understand anything. That was the old system, and wonder-   585
fully interesting it was. I assure you that the amount of things
I and my poor dear sister were taught not to understand was
quite extraordinary. But modern women understand everything, I am told.

563–4 *You can bring tea* added in MS2. In F tea has already been served, and the
   directions differ accordingly.
566 *the Pump Room* associated with the spa's social life as much as its medicinal
   purposes.
569 *I am sorry to say* first appears in PR.
573 *the Higher Education of Women* the appropriateness of university studies for women
   was still a matter of dispute, although the establishment of women's colleges in
   Oxford and Cambridge and the more enlightened policy of London University had
   advanced the cause.
581–2 *and that is not far, is it?* om. LC, BLTS; del. from C but restored in F ('and that
   is not very far, is it?').
585–6 *and wonderfully interesting it was* first appears in PR.

MRS CHEVELEY

Except their husbands. That is the one thing the modern   590
woman never understands.

LADY MARKBY

And a very good thing too, dear, I daresay. It might break up
many a happy home if they did. Not yours, I need hardly say,
Gertrude. You have married a pattern husband. I wish I could
say as much for myself. But since Sir John has taken to   595
attending the debates regularly, which he never used to do in
the good old days, his language has become quite impossible.
He always seems to think that he is addressing the House, and
consequently whenever he discusses the state of the agricul-
tural labourer, or the Welsh Church, or something quite   600
improper of that kind, I am obliged to send all the servants
out of the room. It is not pleasant to see one's own butler, who
has been with one for twenty-three years, actually blushing at
the sideboard, and the footmen making contortions in corners
like persons in circuses. I assure you my life will be quite   605
ruined unless they send John at once to the Upper House. He
won't take any interest in politics then, will he? The House
of Lords is so sensible. An assembly of gentlemen. But in his
present state, Sir John is really a great trial. Why, this
morning before breakfast was half over, he stood up on the   610
hearthrug, put his hands in his pockets, and appealed to the
country at the top of his voice. I left the table as soon as I had
my second cup of tea, I need hardly say. But his violent
language could be heard all over the house! I trust, Gertrude,
that Sir Robert is not like that?   615

LADY CHILTERN

But I am very much interested in politics, Lady Markby. I
love to hear Robert talk about them.

592–615 *And a very good thing . . . like that?* a version of this occurs in MS1 at the
equivalent of I, 98. In F, LC and C 'all over the house' is followed by 'my maid told
me afterwards'. *The Welsh Church* was the object of a controversial measure
proposed by Gladstone, who wished to disestablish the Anglican Church in Wales.
In revisions to C Wilde substituted 'improper' for the typescript's 'uninteresting'.
In BLTS he added (but later deleted) another sentence, to follow 'an assembly of
gentlemen':
  Besides, John has never done anything useful in his life. So his place is with his
  peers.
In the 1880s and 1890s the Liberals considered a call for the abolition of the upper
chamber, provoked by the Lords' blocking the Home Rule bill and other items of
radical legislation.

LADY MARKBY
Well, I hope he is not as devoted to Blue Books as Sir John
is. I don't think they can be quite improving reading for
anyone.   620

MRS CHEVELEY (*Languidly*)
I have never read a Blue Book. I prefer books ... in yellow
covers.

LADY MARKBY (*Genially unconscious*)
Yellow is a gayer colour, is it not? I used to wear yellow a good
deal in my early days, and would do so now if Sir John was
not so painfully personal in his observations, and a man on the   625
question of dress is always ridiculous, is he not?

MRS CHEVELEY
Oh, no! I think men are the only authorities on dress.

LADY MARKBY
Really? One wouldn't say so from the sort of hats they wear,
would one?
                The BUTLER *enters, followed by the* FOOTMAN.
                Tea is set on a small table close to LADY CHILTERN

LADY CHILTERN
May I give you some tea, Mrs Cheveley?   630

MRS CHEVELEY
Thanks.
                The BUTLER *hands* MRS CHEVELEY *a cup of tea on a salver*

LADY CHILTERN
Some tea, Lady Markby?

LADY MARKBY
No thanks, dear. (*The servants go out*) The fact is, I have

618–9 *as Sir John is* MS1 adds 'Half an hour over a Blue Book is sufficient to make Sir
    John a perfect monster'. The reports of parliamentary committees of enquiry, *Blue
    Books* were a byword for methodical, fact-filled, dry publications. The books in
    yellow covers favoured by Mrs C (ll. 621–2) would be French novels, usually sold
    in yellow paper wrappers: they are a familiar Wildean prop. In C Wilde changed
    'improper' to the present reading, 'improving'. In F Mrs Cheveley adds 'They are
    more accurate' after l. 622.
623–6 *I used to . . . is he not?* Cf. the passage in MS and HTC at the equivalent of I, 99–107
    (see note to those lines, above).
627 *authorities on dress* an expertise claimed by Wilde, who espoused the cause of 'rational
    dress' in the 1880s.
629 s.d. in F there are s.d. for the removal of tea at this point.
633–42 *No thanks, dear . . . irreligious* Lady M's remarks on curates were first drafted
    for Act I (cf. note to I, 81). *Lady Brancaster* is the name originally used for Lady
    Bracknell in *Earnest*. The overworked, underpaid and attractive young *curate* was

promised to go round for ten minutes to see poor Lady
Brancaster, who is in very great trouble. Her daughter, quite   635
a well-brought-up girl, too, has actually become engaged to
be married to a curate in Shropshire. It is very sad, very sad
indeed. I can't understand this modern mania for curates. In
my time we girls saw them, of course, running about the place
like rabbits. But we never took any notice of them, I need   640
hardly say. But I am told that nowadays country society is
quite honeycombed with them. I think it most irreligious.
And then the eldest son has quarrelled with his father, and it
is said that when they meet at the club Lord Brancaster always
hides himself behind the money article in *The Times*.   645
However, I believe that is quite a common occurrence
nowadays and that they have to take in extra copies of *The
Times* at all the clubs in St. James's Street; there are so many
sons who won't have anything to do with their fathers, and
so many fathers who won't speak to their sons. I think,   650
myself, it is very much to be regretted.

MRS CHEVELEY
So do I. Fathers have so much to learn from their sons
nowadays.

LADY MARKBY
Really, dear? What?

MRS CHEVELEY
The art of living. The only really Fine Art we have produced   655
in modern times.

LADY MARKBY (*Shaking her head*)
Ah! I am afraid Lord Brancaster knew a good deal about that.

a stock character in Victorian fiction. W.S. Gilbert's *Patience* (1881), in which he
made fun of the aesthetes, was based on his poem 'The Rival Curates', and was to
have concerned the attraction of two churchmen for the love-sick women of a parish:
considerations of taste and the opportunity of more direct satire suggested the
change to poets as a subject.
648–51 *there are so many sons . . . regretted* a version of material originally drafted for
Woman. Cf. Appendix I. In the MS draft of *Earnest* a similar passage occurs:
Mothers, of course, are all right. They pay a chap's bills and don't bother him.
But fathers bother a chap and never pay his bills. I don't know a single chap who
speaks to his father . . . I bet you anything you like that there is not a single chap,
of all the chaps that you and I know, who would be seen walking down St. James's
Street with his own father.
(*Earnest*, I, 612–5, note).
652–70 *So do I . . . And now, Gertrude* om. MS1. ll. 659–70 (from 'You know Lady
Brancaster . . . ') first appear in additions to C. The confounding of the terms in
which 'art' was evaluated in relation to 'life' was one of Wilde's favourite strategies
– notably in 'The Critic as Artist' and 'The Decay of Lying' and in Lord Henry
Wotton's seductive conversations with Dorian Gray.

More than his poor wife ever did. (*Turning to* LADY CHILTERN)
You know Lady Brancaster, don't you, dear?

LADY CHILTERN

Just slightly. She was staying at Langton last autumn, when   660
we were there.

LADY MARKBY

Well, like all stout women, she looks the very picture of
happiness, as no doubt you noticed. But there are many
tragedies in her family, besides this affair of the curate. Her
own sister, Mrs Jekyll, had a most unhappy life; through no   665
fault of her own, I am sorry to say. She ultimately was so
broken-hearted that she went into a convent, or on to the
operatic stage, I forget which. No; I think it was decorative
art-needlework she took up. I know she had lost all sense of
pleasure in life. (*Rising*) And now, Gertrude, if you will allow   670
me, I shall leave Mrs Cheveley in your charge and call back
for her in a quarter of an hour. Or perhaps, dear Mrs
Cheveley, you wouldn't mind waiting in the carriage while I
am with Lady Brancaster. As I intend it to be a visit of
condolence, I shan't stay long.   675

MRS CHEVELEY (*Rising*)

I don't mind waiting in the carriage at all, provided there is
somebody to look at one.

LADY MARKBY

Well, I hear the curate is always prowling about the house.

MRS CHEVELEY

I am afraid I am not fond of girl friends.

LADY CHILTERN (*Rising*)

Oh, I hope Mrs Cheveley will stay here a little. I should like   680
to have a few minutes' conversation with her.

660–1 *She was . . . there* om. LC, BLTS.
662–70 *Well, like all . . . in life* the description of Mrs Jekyll's misfortunes first appears
  as an addition to C. In PR 'as no doubt you noticed' and 'I am sorry to say' are added.
  In F 'besides this affair of the curate' and 'operatic' first appear. In BLTS and LC
  'needlework' is not specified. (It was one of the crafts which Wilde, a disciple of
  William Morris, took seriously.) If Mrs Jekyll was a relation, through her husband,
  of the protagonist of Stevenson's story (published in 1886) her life must have been
  unhappy indeed.
672–83 *Or perhaps . . . pleasure* om. MS1.
674 *I intend it to be* PR restores the phrase from C: other versions read 'It is only'.
676–9 *provided . . . girlfriends* this crude remark, suggesting Mrs C's dislike for the
  competition of younger women, first appears in PR.

MRS CHEVELEY
　　How very kind of you, Lady Chiltern! Believe me, nothing
　　would give me greater pleasure.

LADY MARKBY
　　Ah! no doubt you both have many pleasant reminiscences of
　　your schooldays to talk over together. Good-bye, dear   685
　　Gertrude! Shall I see you at Lady Bonar's tonight? She has
　　discovered a wonderful new genius. He does ... nothing at
　　all, I believe. That is a great comfort, is it not?

LADY CHILTERN
　　Robert and I are dining at home by ourselves tonight, and I
　　don't think I shall go anywhere afterwards. Robert, of course,   690
　　will have to be in the House. But there is nothing interesting
　　on.

LADY MARKBY
　　Dining at home by yourselves? Is that quite prudent? Ah, I
　　forgot, your husband is an exception. Mine is the general rule,
　　and nothing ages a woman so rapidly as having married the   695
　　general rule.
　　　　　　　　　　　　　　　　　　　　　　Exit LADY MARKBY

MRS CHEVELEY
　　Wonderful woman, Lady Markby, isn't she? Talks more and
　　says less than anybody I ever met. She is made to be a public
　　speaker. Much more so than her husband, though he is a
　　typical Englishman, always dull and usually violent.   700

LADY CHILTERN (*Makes no answer, but remains standing. There is
　　a pause. Then the eyes of the two women meet.* LADY CHILTERN
　　looks stern and pale. MRS CHEVELEY *seems rather amused*)
　　Mrs Cheveley, I think it is right to tell you quite frankly that,
　　had I known who you really were, I should not have invited
　　you to my house last night.

MRS CHEVELEY (*With an impertinent smile*)
　　Really?

687 *a wonderful new genius* Doing nothing was claimed by Wilde to be an art in itself,
　　cf. the sub-title of 'The Critic as Artist': 'With some Remarks upon the Importance
　　of Doing Nothing'. In that dialogue Gilbert insists that 'to do nothing at all is the
　　most difficult thing in the world, the most difficult and the most intellectual'
　　(*Intentions*, p. 176/*CW*, p. 1039). The last three sentences of this speech and the
　　two speeches following first appear in F.
693 *Dining at home* F has the s.d. '*Start lowering sun*', presumably referring to the lights
　　behind the windows of the room.
697–700 *Talks more ... usually violent* The first sentence does not appear until F; the
　　rest in PR. The s.d. first appears in PR.

LADY CHILTERN
I could not have done so.   705

MRS CHEVELEY
I see that after all these years you have not changed a bit,
Gertrude.

LADY CHILTERN
I never change.

MRS CHEVELEY (*Elevating her eyebrows*)
Then life has taught you nothing?

LADY CHILTERN
It has taught me that a person who has once been guilty of a   710
dishonest and dishonourable action may be guilty of it a
second time, and should be shunned.

MRS CHEVELEY
Would you apply that rule to everyone?

LADY CHILTERN
Yes, to everyone, without exception.

MRS CHEVELEY
Then I am sorry for you, Gertrude, very sorry for you.   715

LADY CHILTERN
You see now, I am sure, that for many reasons any further
acquaintance between us during your stay in London is quite
impossible?

MRS CHEVELEY (*Leaning back in her chair*)
Do you know, Gertrude, I don't mind your talking morality
a bit. Morality is simply the attitude we adopt towards people   720
whom we personally dislike. You dislike me. I am quite aware
of that. And I have always detested you. And yet I have come
here to do you a service.

LADY CHILTERN (*Contemptuously*)
Like the service you wished to render my husband last night,
I suppose. Thank heaven, I saved him from that.   725

713–8 *Would you apply ... impossible?* First appears in MS2.
719–20 *Do you know ... a bit* Cf. l. 184, above.
722 *And I have always detested you* MS1 reads:
    LADY CHILTERN:
      Yes, I know your true character.
    MRS CHEVELEY
      Perhaps one's true character is what one wishes to be more than what one is.
      But let that pass. You dislike me. I hate you. I have always hated you. And
      yet ...

MRS CHEVELEY (*Starting to her feet*)
  It was you who made him write that insolent letter to me? It
  was you who made him break his promise?

LADY CHILTERN
  Yes.

MRS CHEVELEY
  Then you must make him keep it. I give you till tomorrow
  morning – no more. If by that time your husband does not   730
  solemnly bind himself to help me in this great scheme in
  which I am interested –

LADY CHILTERN
  This fraudulent speculation –

MRS CHEVELEY
  Call it what you choose. I hold your husband in the hollow
  of my hand, and if you are wise you will make him do what   735
  I tell him.

LADY CHILTERN (*Rising and going towards her*)
  You are impertinent. What has my husband to do with you?
  With a woman like you?

MRS CHEVELEY (*With a bitter laugh*)
  In this world like meets with like. It is because your husband
  is himself fraudulent and dishonest that we pair so well   740
  together. Between you and him there are chasms. He and I
  are closer than friends. We are enemies linked together. The
  same sin binds us.

LADY CHILTERN
  How dare you class my husband with yourself? How dare you
  threaten him or me? Leave my house. You are unfit to enter   745
  it.
            SIR ROBERT CHILTERN *enters from behind. He*
        hears his wife's last words, and sees to whom they
                are addressed. He grows deadly pale

MRS CHEVELEY
  Your house! A house bought with the price of dishonour. A
  house, everything in which has been paid for by fraud. (*Turns*
  round and sees SIR ROBERT CHILTERN) Ask him what the origin
  of his fortune is! Get him to tell you how he sold to a   750
  stockbroker a Cabinet secret. Learn from him to what you
  owe your position.

748 *fraud* in F this is the cue for '*Warning for Curtain*'.

LADY CHILTERN
It is not true! Robert! It is not true!

MRS CHEVELEY (*Pointing at him with outstretched finger*)
Look at him! Can he deny it? Does he dare to?

SIR ROBERT CHILTERN
Go! Go at once. You have done your worst now.   755

MRS CHEVELEY
My worst? I have not yet finished with you, with either of you.
I give you both till tomorrow at noon. If by then you don't
do what I bid you to do, the whole world shall know the origin
of Robert Chiltern.
            SIR ROBERT CHILTERN *strikes the bell. Enter* MASON

SIR ROBERT CHILTERN
Show Mrs Cheveley out.   760
            MRS CHEVELEY *starts; then bows with somewhat*
            exaggerated politeness to LADY CHILTERN, *who makes*
            no sign of response. As she passes by SIR ROBERT
            CHILTERN, *who is standing close to the door, she pauses*
            for a moment and looks him straight in the face.
            She then goes out, followed by the servant, who closes
            the door after him. The husband and wife are left
            alone. LADY CHILTERN *stands like someone in a dreadful*
            dream. Then she turns round and looks at her
            husband. She looks at him with strange eyes, as
            though she was seeing him for the first time

LADY CHILTERN
You sold a Cabinet secret for money! You began your life with
fraud! You built up your career on dishonour! Oh, tell me it
is not true! Lie to me! Lie to me! Tell me it is not true!

SIR ROBERT CHILTERN
What this woman said is quite true. But, Gertrude, listen to
me. You don't realize how I was tempted. Let me tell you the   765
whole thing.   *Goes towards her*

756–60 *My worst? . . . out* Mrs C's exit-speech needed some adjustment. It is possible
that Sir Robert's line 'Show Mrs Cheveley out' (added to C) was intended to restore
his 'face' and transfer control of the moment to the actor-manager playing the role.
In MS1 ll. 754–9 are one speech, with no interruption, and begin: 'Look at him!
He does not have the courage even to lie about it. I give you both till tomorrow
morning . . . ' In MS2 'I have not yet finished with you' is added as answer to the
new line for Sir Robert (l. 755). In PR 'with either of you' appears. MS1 omits the
somewhat melodramatic defiance, 'the whole world shall know the origin of Robert
Chiltern'. 'My worst?' first appears in BLTS.
760 s.d. first appears in PR, replacing a simple '*exit*'.

LADY CHILTERN
Don't come near me. Don't touch me. I feel as if you had
soiled me for ever. Oh! what a mask you have been wearing
all these years! A horrible painted mask! You sold yourself for
money. Oh! a common thief were better. You put yourself up   770
to sale to the highest bidder! You were bought in the market.
You lied to the whole world. And yet you will not lie to me.

SIR ROBERT CHILTERN (*Rushing towards her*)
Gertrude! Gertrude!

LADY CHILTERN (*Thrusting him back with outstretched hands*)
No, don't speak! Say nothing! Your voice wakes terrible
memories – memories of things that made me love you –   775
memories of words that made me love you – memories that
now are horrible to me. And how I worshipped you! You were
to me something apart from common life, a thing pure, noble,
honest, without stain. The world seemed to me finer because
you were in it, and goodness more real because you lived. And 780
now – oh, when I think that I made of a man like you my ideal!
the ideal of my life!

SIR ROBERT CHILTERN
There was your mistake. There was your error. The error all
women commit. Why can't you women love us, faults and all?
Why do you place us on monstrous pedestals? We have all feet   785
of clay, women as well as men; but when we men love women,
we love them knowing their weaknesses, their follies, their

767–8 *I feel as if . . . for ever* in MS1 the idea is expressed more crudely: 'I feel as if you
have touched me too much, you have soiled me for ever.' In F the line does not appear
and the speech begins 'Don't. Oh! what a mask . . . '. The horrible *painted mask*
recalls a number of instances of the theme in Wilde's work, including Mrs Erlynne's
description of her life as an 'outcast': 'afraid every moment lest the mask should be
stripped from one's face' (*LWF*, III, 149-50). Cf. also 'The Decay of Lying': 'In
point of fact what is interesting about people in "good society" . . . is the mask that
each one of them wears, not the reality that lies behind the mask'. (*Intentions*,
p. 15/*CW*, p. 975.)
774 *No, don't speak* MS1 precedes this with 'Life becomes bitter in one's mouth'.
782 *the ideal of my life!* first appears in PR.
783–814 *There was your mistake . . . have ruined mine!* very few changes were made in this
speech after MS1. Versions before PR read 'humane' for 'human' (l. 795); MS1 has
'from the altar on which your vanity had placed me. I had not the courage to show
you my wounds' after 'come down' (l. 798); 'terrible' in PR replaces the earlier
'horrible'; LC simplifies 'terrible shame, the mockery of the world, a lonely
dishonoured death' to 'horrible death'. In LC and earlier versions 'Let women make
no more ideals of men' is followed by 'in your life' and the next verb and its subject
are in the second person ('Don't put them . . . or you may ruin . . . '). 'You whom
I have so wildly loved' first appears in PR. In F 'some day' (ll. 810–1) is followed
by the s.d. '(*Pause, goes up stage, then turns to Lady C*)'. The final s.d. first appears
in PR, replacing the simple exit marked in earlier versions.

imperfections, love them all the more, it may be, for that
reason. It is not the perfect, but the imperfect, who have need
of love. It is when we are wounded by our own hands, or by   790
the hands of others, that love should come to cure us   else
what use is love at all? All sins, except a sin against itself, Love
should forgive. All lives, save loveless lives, true Love should
pardon. A man's love is like that. It is wider, larger, more
human than a woman's. Women think that they are making   795
ideals of men. What they are making of us are false idols
merely. You made your false idol of me, and I had not the
courage to come down, show you my wounds, tell you my
weaknesses. I was afraid that I might lose your love, as I have
lost it now. And so, last night you ruined my life for me – yes,   800
ruined it! What this woman asked of me was nothing
compared to what she offered to me. She offered security,
peace, stability. The sin of my youth, that I had thought was
buried, rose up in front of me, hideous, horrible, with its
hands at my throat. I could have killed it for ever, sent it back   805
into its tomb, destroyed its record, burned the one witness
against me. You prevented me. No one but you, you know
it. And now what is there before me but public disgrace, ruin,
terrible shame, the mockery of the world, a lonely dishonoured life, a lonely dishonoured death, it may be, some   810
day? Let women make no more ideals of men! let them not
put them on altars and bow before them, or they may ruin
other lives as completely as you – you whom I have so wildly
loved – have ruined mine!

He passes from the room. LADY CHILTERN *rushes*
towards him, but the door is closed when she reaches
it. Pale with anguish, bewildered, helpless, she
sways like a plant in the water. Her hands, outstretched,
seem to tremble in the air like blossoms in
the wind. Then she flings herself down beside a sofa
and buries her face. Her sobs are like the sobs of a child

ACT-DROP

Act III

The Library in LORD GORING's *house.*
An Adam room. On the right is the door leading
into the hall. On the left, the door of the smoking-room.
A pair of folding doors at the back open into
the drawing-room. The fire is lit. PHIPPS, *the butler,*
is arranging some newspapers on the writing-table.
The distinction of PHIPPS *is his impassivity. He has*
been termed by enthusiasts the Ideal Butler. The
Sphinx is not so incommunicable. He is a mask
with a manner. Of his intellectual or emotional life
history knows nothing. He represents the dominance of form.
Enter LORD GORING *in evening dress with a buttonhole.*
He is wearing a silk hat and Inverness cape.
White-gloved, he carries a Louis Seize cane. His
are all the delicate fopperies of Fashion. One sees
that he stands in immediate relation to modern life,
makes it indeed, and so masters it. He is the first
well-dressed philosopher in the history of thought

LORD GORING
Got my second buttonhole for me, Phipps?

PHIPPS
Yes, my lord.
Takes his hat, cane and cape, and presents new buttonhole on
salver

1 s.d. first appears in PR, with details added to the proof. In LC the s.d. is 'LORD
  GORING'S *rooms.* PHIPPS *discovered. Enter* LORD GORING.' In F there is business
  establishing Phipps' ascendancy over his fellow servant:
         PHIPPS and HAROLD discovered – Business. HAROLD opens blotter on table, moves
         cigarette stand on table table, R., also arranges papers on table, L. PHIPPS shuts
         blotter, puts cigarette stand in former position, rearranges papers.
      There is a warning: '*Note* Brooch in drawer of table, R.' Wilde added '*by enthusiasts*'
  and '*White-gloved ... thought*' to PR. The room is decorated by *Robert Adam*
  (corrected from 1st ed's 'Adams') (1728-92), British architect and interior designer.
  On the *Sphinx* cf. note to *Woman*, I, 439-40. Wilde himself affected a *Louis Seize* cane
  and claimed in *De Profundis* to have 'stood in symbolic relations to the art and culture
  of my age' (cf. 'The Author', p. ix, above). It is difficult not to see this s.d. as the
  author's comment on himself as he was before his downfall.
      MS begins with a short soliloquy by Lord G, who is reading a letter on pink paper.
  Lord C enters and remarks that he usually finds his son 'lolling about other people's
  houses.' His son replies: 'I don't loll, father. I don't know how to loll. But I prefer
  other people's houses to my own. I prefer everything that other people have to what
  I have. I am afraid, father that I have terrible communistic tendencies in me. It comes
  from my never having had time to study the question of property'. MS then moves
  to l. 63. In BLTS the passage is deleted and transferred to l. 60.
2 s.d. *cane* added to PR.

LORD GORING
Rather distinguished thing, Phipps. I am the only person of
the smallest importance in London at present who wears a
buttonhole.   5

PHIPPS
Yes, my lord. I have observed that.

LORD GORING (*Taking out old buttonhole*)
You see, Phipps, Fashion is what one wears oneself. What is
unfashionable is what other people wear.

PHIPPS
Yes, my lord.

LORD GORING
Just as vulgarity is simply the conduct of other people.   10

PHIPPS
Yes, my lord.

LORD GORING (*Putting in new buttonhole*)
And falsehoods the truths of other people.

PHIPPS
Yes, my lord.

LORD GORING
Other people are quite dreadful. The only possible society is
oneself.   15

PHIPPS
Yes, my lord.

LORD GORING
To love oneself is the beginning of a life-long romance,
Phipps.

PHIPPS
Yes, my lord.

LORD GORING (*Looking at himself in the glass*)
Don't think I quite like this buttonhole, Phipps. Makes me   20

3–6 *Rather . . . Yes, my lord* the sequence first appears in F (which om. ll. 12–3, 17–9).
On *button-holes*, cf. 'Phrases and Philosophies for the Use of the Young' (*CW*, pp.
1205-6): 'A really well-made button-hole is the only link between Art and Nature';
in *Earnest* Algernon tells Cecily: 'I never have any appetite unless I have a button-hole
first' (II, 172-3).
17–28 *To love oneself . . . Phipps* Cf. note to I, 267–9, above.

look a little too old. Makes me almost in the prime of life, eh, Phipps?

PHIPPS
I don't observe any alteration in your lordship's appearance.

LORD GORING
You don't, Phipps?

PHIPPS
No, my lord.   25

LORD GORING
I am not quite sure. For the future a more trivial buttonhole, Phipps, on Thursday evenings.

PHIPPS
I will speak to the florist, my lord. She has had a loss in her family lately, which perhaps accounts for the lack of triviality your lordship complains of in the buttonhole.   30

LORD GORING
Extraordinary thing about the lower classes in England – they are always losing their relations.

PHIPPS
Yes, my lord! They are extremely fortunate in that respect.

LORD GORING (*Turns round and looks at him.* PHIPPS *remains impassive*)
Hum! Any letters, Phipps?

PHIPPS
Three, my lord.   *Hands letters on a salver*   35

LORD GORING (*Takes letters*)
Want my cab round in twenty minutes.

PHIPPS
Yes, my lord.   *Goes towards door*

LORD GORING (*Holds up letter in pink envelope*)
Ahem! Phipps, when did this letter arrive?

PHIPPS
It was brought by hand just after your lordship went to the Club.   40

21 *in the prime of life* in BLTS Wilde altered 'look quite middle-aged' to 'middle-aged', which was adopted in C and LC. The present phrase first appears in F.
28–34 *I will speak ... Phipps?* added to BLTS.
31 *lower classes* (lower middle classes LC; middle classes C, BLTS.)
34 s.d. *Turns ... impassive* first appears in PR.

LORD GORING

That will do. (*Exit* PHIPPS) Lady Chiltern's handwriting on
Lady Chiltern's pink notepaper. That is rather curious. I
thought Robert was to write. Wonder what Lady Chiltern has
got to say to me? (*Sits at bureau and opens letter, and reads it*)
'I want you. I trust you. I am coming to you. Gertrude.' (*Puts*   45
*down the letter with a puzzled look. Then takes it up, and reads
it again slowly*) 'I want you. I trust you. I am coming to you.'
So she has found out everything! Poor woman! Poor woman!
(*Pulls out watch and looks at it.*) But what an hour to
call! Ten o'clock! I shall have to give up going to the
Berkshires'. However, it is always nice to be expected, and   50
not to arrive. I am not expected at the Bachelors', so I shall
certainly go there. Well, I will make her stand by her husband. That is the only thing for her to do. That is the only
thing for any woman to do. It is the growth of the moral sense
in women that makes marriage such a hopeless, one-sided   55
institution. Ten o'clock. She should be here soon. I must tell
Phipps I am not in to anyone else.
              Goes towards bell
              Enter PHIPPS

PHIPPS
Lord Caversham.

LORD GORING
Oh, why will parents always appear at the wrong time? Some
extraordinary mistake in nature, I suppose. (*Enter* LORD   60
CAVERSHAM) Delighted to see you, my dear father.
              Goes to meet him

LORD CAVERSHAM
Take my cloak off.

LORD GORING
Is it worth while, father?

LORD CAVERSHAM
Of course it is worth while, sir. Which is the most comfortable
chair?   65

41–57 *That will do . . . anyone else* LC and earlier versions of this speech are simpler,
     without the repetition of the letter's contents and the reflections on the 'growth of
     moral sense in women'. In LC Lord G anticipates giving Lady C 'a good lecture'.
     In C he (somewhat incongruously) speaks of her having 'stepped right into the little
     trap [he] laid for her' and intends 'teaching her a salutary lesson when she arrives'
     (derives from additions to BLTS). He also remarks that he will not try any more
     'psychological experiments' – 'At least not on women, they are far too clever for
     me'.
59–60 *Some . . . suppose* first appears in C, which adds material from the beginning of
     the act in MS; F om. this sentence.

LORD GORING
This one, father. It is the chair I use myself, when I have
visitors.

LORD CAVERSHAM
Thank ye. No draught, I hope, in this room?

LORD GORING
No, father.

LORD CAVERSHAM (*Sitting down*)
Glad to hear it. Can't stand draughts. No draughts at home.   70

LORD GORING
Good many breezes, father.

LORD CAVERSHAM
Eh? Eh? Don't understand what you mean. Want to have a
serious conversation with you, sir.

LORD GORING
My dear father! At this hour?

LORD CAVERSHAM
Well, sir, it is only ten o'clock. What is your objection to the   75
hour? I think the hour is an admirable hour!

LORD GORING
Well, the fact is, father, this is not my day for talking
seriously. I am very sorry, but it is not my day.

LORD CAVERSHAM
What do you mean, sir?

LORD GORING
During the season, father, I only talk seriously on the first   80
Tuesday in every month, from four to seven.

LORD CAVERSHAM
Well, make it Tuesday, sir, make it Tuesday.

LORD GORING
But it is after seven, father, and my doctor says I must not
have any serious conversation after seven. It makes me talk
in my sleep.   85

71 *breezes* quarrels, disagreements (slang).
76 *an admirable hour!* in MS Lord C proposes his own company for his son—'much
   more profitable for you, much more improving for your character'. Lord G replies
   'I don't want my character improved, I am perfectly satisfied with it as it is'.
77–8 *not my day for talking seriously* analogous to the practice of appointing a regular day
   on which a hostess would be 'at home' to receive afternoon visitors. (Cf. I, 35–6 'You
   know we are always at home on Wednesdays'.)

LORD CAVERSHAM
Talk in your sleep, sir? What does that matter? You are not
married.

LORD GORING
No, father, I am not married.

LORD CAVERSHAM
Hum! That is what I have come to talk to you about, sir. You
have got to get married, and at once. Why, when I was your   90
age, sir, I had been an inconsolable widower for three months,
and was already paying my addresses to your admirable
mother. Dammc, sir, it is your duty to get married. You can't
be always living for pleasure. Every man of position is married
nowadays. Bachelors are not fashionable any more. They are   95
a damaged lot. Too much is known about them. You must get
a wife, sir. Look where your friend Robert Chiltern has got
to by probity, hard work, and a sensible marriage with a good
woman. Why don't you imitate him, sir? Why don't you take
him for your model?   100

LORD GORING
I think I shall, father.

LORD CAVERSHAM
I wish you would, sir. Then I should be happy. At present I
make your mother's life miserable on your account. You are
heartless, sir, quite heartless.

LORD GORING
I hope not, father.   105

LORD CAVERSHAM
And it is high time for you to get married. You are thirty-four
years of age, sir.

89–100 *Hum! ... model?* in MS Lord C had been 'divorced twice'. The reference to his
being a widower first appears in C, where the mother of Lord G is 'sainted' rather
than 'admirable'. The customary period of mourning for a widower was one year,
during which black clothes would be worn. In MS and BLTS the reasons for urging
marriage on Lord G are frankly selfish:
    You don't suppose I want the property to go to my damned nephew, do you? You
    don't suppose I want your idiotic cousin to have the title. I hate all my relations.
    It is only human nature to hate one's relations. A man who doesn't hate his
    relations has no regard for his own flesh and blood ...
Lord G insists that 'pleasure, or the prospect of it, is the only thing that would induce
[him] to marry at all', and resists his father's appeal to his 'duty to [his] name and
race'. The passage was abbreviated in revisions to BLTS; the reference to 'name and
race' does not appear after C.
106 etc. in LC Lord G is 36, but admits to $33^1/_2$; in C he is 36 ($34^1/_2$); and in MS and
BLTS he is 38 ($34^1/_2$).

LORD GORING
Yes, father, but I only admit to thirty-two – thirty-one and
a half when I have a really good buttonhole. This buttonhole
is not ... trivial enough.   110

LORD CAVERSHAM
I tell you you are thirty-four, sir. And there is a draught in
your room, besides, which makes your conduct worse. Why
did you tell me there was no draught, sir? I feel a draught, sir,
I feel it distinctly.

LORD GORING
So do I, father. It is a dreadful draught. I will come and see   115
you tomorrow, father. We can talk over anything you like. Let
me help you on with your cloak, father.

LORD CAVERSHAM
No, sir; I have called this evening for a definite purpose, and
I am going to see it through at all costs to my health or yours.
Put down my cloak, sir.   120

LORD GORING
Certainly, father. But let us go into another room. (*Rings bell*)
There is a dreadful draught here. (*Enter* PHIPPS) Phipps, is
there a good fire in the smoking-room?

PHIPPS
Yes, my lord.

LORD GORING
Come in there, father. Your sneezes are quite heart-rend-   125
ing.

LORD CAVERSHAM
Well, sir, I suppose I have a right to sneeze when I choose?

LORD GORING (*Apologetically*)
Quite so, father. I was merely expressing sympathy.

LORD CAVERSHAM
Oh, damn sympathy. There is a great deal too much of that
sort of thing going on nowadays.   130

LORD GORING
I quite agree with you, father. If there was less sympathy in

131–8 *If there was ... puppy!* first appears in F (which om. the last speech and reads
   'sorrow' for 'trouble' in 1. 132); ll.136–7 ('Do you always ... attentively') were
   transferred from the drafts of *Earnest*, Act I (1.276). The lines may have been spoken
   in performances of *Earnest*; they do not appear in Smithers' edition of the play and
   the promptbook compiled by Alexander, but are found in the licensing copy and
   earlier versions.

the world there would be less trouble in the world.

LORD CAVERSHAM (*Going towards the smoking-room*)
    That is a paradox, sir. I hate paradoxes.

LORD GORING
    So do I, father. Everybody one meets is a paradox nowadays.
    It is a great bore. It makes society so obvious.   135

LORD CAVERSHAM (*Turning round, and looking at his son beneath his bushy eyebrows*)
    Do you always really understand what you say, sir?

LORD GORING (*After some hesitation*)
    Yes, father, if I listen attentively.

LORD CAVERSHAM (*Indignantly*)
    If you listen attentively! ... Conceited young puppy!
        Goes off grumbling into the smoking-room. PHIPPS
               enters

LORD GORING
    Phipps, there is a lady coming to see me this evening on
    particular business. Show her into the drawing-room when   140
    she arrives. You understand?

PHIPPS
    Yes, my lord.

LORD GORING
    It is a matter of the gravest importance, Phipps.

PHIPPS
    I understand, my lord.

LORD GORING
    No one else is to be admitted, under any circumstances.   145

PHIPPS
    I understand, my lord.

                              Bell rings

LORD GORING
    Ah! that is probably the lady. I shall see her myself.
        Just as he is going towards the door LORD CAVERSHAM
           enters from the smoking-room

LORD CAVERSHAM
    Well, sir? am I to wait attendance on you?

147 *Ah!* ... *myself* in F Lord G remarks 'For a lady she is wonderfully punctual'. In
    versions before F the badinage with Lord C is longer.

LORD GORING (*Considerably perplexed*)
In a moment, father. Do excuse me. (LORD CAVERSHAM *goes
back*) Well, remember my instructions, Phipps – into that   150
room.

PHIPPS
Yes, my lord.
LORD GORING *goes into the smoking-room.* HAROLD, *the footman,
shows* MRS CHEVELEY *in. Lamia-like, she is in green and silver.
She has a cloak of black satin, lined with dead rose-leaf silk*

HAROLD
What name, madam?

MRS CHEVELEY (*To* PHIPPS, *who advances towards her*)
Is Lord Goring not here? I was told he was at home?

PHIPPS
His lordship is engaged at present with Lord Caversham,   155
madam.
Turns a cold, glassy eye on HAROLD, *who at once retires*

MRS CHEVELEY (*To herself*)
How very filial!

PHIPPS
His lordship told me to ask you, madam, to be kind enough
to wait in the drawing-room for him. His lordship will come
to you there.   ·   160

MRS CHEVELEY (*With a look of surprise*)
Lord Goring expects me?

PHIPPS
Yes, madam.

MRS CHEVELEY
Are you quite sure?

152 *Yes, my lord* in MS and BLTS Phipps has a brief soliloquy:
        Wonder who the lady coming to see him on important business is? Hope he is
        not going to be married. Hate women about a home. They are so inquisitive.
        In BLTS Wilde deleted this and drafted an alternative:
        Hope he is going to be married. I like a well-dressed woman about the house. They
        set off a dinner table so well. Besides, if a man is married he doesn't dine at home
        quite so often. Bachelors nowadays are far too domestic.
        This was also deleted.
152 s.d. *Lamia-like* Cf. the woman in serpent's shape of Keats' poem 'Lamia': 'a gordian
        shape of dazzling hue/Vermilion-spotted, golden, green and blue' and covered in
        'silver mail, and golden brede' (I, 48–9; 158).
157 *How very filial*! first appears in PR: another jibe at social institutions (Cf. I,
        193–7).

PHIPPS
His lordship told me that if a lady called I was to ask her to
wait in the drawing-room. (*Goes to the door of the drawing-room*   165
and opens it) His lordship's directions on the subject were very
precise.

MRS CHEVELEY (*To herself*)
How thoughtful of him! To expect the unexpected shows a
thoroughly modern intellect. (*Goes towards the drawing-room
and looks in*) Ugh! How dreary a bachelor's drawing-room   170
always looks. I shall have to alter all this. (PHIPPS *brings the
lamp from the writing-table*) No, I don't care for that lamp. It
is far too glaring. Light some candles.

PHIPPS (*Replaces lamp*)
Certainly, madam.

MRS CHEVELEY
I hope the candles have very becoming shades.   175

PHIPPS
We have had no complaints about them, madam, as yet.
Passes into the drawing-room and begins to light the candles

MRS CHEVELEY (*To herself*)
I wonder what woman he is waiting for tonight. It will be
delightful to catch him. Men always look so silly when they
are caught. And they are always being caught. (*Looks about
room and approaches the writing-table*) What a very interesting   180
room! What a very interesting picture! Wonder what his
correspondence is like. (*Takes up letters*) Oh, what a very
uninteresting correspondence! Bills and cards, debts and
dowagers! Who on earth writes to him on pink paper? How

168–9 *To expect . . . intellect* first appears in F ('a good deal of intellect').
169 s.d. in F the s.d. specifies '*lights down in drawing-room*' when the door is opened and
'*White lights up in drawing-room*' as the candles are lit. After the shades have been
put on there is '*Rose pink light in drawing-room*'.
170 *dreary* altered from 'horrid' in revision to BLTS.
176 *as yet* added to PR.
177–95 *I wonder . . . coming to you.*' F and LC om. 'Bills and cards, debts and dowagers'.
It derives from an addition to BLTS (adopted in C):
  Poor Arthur, he is always being scrambled for by creditors and countesses. With
  all his faults he is still remarkably modern (*Takes up looking-glass.*) and he wears
  well, too. Almost as well as I do.
LC and earlier versions add 'some romantic girl, I suppose' after 'who . . . pink
paper?' 'Romance . . . settlement' first appears in F. In LC, C, BLTS and MS 'How
I detest that woman' is followed by:
  She separated us once. I suppose she is trying to separate us again. I think I had
  better read it. I hate reading horrid things about myself, and I am invariably doing
  it. How perverse we all are nowadays.

silly to write on pink paper! It looks like the beginning of a   185
middle-class romance. Romance should never begin with
sentiment. It should begin with science and end with a
settlement. (*Puts letter down, then takes it up again*) I know that
handwriting. That is Gertrude Chiltern's. I remember it
perfectly. The ten commandments in every stroke of the pen,   190
and the moral law all over the page. Wonder what Gertrude
is writing to him about? Something horrid about me, I
suppose. How I detest that woman! (*Reads it*) 'I trust you. I
want you. I am coming to you. Gertrude.' 'I trust you. I want
you. I am coming to you.'   195

> *A look of triumph comes over her face. She is*
> *just about to steal the letter, when* PHIPPS *comes in*

PHIPPS
The candles in the drawing-room are lit, madam, as you
directed.

MRS CHEVELEY
Thank you.
> *Rises hastily, and slips the letter under a large silver-cased*
> *blotting-book that is lying on the table*

PHIPPS
I trust the shades will be to your liking, madam. They are the
most becoming we have. They are the same as his lordship   200
uses himself when he is dressing for dinner.

MRS CHEVELEY (*With a smile*)
Then I am sure they will be perfectly right.

PHIPPS (*Gravely*)
Thank you, madam.
> MRS CHEVELEY *goes into the drawing-room.*
> PHIPPS *closes the door and retires. The door is then*
> *slowly opened, and* MRS CHEVELEY *comes out and creeps*
> *stealthily towards the writing-table. Suddenly voices*
> *are heard from the smoking-room.* MRS CHEVELEY
> *grows pale, and stops. The voices grow louder, and*
> *she goes back into the drawing-room, biting her lip.*
> *Enter* LORD GORING *and* LORD CAVERSHAM

---

198 s.d. *and slips . . . table* first appears in PR: F notes '*places pink letter on table and closes
the lid of the blotter over it, down stage, so as to hide it, the pink envelope is left on corner
of table below blotter*'.

203 s.d. PHIPPS . . . *biting her lip* Wilde added a speech to BLTS making the motives and
actions clear:
    I should like to have that letter! It might be useful when Lady Chiltern arrives.
    (*Hears voices and and retreats*) I can't! What a disappointment!
This does not appear in LC or F.

LORD GORING (*Expostulating*)
My dear father, if I am to get married, surely you will allow
me to choose the time, place, and person? Particularly the   205
person.

LORD CAVERSHAM (*Testily*)
That is a matter for me, sir. You would probably make a very
poor choice. It is I who should be consulted, not you. There
is property at stake. It is not a matter for affection. Affection
comes later on in married life.   210

LORD GORING
Yes. In married life affection comes when people thoroughly
dislike each other, father, doesn't it?
                Puts on LORD CAVERSHAM'S *cloak for him*

LORD CAVERSHAM
Certainly, sir. I mean certainly not, sir. You are talking very
foolishly tonight. What I say is that marriage is a matter for
common sense.   215

LORD GORING
But women who have common sense are so curiously plain,
father, aren't they? Of course I only speak from hearsay.

LORD CAVERSHAM
No woman, plain or pretty, has any common sense at all, sir.
Common sense is the privilege of our sex.

LORD GORING
Quite so. And we men are so self-sacrificing that we never use   220
it, do we, father?

LORD CAVERSHAM
I use it, sir. I use nothing else.

LORD GORING
So my mother tells me.

---

207 *That this a matter for me, sir* usually a mother's prerogative with regard to her
    daughter. Cf. Lady Bracknell's insistence on it (*Earnest*, I, 465-470 and III, 71
    etc.).
207–8 *a very poor choice* F indicates '*First coat business*' and has s.d. throughout the
    exchange for this, but does not describe the action.
209–15 *Affection ... common sense* first appears, in a slightly different form (with
    'sentiment' for 'affection') in F.
217 *Of course ... hearsay* BLTS reads 'There is always something wrong about their
    complexions', to which Wilde added in manuscript 'They always look like
    second-hand dictionaries'. The second sentence survived into LC and F.

LORD CAVERSHAM
   It is the secret of your mother's happiness. You are very
   heartless, sir, very heartless.   225

LORD GORING
   I hope not, father.
   Goes out for a moment [with LORD CAVERSHAM]. *Then returns,
   looking rather put out, with* SIR ROBERT CHILTERN

SIR ROBERT CHILTERN
   My dear Arthur, what a piece of good luck meeting you on
   the doorstep! Your servant had just told me you were not at
   home. How extraordinary!

LORD GORING
   The fact is, I am horribly busy tonight, Robert, and I gave   230
   orders I was not at home to anyone. Even my father had a
   comparatively cold reception. He complained of a draught the
   whole time.

SIR ROBERT CHILTERN
   Ah! you must be at home to me, Arthur. You are my best
   friend. Perhaps by tomorrow you will be my only friend. My   235
   wife has discovered everything.

LORD GORING
   Ah! I guessed as much!

SIR ROBERT CHILTERN (*Looking at him*)
   Really! How?

LORD GORING (*After some hesitation*)
   Oh, merely by something in the expression of your face as you
   came in. Who told her?   240

SIR ROBERT CHILTERN
   Mrs Cheveley herself. And the woman I love knows that I
   began my career with an act of low dishonesty, that I built up
   my life upon sands of shame – that I sold, like a common

224–5 *It is . . . heartless* MS has a longer version. In BLTS Wilde added the reminder:
   'You were engaged once to a charming girl and jilted her after a week' – adopted
   in C ('someone' for 'a charming girl') but not in LC.
226 s.d. Wilde corrects an erroneous s.d. in PR ('*Enter* MRS CHEVELEY. *Then enter* LORD
   GORING *and* SIR ROBERT CHILTERN').
231–3 *Even . . . time* first appears in PR.
237 *Ah! I guessed as much!* F has '*business with envelope*' before this line and '*Lord G.
   puts pink envelope in his pocket*' after it.
242 *low dishonesty* 1st ed., PR, F (dishonour LC, BLTS, C; dishonesty MS). Earlier
   versions include an account by Sir Robert of the circumstances under which his wife
   learned the secret from Mrs C: Wilde (or Waller) evidently decided that this was
   unnecessary, since the audience witnessed the incident in Act II.

huckster, the secret that had been intrusted to me as a man
of honour. I thank heaven poor Lord Radley died without   245
knowing that I betrayed him. I would to God I had died before
I had been so horribly tempted, or had fallen so low.

Burying his face in his hands

LORD GORING (*After a pause*)
You have heard nothing from Vienna yet, in answer to your
wire?

SIR ROBERT CHILTERN (*Looking up*)
Yes; I got a telegram from the first secretary at eight o'clock   250
tonight.

LORD GORING
Well?

SIR ROBERT CHILTERN
Nothing is absolutely known against her. On the contrary, she
occupies a rather high position in society. It is a sort of open
secret that Baron Arnheim left her the greater portion of his   255
immense fortune. Beyond that I can learn nothing.

LORD GORING
She doesn't turn out to be a spy, then?

SIR ROBERT CHILTERN
Oh! spies are of no use nowadays. Their profession is over.
The newspapers do their work instead.

LORD GORING
And thunderingly well they do it.   260

SIR ROBERT CHILTERN
Arthur, I am parched with thirst. May I ring for something?
Some hock and seltzer?

248–56 *You have heard ... learn nothing* first appears in F.
253–4 *Nothing ... in society* PR (All that is known about her is ... F).
257–9 *She doesn't ... they do it* first appears in PR. There may be an oblique reference
    to the conduct of *The Times* (known as 'The Thunderer') in the Parnell Case (1887).
    Letters, later shown to be forged, had been procured which purported to show that
    the Irish politician Charles Stuart Parnell approved of the Phoenix Park murders.
262 *hock and seltzer* the mixture of hock and soda-water was a favourite restorative, used
    by Dorian Gray (*DG*, p. 149 / *CW*, p. 116) and Lord Byron:
        'And for the future – (But I write this reeling,
        Having got drunk exceedingly today,
        So that I seem to stand upon the ceiling)
        I say – the future is a serious matter –
        And so – for God's sake – hock and soda-water!'
    (*Don Juan*, fragment on the back of the MS of Canto I).

LORD GORING
  Certainly. Let me.   *Rings the bell*

SIR ROBERT CHILTERN
  Thanks! I don't know what to do, Arthur, I don't know what
  to do, and you are my only friend. But what a friend you are   265
  – the one friend I can trust. I can trust you absolutely, can't
  I?
                    Enter PHIPPS

LORD GORING
  My dear Robert, of course. Oh! (*To* PHIPPS) Bring some hock
  and seltzer.

PHIPPS
  Yes, my lord.   270

LORD GORING
  And Phipps!

PHIPPS
  Yes, my lord.

LORD GORING
  Will you excuse me for a moment, Robert? I want to give some
  directions to my servant.

SIR ROBERT CHILTERN
  Certainly.   275

LORD GORING
  When that lady calls, tell her that I am not expected home this
  evening. Tell her that I have been suddenly called out of town.
  You understand?

PHIPPS
  The lady is in that room, my lord. You told me to show her
  into that room, my lord.   280

LORD GORING
  You did perfectly right. (*Exit* PHIPPS) What a mess I am in.
  No; I think I shall get through it. I'll give her a lecture through
  the door. Awkward thing to manage, though.

SIR ROBERT CHILTERN
  Arthur, tell me what I should do. My life seems to have

---

265 *my only friend. But what a friend you are* this, and the final sentence of the speech,
    first appear in PR.
281–3 *What a mess ... manage, though* added to BLTS and included in C and LC; om.
    F.

crumbled about me. I am a ship without a rudder in a night   285
without a star.

LORD GORING
Robert, you love your wife, don't you?

SIR ROBERT CHILTERN
I love her more than anything in the world. I used to think
ambition the great thing. It is not. Love is the great thing in
the world. There is nothing but love, and I love her. But I am   290
defamed in her eyes. I am ignoble in her eyes. There is a wide
gulf between us now. She has found me out, Arthur, she has
found me out.

LORD GORING
Has she never in her life done some folly – some indiscretion
– that she should not forgive your sin?   295

SIR ROBERT CHILTERN
My wife! Never! She does not know what weakness or
temptation is. I am of clay like other men. She stands apart
as good women do – pitiless in her perfection – cold and stern
and without mercy. But I love her, Arthur. We are childless,
and I have no one else to love, no one else to love me. Perhaps   300
if God had sent us children she might have been kinder to me.
But God has given us a lonely house. And she has cut my heart
in two. Don't let us talk of it. I was brutal to her this evening.
But I suppose when sinners talk to saints they are brutal
always. I said to her things that were hideously true, on my   305
side, from my standpoint, from the standpoint of men. But
don't let us talk of that.

LORD GORING
Your wife will forgive you. Perhaps at this moment she is
forgiving you. She loves you, Robert. Why should she not
forgive?   310

SIR ROBERT CHILTERN
God grant it! God grant it! (*Buries his face in his hands*) But
there is something more I have to tell you, Arthur.
Enter PHIPPS *with drinks*

PHIPPS (*Hands hock and seltzer to* SIR ROBERT CHILTERN)
Hock and seltzer, sir.

285 *a ship without a rudder* F and MS read 'as a ship without a rudder'.
292–3 *She . . . out* om. F.
294–5 *Has she . . . sin?* F and LC transpose ll.308–11 to this point. MS, C read 'or worse
    than folly' for 'some indiscretion'.
298–9 *cold and stern and without mercy* om. F.

SIR ROBERT CHILTERN
   Thank you.

LORD GORING
   Is your carriage here, Robert?   315

SIR ROBERT CHILTERN
   No; I walked from the club.

LORD GORING
   Sir Robert will take my cab, Phipps.

PHIPPS
   Yes, my lord.   *Exit*

LORD GORING
   Robert, you don't mind my sending you away?

SIR ROBERT CHILTERN
   Arthur, you must let me stay for five minutes. I have made   320
   up my mind what I am going to do tonight in the House. The
   debate on the Argentine Canal is to begin at eleven. (*A chair
   falls in the drawing-room*) What is that?

LORD GORING
   Nothing.

SIR ROBERT CHILTERN
   I heard a chair fall in the next room. Someone has been   325
   listening.

LORD GORING
   No, no; there is no one there.

SIR ROBERT CHILTERN
   There is someone. There are lights in the room, and the door
   is ajar. Someone has been listening to every secret of my life.
   Arthur, what does this mean?   330

LORD GORING
   Robert, you are excited, unnerved. I tell you there is no one
   in that room. Sit down, Robert.

SIR ROBERT CHILTERN
   Do you give me your word that there is no one there?

LORD GORING
   Yes.

320–2 *I have made up . . . eleven* first appears in F; LC, C, BLTS and MS provide another
   reference to the information expected from Lord Berkshire (cf. note to II, 212–3,
   above) and to Mrs C's 'confession'.

SIR ROBERT CHILTERN
  Your word of honour?   *Sits down*   335

LORD GORING
  Yes.

SIR ROBERT CHILTERN (*Rises*)
  Arthur, let me see for myself.

LORD GORING
  No, no.

SIR ROBERT CHILTERN
  If there is no one there why should I not look in that room?
  Arthur, you must let me go into that room and satisfy myself.   340
  Let me know that no eavesdropper has heard my life's secret.
  Arthur, you don't realize what I am going through.

LORD GORING
  Robert, this must stop. I have told you that there is no one
  in that room – that is enough.

SIR ROBERT CHILTERN (*Rushes to the door of the room*)
  It is not enough. I insist on going into this room. You have   345
  told me there is no one there, so what reason can you have for
  refusing me?

LORD GORING
  For God's sake, don't! There is someone there. Someone
  whom you must not see.

SIR ROBERT CHILTERN
  Ah, I thought so!   350

LORD GORING
  I forbid you to enter that room.

SIR ROBERT CHILTERN
  Stand back. My life is at stake. And I don't care who is there.
  I will know who it is to whom I have told my secret and my
  shame.
                                                        Enters room

LORD GORING
  Great Heavens! his own wife!   355

345–71 *It is not enough ... word of honour* F has a simpler version of the sequence,
  culminating in Lord G's protest: 'But Robert, you know perfectly well that Lady
  Chiltern -' and the angry reply, 'I think, sir, that we had better leave my wife's name
  out of the question'. PR seems closer to BLTS than to F in this passage.

SIR ROBERT CHILTERN *comes back, with a look of*
scorn and anger on his face

SIR ROBERT CHILTERN
What explanation have you to give me for the presence of that
woman here?

LORD GORING
Robert, I swear to you on my honour that that lady is stainless
and guiltless of all offence towards you.

SIR ROBERT CHILTERN
She is a vile, an infamous thing!   360

LORD GORING
Don't say that, Robert! It was for your sake she came here.
It was to try and save you she came here. She loves you and
no one else.

SIR ROBERT CHILTERN
You are mad. What have I to do with her intrigues with you?
Let her remain your mistress! You are well suited to each   365
other. She, corrupt and shameful – you, false as a friend,
treacherous as an enemy even –

LORD GORING
It is not true, Robert. Before heaven, it is not true. In her
presence and in yours I will explain all.

SIR ROBERT CHILTERN
Let me pass, sir. You have lied enough upon your word of   370
honour.
          SIR ROBERT CHILTERN *goes out.* LORD GORING *rushes*
          to the door of the drawing-room, when MRS CHEVELEY
          comes out, looking radiant and much amused

MRS CHEVELEY (*With a mock curtsey*)
Good evening, Lord Goring!

LORD GORING
Mrs Cheveley! Great Heavens! ... May I ask what you were
doing in my drawing-room?

---

369 *I will explain all* LC and earlier versions add a further exchange in which Lord G
  insists on the woman's being 'pure and good and gentle' and Sir Robert tells him
  that he hopes never to see either of them again.

MRS CHEVELEY
   Merely listening. I have a perfect passion for listening through   375
   keyholes. One always hears such wonderful things through
   them.

LORD GORING
   Doesn't that sound rather like tempting Providence?

MRS CHEVELEY
   Oh! surely Providence can resist temptation by this time.
   Makes a sign to him to take her cloak off, which he does

LORD GORING
   I am glad you have called. I am going to give you some good   380
   advice.

MRS CHEVELEY
   Oh! pray don't. One should never give a woman anything that
   she can't wear in the evening.

LORD GORING
   I see you are quite as wilful as you used to be.

MRS CHEVELEY
   Far more! I have greatly improved. I have had more   385
   experience.

LORD GORING
   Too much experience is a dangerous thing. Pray have a
   cigarette. Half the pretty women in London smoke cigarettes.
   Personally I prefer the other half.

375–7 *Merely listening . . . through them* MS reads:
   We often pay after dinner calls in Vienna. It is quite the thing to do. So I thought
   I would pay you one, and your servant asked me to wait in your drawing-room,
   so I waited. I was so sorry Gertrude Chiltern did not join me. It would have been
   a delightful meeting. I was bored to death till you and the admirable Sir Robert
   began to talk about me – then I listened.
   Lord G replies, 'What do you mean by saying Lady Chiltern didn't join you?'. This
   is followed by a note asking the typist to leave a space. In BLTS this instruction
   is followed, and Wilde has filled in the gap with manuscript additions, including
   ll. 378–9 'Doesn't that . . . by this time'). The MS equivalent of the scene that
   follows differs considerably from the present edition. Goring trades Mrs C's written
   'confession' of dishonesty for the incriminating letter, and burns them both. There
   is no mention of the brooch, which does not appear until the F typescript.
385–92 *I have had . . . discovered* Cf. Appendix I for revisions to this passage. The
   epigram on the two duties of women ('and a woman's . . . discovered') adapts a *bon
   mot* that appears in F's version of Act II (see note to II, 440–66).
      In MS and BLTS Lord G announces his intention of showing the 'confession' of
   Mrs C to his uncle (at the embassy in Vienna) and Lady M, thus ensuring that Mrs
   C will be ostracised there. She accuses him directly of being Lady C's lover.

MRS CHEVELEY
 Thanks. I never smoke. My dressmaker wouldn't like it, and   390
 a woman's first duty in life is to her dressmaker, isn't it? What
 the second duty is, no one has as yet discovered.

LORD GORING
 You have come here to sell me Robert Chiltern's letter,
 haven't you?

MRS CHEVELEY
 To offer it to you on conditions. How did you guess that?   395

LORD GORING
 Because you haven't mentioned the subject. Have you got it
 with you?

MRS CHEVELEY (*Sitting down*)
 Oh, no! A well-made dress has no pockets.

LORD GORING
 What is your price for it?

MRS CHEVELEY
 How absurdly English you are! The English think that a   400
 cheque-book can solve every problem in life. Why, my dear
 Arthur, I have very much more money than you have, and
 quite as much as Robert Chiltern has got hold of. Money is
 not what I want.

LORD GORING
 What do you want then, Mrs Cheveley?   405

MRS CHEVELEY
 Why don't you call me Laura?

LORD GORING
 I don't like the name.

MRS CHEVELEY
 You used to adore it.

LORD GORING
 Yes: that's why.
 MRS CHEVELEY *motions to him to sit down beside her. He smiles,*
                      and does so

MRS CHEVELEY
 Arthur, you loved me once.   410

406 *Why don't you call me Laura?* an intimacy appropriate only between close relatives,
    married couples and those engaged to be married: Mrs C is taunting him with a
    reference to their engagement.

LORD GORING
  Yes.

MRS CHEVELEY
  And you asked me to be your wife.

LORD GORING
  That was the natural result of my loving you.

MRS CHEVELEY
  And you threw me over because you saw, or said you saw,
  poor old Lord Mortlake trying to have a violent flirtation with   415
  me in the conservatory at Tenby.

LORD GORING
  I am under the impression that my lawyer settled that matter
  with you on certain terms . . . dictated by yourself.

MRS CHEVELEY
  At that time I was poor; you were rich.

LORD GORING
  Quite so. That is why you pretended to love me.   420

MRS CHEVELEY (*Shrugging her shoulders*)
  Poor old Lord Mortlake, who had only two topics of
  conversation, his gout and his wife! I never could quite make
  out which of the two he was talking about. He used the most
  horrible language about them both. Well, you were silly,
  Arthur. Why, Lord Mortlake was never anything more to me   425
  than an amusement. One of those utterly tedious amusements
  one only finds at an English country house on an English
  country Sunday. I don't think anyone at all morally respon-

---

411 *Yes* LC adds 'I have done many foolish things in my life. That was the most
    foolish'.
414–6 *because . . . Tenby* om. F. In LC she accuses Lord G of throwing her over 'without
    a word of warning', of giving no explanation and refusing to see her. Later in this
    version we are given more circumstantial details of the flirtation in question,
    including the rather crude admonition: 'Mrs Cheveley, you had not quite realized
    that conservatories have glass walls. They are not like boudoirs. They are not so
    convenient.' In the subsequent description of Tenby, C (following revisions to
    BLTS) included remarks on the English Country House later transferred to Act I
    (ll. 372–5). Mrs C had been seen sitting on Lord Mortlake's knees, kissing him;
    she offers flippant reasons for this behaviour ('And I never could live without at least
    one flirtation a day').
417–8 *my lawyer . . . terms* too honourable to let it be thought that a lady had given
    grounds for the breaking-off of an engagement, Lord Goring took the responsibility
    upon himself. The 'terms' would be a financial settlement to avoid the possibility
    of his being sued for breach of promise of marriage.
428–9 *I don't think . . . country house* first appears in F. The tedium of English country
    life is a theme of the first act of *Woman*.

sible for what he or she does at an English country house.

LORD GORING
Yes. I know lots of people think that.   430

MRS CHEVELEY
I loved you, Arthur.

LORD GORING
My dear Mrs Cheveley, you have always been far too clever
to know anything about love.

MRS CHEVELEY
I did love you. And you loved me. You know you loved me;
and love is a very wonderful thing. I suppose that when a man   435
has once loved a woman, he will do anything for her, except
continue to love her?

Puts her hand on his

LORD GORING (*Taking his hand away quietly*)
Yes: except that.

MRS CHEVELEY (*After a pause*)
I am tired of living abroad. I want to come back to London.
I want to have a charming house here. I want to have a salon.   440
If one could only teach the English how to talk, and the Irish
how to listen, society here would be quite civilized. Besides,
I have arrived at the romantic stage. When I saw you last night
at the Chilterns', I knew you were the only person I had ever
cared for, if I ever have cared for anybody, Arthur. And so,   445
on the morning of the day you marry me, I will give you
Robert Chiltern's letter. That is my offer. I will give it to you
now, if you promise to marry me.

LORD GORING
Now?

MRS CHEVELEY (*Smiling*)
Tomorrow.   450

LORD GORING
Are you really serious?

439 *I am tired of living abroad* . . . LC's version of the remainder of this act, which is based
    on C, includes some of the material printed here but om. 11. 439–51 ('I am tired
    . . . really serious?'), 461–84 ('Do you think . . : true character') and 500–96 (Well,
    Arthur, . . . With pleasure'). F's version approximates to that of PR.
440–5 *I want to have . . . And so* om. F. The ideal of a *salon*, in which the hostess would
    attract to her drawing-room the cream of intellectual society, was difficult to achieve.
    Wilde said of the rich, homosexual Russian emigré André Raffalovich that he came
    to London intending to found a *salon* and only succeeded in founding a saloon
    (*Letters*, p. 173, note).

MRS CHEVELEY
  Yes, quite serious.

LORD GORING
  I should make you a very bad husband.

MRS CHEVELEY
  I don't mind bad husbands. I have had two. They amused me
  immensely.   455

LORD GORING
  You mean that you amused yourself immensely, don't you?

MRS CHEVELEY
  What do you know about my married life?

LORD GORING
  Nothing: but I can read it like a book.

MRS CHEVELEY
  What book?

LORD GORING (*Rising*)
  The Book of Numbers.   460

MRS CHEVELEY
  Do you think it quite charming of you to be so rude to a
  woman in your own house?

LORD GORING
  In the case of very fascinating women, sex is a challenge, not
  a defence.

MRS CHEVELEY
  I suppose that is meant for a compliment. My dear Arthur,   465
  women are never disarmed by compliments. Men always are.
  That is the difference between the two sexes.

LORD GORING
  Women are never disarmed by anything, as far as I know
  them.

MRS CHEVELEY (*After a pause*)
  Then you are going to allow your greatest friend, Robert   470
  Chiltern, to be ruined, rather than marry someone who really
  has considerable attractions left. I thought you would have
  risen to some great height of self-sacrifice, Arthur. I think you

---

461-9 *Do you think . . . as I know them* first appears in PR. Lines 463-4 ('In the case of
  a very fascinating woman . . . ') are adapted from material originally drafted for Act
  II.

should. And the rest of your life you could spend in
contemplating your own perfections. 475

LORD GORING

Oh! I do that as it is. And self-sacrifice is a thing that should
be put down by law. It is so demoralizing to the people for
whom one sacrifices oneself. They always go to the bad.

MRS CHEVELEY

As if anything could demoralize Robert Chiltern! You seem
to forget that I know his real character. 480

LORD GORING

What you know about him is not his real character. It was an
act of folly done in his youth, dishonourable, I admit,
shameful, I admit, unworthy of him, I admit, and therefore
... not his true character.

MRS CHEVELEY

How you men stand up for each other! 485

LORD GORING

How you women war against each other!

MRS CHEVELEY (*Bitterly*)

I only war against one woman, against Gertrude Chiltern. I
hate her. I hate her now more than ever.

LORD GORING

Because you have brought a real tragedy into her life, I
suppose. 490

MRS CHEVELEY (*With a sneer*)

Oh, there is only one real tragedy in a woman's life. The fact
that her past is always her lover, and her future invariably her
husband.

LORD GORING

Lady Chiltern knows nothing of the kind of life to which you
are alluding. 495

MRS CHEVELEY

A woman whose size in gloves is seven and three-quarters
never knows much about anything. You know Gertrude has

476–8 *And self-sacrifice ... sacrifices oneself* this anticipates Lord G's interview with Lady
C near the end of Act IV (ll. 393–436).
489–98 *Because ... seven and three-quarters?* added to BLTS with variations of detail. In
a line deleted from C Mrs C remarks that 'I don't mind her having a large heart,
but I can't stand large hands'. After l. 499 both BLTS and C move to the equivalent
of l. 595: the letters have been burned, and the bracelet incident is absent.

always worn seven and three-quarters? That is one of the
reasons why there was never any moral sympathy between us
... Well, Arthur, I suppose this romantic interview may be   500
regarded as at an end. You admit it was romantic, don't you?
For the privilege of being your wife I was ready to surrender
a great prize, the climax of my diplomatic career. You decline.
Very well. If Sir Robert doesn't uphold my Argentine scheme,
I expose him. *Voilà tout.*   505

LORD GORING
You mustn't do that. It would be vile, horrible, infamous.

MRS CHEVELEY (*Shrugging her shoulders*)
Oh! don't use big words. They mean so little. It is a
commercial transaction. That is all. There is no good mixing
up sentimentality in it. I offered to sell Robert Chiltern a
certain thing. If he won't pay me my price, he will have to pay 510
the world a greater price. There is no more to be said. I must
go. Good-bye. Won't you shake hands?

LORD GORING
With you? No. Your transaction with Robert Chiltern may
pass as a loathsome commercial transaction of a loathsome
commercial age; but you seem to have forgotten that you who 515
came here tonight to talk of love, you whose lips desecrated
the word love, you to whom the thing is a book closely sealed,
went this afternoon to the house of one of the most noble and
gentle women in the world to degrade her husband in her eyes,
to try and kill her love for him, to put poison in her heart, and 520
bitterness in her life, to break her idol and, it may be, spoil
her soul. That I cannot forgive you. That was horrible. For
that there can be no forgiveness.

MRS CHEVELEY
Arthur, you are unjust to me. Believe me, you are quite unjust
to me. I didn't go to taunt Gertrude at all. I had no idea of 525

501–4 *You admit . . . Very well* first appears in PR.
505 *Voilà tout* altered in PR from its English equivalent 'That is all'.
506 *You mustn't* altered from 'Don't' in PR.
507–12 *It is a commercial . . . I must go* first appears in PR.
513–7 *Your transaction . . . sealed* first appears in PR (F begins 'You went this afternoon
. . . '), as do ll. 520–2 (to try . . . her soul'), 522–3 ('That I cannot . . . forgiveness'),
524 ('you are unjust to me') and 529–35 ('If you don't . . . the whole thing'). These
differences between PR and F might indicate that copy for PR was based on a fuller
version predating F (and simplified for performance by the compiler of F) or that
Wilde added to the rhetorical intensity of the passage in 1898–99 when he prepared
it for the printer. Only the last of the additions seems designed to clarify the play's
action.

doing anything of the kind when I entered. I called with Lady
Markby simply to ask whether an ornament, a jewel, that I
lost somewhere last night, had been found at the Chilterns'.
If you don't believe me, you can ask Lady Markby. She will
tell you it is true. The scene that occurred happened after 530
Lady Markby had left, and was really forced on me by
Gertrude's rudeness and sneers. I called, oh! – a little out of
malice if you like – but really to ask if a diamond brooch of
mine had been found. That was the origin of the whole
thing. 535

LORD GORING
A diamond snake-brooch with a ruby?

MRS CHEVELEY
Yes. How do you know?

LORD GORING
Because it is found. In point of fact, I found it myself, and
stupidly forgot to tell the butler anything about it as I was
leaving. (*Goes over to the writing-table and pulls out the drawers*) 540
It is in this drawer. No, that one. This is the brooch, isn't
it?

Holds up the brooch

MRS CHEVELEY
Yes. I am so glad to get it back. It was . . . a present.

LORD GORING
Won't you wear it?

MRS CHEVELEY
Certainly, if you pin it in. (LORD GORING *suddenly clasps it on* 545
her arm) Why do you put it on as a bracelet? I never knew it
could be worn as a bracelet.

LORD GORING
Really?

MRS CHEVELEY (*Holding out her handsome arm*)
No; but it looks very well on me as a bracelet, doesn't it?

LORD GORING
Yes; much better than when I saw it last. 550

MRS CHEVELEY
When did you see it last?

536 *with a ruby* (with ruby eyes F)
549 s.d. *holding . . . arm* added to PR.

LORD GORING (*Calmly*)
Oh, ten years ago, on Lady Berkshire, from whom you stole
it.

MRS CHEVELEY (*Starting*)
What do you mean?

LORD GORING
I mean that you stole that ornament from my cousin, Mary　555
Berkshire, to whom I gave it when she was married. Suspicion
fell on a wretched servant, who was sent away in disgrace. I
recognized it last night. I determined to say nothing about it
till I had found the thief. I have found the thief now, and I
have heard her own confession.　　　　　　　　　　　560

MRS CHEVELEY (*Tossing her head*)
It is not true.

LORD GORING
You know it is true. Why, thief is written across your face at
this moment.

MRS CHEVELEY
I will deny the whole affair from beginning to end. I will say
that I have never seen this wretched thing, that it was never　565
in my possession.
　　　　　MRS CHEVELEY *tries to get the bracelet off her arm,*
　　　　　but fails. LORD GORING *looks on amused. Her thin*
　　　　　fingers tear at the jewel to no purpose. A curse
　　　　　　　　　breaks from her

LORD GORING
The drawback of stealing a thing, Mrs Cheveley, is that one
never knows how wonderful the thing that one steals is. You
can't get that bracelet off, unless you know where the spring
is. And I see you don't know where the spring is. It is rather　570
difficult to find.

MRS CHEVELEY
You brute! You coward!
　　　　　　She tries again to unclasp the bracelet, but fails

LORD GORING
Oh! don't use big words. They mean so little.

---

560 s.d. added to PR by Wilde together with subsequent s.d. at 11. 566 (*Her thin . . .*
　　from her), 574, 578 and 581.
567–8 *The drawback . . . steals is* added in manuscript to F.

MRS CHEVELEY (*Again tears at the bracelet in a paroxysm of rage,
with inarticulate sounds. Then stops, and looks at* LORD
GORING)
What are you going to do?

LORD GORING
I am going to ring for my servant. He is an admirable servant.   575
Always comes in the moment one rings for him. When he
comes I will tell him to fetch the police.

MRS CHEVELEY (*Trembling*)
The police? What for?

LORD GORING
Tomorrow the Berkshires will prosecute you. That is what the
police are for.   580

MRS CHEVELEY (*Is now in an agony of physical terror. Her face is
distorted. Her mouth awry. A mask has fallen from her. She is,
for the moment, dreadful to look at*)
Don't do that. I will do anything you want. Anything in the
world you want.

LORD GORING
Give me Robert Chiltern's letter.

MRS CHEVELEY
Stop! Stop! Let me have time to think.

LORD GORING
Give me Robert Chiltern's letter.   585

MRS CHEVELEY
I have not got it with me. I will give it to you tomorrow.

LORD GORING
You know you are lying. Give it to me at once. (MRS CHEVELEY
pulls the letter out, and hands it to him. She is horribly pale.) This
is it?

MRS CHEVELEY (*In a hoarse voice*)
Yes.   590

LORD GORING (*Takes the letter, examines it, sighs, and burns it over
the lamp*)
For so well-dressed a woman, Mrs Cheveley, you have
moments of admirable common sense. I congratulate you.

576–7 *Always . . . are for* (And have you given in charge for theft F).
586–90 *I have not . . . Yes* F has 'Yes! yes!' followed by the s.d. '*Bus. – gives letter. Lord
    G. takes bracelet off*'.

MRS CHEVELEY (*Catches sight of* LADY CHILTERN's *letter, the cover of which is just showing from under the blotting-book*)
Please get me a glass of water.

LORD GORING
Certainly.
Goes to the corner of the room and pours out a glass of water. While his back is turned MRS CHEVELEY *steals* LADY CHILTERN's *letter. When* LORD GORING *returns with the glass she refuses it with a gesture*

MRS CHEVELEY
Thank you. Will you help me on with my cloak?   595

LORD GORING
With pleasure.

Puts her cloak on

MRS CHEVELEY
Thanks. I am never going to try to harm Robert Chiltern again.

LORD GORING
Fortunately you have not the chance, Mrs Cheveley.

MRS CHEVELEY
Well, if even I had the chance, I wouldn't. On the contrary,   600
I am going to render him a great service.

LORD GORING
I am charmed to hear it. It is a reformation.

MRS CHEVELEY
Yes. I can't bear so upright a gentleman, so honourable an English gentleman, being so shamefully deceived, and so –

LORD GORING
Well?   605

MRS CHEVELEY
I find that somehow Gertrude Chiltern's dying speech and confession has strayed into my pocket.

---

593 s.d. F has a practical, prompter's version of this s.d.: '*Shows by her expression that she remembers the pink letter under the blotter*'.
597 *Thanks* . . . from this point LC, BLTS, C and MS differ only in minor details from F, PR and 1st ed.
605–7 *Well? . . . pocket* om. F, LC. The lines are found in BLTS and MS ('What do you mean?' for 'Well?') and are deleted in C. The phrase 'dying speech and confession' recalls the 'confession' of Mrs C that figures in early drafts.

LORD GORING
What do you mean?

MRS CHEVELEY (*With a bitter note of triumph in her voice.*)
I mean that I am going to send Robert Chiltern the love letter
his wife wrote to you tonight.   610

LORD GORING
Love letter?

MRS CHEVELEY (*Laughing*)
'I want you. I trust you. I am coming to you. Gertrude.'
          LORD GORING *rushes to the bureau and takes up the
          envelope, finds it empty, and turns round*

LORD GORING
You wretched woman, must you always be thieving? Give me
back that letter. I'll take it from you by force. You shall not
leave my room till I have got it.   615
          He rushes towards her, but MRS CHEVELEY *at once
          puts her hand on the electric bell that is on the table.
          The bell sounds with shrill reverberations, and* PHIPPS
          enters

MRS CHEVELEY (*After a pause*)
Lord Goring merely rang that you should show me out.
Good-night, Lord Goring!
          Goes out, followed by PHIPPS. *Her face is illumined
          with evil triumph. There is joy in her eyes.
          Youth seems to have come back to her. Her last
          glance is like a swift arrow.* LORD GORING *bites his
          lip, and lights a cigarette*

ACT-DROP

611–12 *Love Letter? . . . Gertrude* om. BLTS, MS. In F Lord G has put the pink envelope
          in his pocket. He examines it now and finds it to be empty.
613 *You wretched woman* om. BLTS, MS; in C 'miserable' is del. and 'unfortunate'
          substituted; *must you . . . thieving?* om. F.
614–5 *You shall not . . . got it* om. F.
615 s.d. *The bell . . . reverberations* added to PR.
617 s.d. *Her face . . . a swift arrow* added to PR.

Act IV

Scene – Same as Act II
LORD GORING *is standing by the fireplace with his
hands in his pockets. He is looking rather bored*

LORD GORING (*Pulls out his watch, inspects it, and rings the bell*)
It is a great nuisance. I can't find anyone in this house to talk
to. And I am full of interesting information. I feel like the
latest edition of something or other.
Enter SERVANT

JAMES
Sir Robert is still at the Foreign Office, my lord.

LORD GORING
Lady Chiltern not down yet?   5

JAMES
Her ladyship has not yet left her room. Miss Chiltern has just
come in from riding.

LORD GORING (*To himself*)
Ah! that is something.

JAMES
Lord Caversham has been waiting some time in the library for
Sir Robert. I told him your lordship was here.   10

LORD GORING
Thank you. Would you kindly tell him I've gone?

JAMES (*Bowing*)
I shall do so, my lord.
Exit SERVANT

---

1 s.d. *Scene* in F, LC, C and MS the act begins with a different sequence and is set in
Lady C's boudoir. Mabel tells Lady C about Sir Robert's speech (11. 50–5 in the
present text) and complains that Lord G failed to keep his appointment with her.
When he arrives, Lord G is reproached with his discourtesy. He asks to speak to Lady
C alone. She tells him that she has decided to stand by her husband, and is assured
that the incriminating letter has been burned (1. 201 etc.). The present arrangement
appears in BLTS and PR. In BLTS the first sentence only of the s.d. is included.
1 *this house* (this extraordinary house BLTS).
1–3 *to talk . . . or other* om. BLTS.
4 *Sir Robert . . . Office* In BLTS this is a question, to which James replies 'Yes, my
lord'.

LORD GORING
Really, I don't want to meet my father three days running. It
is a great deal too much excitement for any son. I hope to
goodness he won't come up. Fathers should be neither seen   15
nor heard. That is the only proper basis for family life.
Mothers are different. Mothers are darlings.
*Throws himself down into a chair, picks up a paper and begins
to read it*
Enter LORD CAVERSHAM

LORD CAVERSHAM
Well, sir, what are you doing here? Wasting your time as
usual, I suppose?

LORD GORING (*Throws down paper and rises*)
My dear father, when one pays a visit it is for the purpose of   20
wasting other people's time, not one's own.

LORD CAVERSHAM
Have you been thinking over what I spoke to you about last
night?

LORD GORING
I have been thinking about nothing else.

LORD CAVERSHAM
Engaged to be married yet?   25

LORD GORING (*Genially*)
Not yet: but I hope to be before lunch-time.

LORD CAVERSHAM (*Caustically*)
You can have till dinner-time if it would be of any convenience
to you.

LORD GORING
Thanks awfully, but I think I'd sooner be engaged before
lunch.   30

LORD CAVERSHAM
Humph! Never know when you are serious or not.

LORD GORING
Neither do I father.

A pause

LORD CAVERSHAM
I suppose you have read *The Times* this morning?

15-7 *Fathers ... different* om. BLTS.

LORD GORING (*Airily*)
The Times? Certainly not. I only read *The Morning Post*. All
that one should know about modern life is where the   35
Duchesses are; anything else is quite demoralizing.

LORD CAVERSHAM
Do you mean to say you have not read *The Times'* leading
article on Robert Chiltern's career?

LORD GORING
Good heavens! No. What does it say?

LORD CAVERSHAM
What should it say, sir? Everything complimentary, of   40
course. Chiltern's speech last night on this Argentine Canal
Scheme was one of the finest pieces of oratory ever delivered
in the House since Canning.

LORD GORING
Ah! Never heard of Canning. Never wanted to. And did ...
did Chiltern uphold the scheme?   45

LORD CAVERSHAM
Uphold it, sir? How little you know him! Why, he denounced
it roundly, and the whole system of modern political finance.
This speech is the turning-point in his career, as *The Times*
points out. You should read this article, sir. (*Opens* The
Times) 'Sir Robert Chiltern ... most rising of all our young   50
statesmen ... Brilliant orator ... Unblemished career ...
Well-known integrity of character ... Represents what is best
in English public life ... Noble contrast to the lax morality

---

34 *The Times?* om. BLTS, which continues: 'Certainly not, father. Nothing ages one so
   rapidly as reading the *Times*'. In LC and earlier texts these opinions are relayed by
   Mabel, who attributes them to Lord G. As she leafs through the paper she
   remarks:
       Wish there were not so many pages in *The Times* – I can never find anything but
       the letters from the country clergy, and the reports of the university extension
       scheme, and they are so demoralizing for a young girl.
   A manuscript s.d. in F has her *'sitting on couch, L. throwing sheets of the paper about
   in vain endeavour to find the speech.'*.
43 *Canning* George Canning (1770-1827), statesman and orator. The references to
   Canning first appear in PR.
46–55 *Uphold ... of you, sir* in LC and earlier versions, Mabel reads the excerpts from
   the report, including '"ethical something" ... Ah! that is too long a word for me.
   Besides, I don't know what ethical means'. In BLTS Lord C is more emphatic in his
   denunciation of the canal scheme: 'Why, he didn't leave a drop of water in the whole
   damned concern. The thing is a fraud, and a very infamous fraud, and he denounced
   it roundly ...'. See Appendix I for the BLTS continuation of the dialogue after this
   speech.

so common among foreign politicians.' They will never say
that of you, sir.   55

LORD GORING
I sincerely hope not, father. However, I am delighted at what
you tell me about Robert, thoroughly delighted. It shows he
has got pluck.

LORD CAVERSHAM
He has got more than pluck, sir, he has got genius.

LORD GORING
Ah! I prefer pluck. It is not so common, nowadays, as genius   60
is.

LORD CAVERSHAM
I wish you would go into Parliament.

LORD GORING
My dear father, only people who look dull ever get into the
House of Commons, and only people who are dull ever
succeed there.   65

LORD CAVERSHAM
Why don't you try to do something useful in life?

LORD GORING
I am far too young.

LORD CAVERSHAM (*Testily*)
I hate this affectation of youth, sir. It is a great deal too
prevalent nowadays.

LORD GORING
Youth isn't an affectation. Youth is an art.   70

68 *this affectation of youth* Wilde frequently expressed his preference for the company
of the young, statements which sometimes touched dangerously on his sexual
preferences and which were turned against him at his trials. Cf., for example, among
his 'Phrases and Philosophies for the Use of the Young': 'The old believe everything;
the middle-aged suspect everything; the young know everything' (*CW*, p. 1206). A
similar collection, 'A Few Maxims for the Instruction of the Over-educated' (*Saturday
Review*, 1891), includes 'Those whom the gods love grow young'. Asked in cross-
examination 'What enjoyment was it to you to entertain grooms and coachmen [to
expensive meals]?' Wilde replied: 'The pleasure to me was being with those who are
young, bright, happy, careless, and free. I do not like the sensible and I do not like the
old' (H. Montgomery Hyde, *The Trials of Oscar Wilde*, New York, 1973, p. 127). See
also Lord Illingworth's praise of the virtues of youth in *Woman* (III, 12–20).

LORD CAVERSHAM
Why don't you propose to that pretty Miss Chiltern?

LORD GORING
I am of a very nervous disposition, especially in the morning.

LORD CAVERSHAM
I don't suppose there is the smallest chance of her accepting you.   75

LORD GORING
I don't know how the betting stands today.

LORD CAVERSHAM
If she did accept you she would be the prettiest fool in England.

LORD GORING
That is just what I should like to marry. A thoroughly sensible wife would reduce me to a condition of absolute idiocy in less   80
than six months.

LORD CAVERSHAM
You don't deserve her, sir.

LORD GORING
My dear father, if we men married the women we deserved, we should have a very bad time of it.
                              Enter MABEL CHILTERN

MABEL CHILTERN
Oh! ... How do you do, Lord Caversham? I hope Lady   85
Caversham is quite well?

LORD CAVERSHAM
Lady Caversham is as usual, as usual.

LORD GORING
Good morning, Miss Mabel!

MABEL CHILTERN (*Taking no notice at all of* LORD GORING, *and addressing herself exclusively to* LORD CAVERSHAM)
And Lady Caversham's bonnets ... are they at all better?

---

76 *I don't ... today* BLTS adds 'I have not been to the club today', which may have seemed to imply too strongly that Mabel's name really is bandied about the club world in an ungentlemanly fashion.
77–81 *If she did ... six months* used later in the act in LC and earlier versions.

LORD CAVERSHAM
They have had a serious relapse, I am sorry to say.   90

LORD GORING
Good morning, Miss Mabel!

MABEL CHILTERN (*To* LORD CAVERSHAM)
I hope an operation will not be necessary.

LORD CAVERSHAM (*Smiling at her pertness*)
If it is we shall have to give Lady Caversham a narcotic.
Otherwise she would never consent to have a feather
touched.   95

LORD GORING (*With increased emphasis*)
Good morning, Miss Mabel!

MABEL CHILTERN (*Turning round with feigned surprise*)
Oh, are you here? Of course you understand that after your
breaking your appointment I am never going to speak to you
again.

LORD GORING
Oh, please don't say such a thing. You are the one person in   100
London I really like to have to listen to me.

MABEL CHILTERN
Lord Goring, I never believe a single word that either you or
I say to each other.

LORD CAVERSHAM
You are quite right, my dear, quite right ... as far as he is
concerned, I mean.   105

MABEL CHILTERN
Do you think you could possibly make your son behave a little
better occasionally? Just as a change.

LORD CAVERSHAM
I regret to say, Miss Chiltern, that I have no influence at all
over my son. I wish I had. If I had, I know what I would make
him do.   110

90–7 *They have had ... Oh, are you here?* om. BLTS, which (with MS and C) has a
    different version of the conversation. Lord G, told by Mabel that she 'got a great deal
    of sympathy, especially from Mr Trafford' on account of her fruitless wait for him
    in the Park, excuses himself.
        ... I was terribly engaged this morning. I was asleep, in fact, till ten. And when
    I woke up, I found that my horse had gone lame. I went a little lame myself.
    Everything, in fact, went quite lame.

MABEL CHILTERN
  I am afraid that he has one of those terribly weak natures that
  are not susceptible to influence.

LORD CAVERSHAM
  He is very heartless, very heartless.

LORD GORING
  It seems to me that I am a little in the way here.

MABEL CHILTERN
  It is very good for you to be in the way, and to know what   115
  people say of you behind your back.

LORD GORING
  I don't at all like knowing what people say of me behind my
  back. It makes me far too conceited.

LORD CAVERSHAM
  After that, my dear I really must bid you good morning.

MABEL CHILTERN
  Oh! I hope you are not going to leave me all alone with Lord   120
  Goring? Especially at such an early hour in the day.

LORD CAVERSHAM
  I am afraid I can't take him with me to Downing Street. It is
  not the Prime Minister's day for seeing the unemployed.
           Shakes hands with MABEL CHILTERN, *takes up his hat*
           and stick, and goes out, with a parting glare of indignation
                                                     at LORD GORING

MABEL CHILTERN (*Takes up roses and begins to arrange them in a*
  bowl on the table)
  People who don't keep their appointments in the Park are
  horrid.   125

LORD GORING
  Detestable.

MABEL CHILTERN
  I am glad you admit it. But I wish you wouldn't look so
  pleased about it.

122–3 *I am afraid ... unemployed* BLTS follows up Lord G's reference (later deleted)
    to his horse, at ll.90–7. Concern about the *unemployed* as a group, and as a political
    force, had come to a head in the Trafalgar Square riot in 1886. It was a commonplace
    of the conservative press (including *Punch*) that only workshy ne'er-do-wells took
    part, and *The Times* used inverted commas for the collective noun – 'the
    unemployed' – in its report of the disturbance. The s.d. after this speech, and at
    l. 124, first appear in PR.

LORD GORING
  I can't help it. I always look pleased when I am with you.

MABEL CHILTERN (*Sadly*)
  Then I suppose it is my duty to remain with you?   130

LORD GORING
  Of course it is.

MABEL CHILTERN
  Well, my duty is a thing I never do, on principle. It always
  depresses me. So I am afraid I must leave you.

LORD GORING
  Please don't, Miss Mabel. I have something very particular to
  say to you.   135

MABEL CHILTERN (*Rapturously*)
  Oh! is it a proposal?

LORD GORING (*Somewhat taken aback*)
  Well, yes, it is – I am bound to say it is.

MABEL CHILTERN (*With a sigh of pleasure*)
  I am so glad. That makes the second today.

LORD GORING (*Indignantly*)
  The second today? What conceited ass has been impertinent
  enough to dare to propose to you before I had proposed to   140
  you?

MABEL CHILTERN
  Tommy Trafford, of course. It is one of Tommy's days for
  proposing. He always proposes on Tuesdays and Thursdays,
  during the season.

LORD GORING
  You didn't accept him, I hope?   145

MABEL CHILTERN
  I make it a rule never to accept Tommy. That is why he goes
  on proposing. Of course, as you didn't turn up this morning,
  I very nearly said yes. It would have been an excellent lesson
  both for him and for you if I had. It would have taught you
  both better manners.   150

---

130 *Then . . . you?* (In that case, I will certainly leave you BLTS). The s.d. here, and
   at ll. 136, 137, 139, and 158 first appear in PR.
142–3 *It is . . . season* Cf. note to Act III, ll. 76–7. The last three words do not appear
   in BLTS.

LORD GORING
Oh! bother Tommy Trafford. Tommy is a silly little ass. I love you.

MABEL CHILTERN
I know. And I think you might have mentioned it before. I am sure I have given you heaps of opportunities.

LORD GORING
Mabel, do be serious. Please be serious.   155

MABEL CHILTERN
Ah! that is the sort of thing a man always says to a girl before he has been married to her. He never says it afterwards.

LORD GORING (*Taking hold of her hand*)
Mabel, I have told you that I love you. Can't you love me a little in return?

MABEL CHILTERN
You silly Arthur! If you knew anything about . . . anything,   160
which you don't, you would know that I adore you. Everyone in London knows it except you. It is a public scandal the way I adore you. I have been going about for the last six months telling the whole of society that I adore you. I wonder you consent to have anything to say to me. I have no character left   165
at all. At least, I feel so happy that I am quite sure I have no character left at all.

LORD GORING (*Catches her in his arms and kisses her. Then there is a pause of bliss*)
Dear! Do you know I was awfully afraid of being refused!

MABEL CHILTERN (*Looking up at him*)
But you never have been refused yet by anybody, have you Arthur? I can't imagine anyone refusing you.   170

LORD GORING (*After kissing her again*)
Of course I'm not nearly good enough for you, Mabel.

156–7 *Ah! . . . afterwards* BLTS adds: 'I wish you wouldn't say those sort of things to me. They don't come well from you at all'. The revision concentrates attention on the references to marriage and 'seriousness', without the distracting reference to Lord G's reputation.

160 *Anything about . . . anything* (Anything about women BLTS).

162 *a public scandal* This phrase, present in all versions of the proposal sequence (which LC, C, F and MS place at the end of the act) reiterates the comic variation on the scandal theme (cf. Lady M's speech at II, 536, etc., Mabel's references to the *tableaux vivants*, etc.). The s.d. before l. 168 first appears in PR.

MABEL CHILTERN (*Nestling close to him*)
I am so glad, darling. I was afraid you were.

LORD GORING (*After some hesitation*)
And I'm ... I'm a little over thirty.

MABLE CHILTERN
Dear, you look weeks younger than that.

LORD GORING (*Enthusiastically*)
How sweet of you to say so! ... And it is only fair to tell you   175
frankly that I am fearfully extravagant.

MABEL CHILTERN
But so am I, Arthur. So we're sure to agree. And now I must
go and see Gertrude.

LORD GORING
Must you really?   *Kisses her*

MABEL CHILTERN
Yes.   180

LORD GORING
Then do tell her I want to talk to her particularly. I have been
waiting here all the morning to see either her or Robert.

MABEL CHILTERN
Do you mean to say you didn't come here expressly to propose
to me?

LORD GORING (*Triumphantly*)
No; that was a flash of genius.   185

MABEL CHILTERN
Your first.

LORD GORING (*With determination*)
My last.

MABEL CHILTERN
I am delighted to hear it. Now don't stir. I'll be back in five

---

175–6 *And it is . . . extravagant* om. BLTS, which has an extended version of the
dialogue: see Appendix I.
188 *I am delighted to hear it* BLTS has a longer version of this speech:
    I am very glad to hear it. I certainly don't want to marry a man of genius. I'd be
    very unhappy with him. I like you. You have no past: and no future. You are a
    perfect darling. Just the sort of man every girl should marry.
    Lord G replies: 'I hope they won't, darling. I don't want to marry anyone but you'.
    Mabel's next speech begins, 'I'll take very great precautions that you don't', and
    picks up with 'I'll be back in five minutes ... '.

minutes. And don't fall into any temptations while I am
away.   190

LORD GORING
Dear Mabel, while you are away, there are none. It makes me
horribly dependent on you.
                    Enter LADY CHILTERN

LADY CHILTERN
Good morning, dear! How pretty you are looking!

MABEL CHILTERN
How pale you are looking, Gertrude! It is most becoming!

LADY CHILTERN
Good morning, Lord Goring!   195

LORD GORING (*Bowing*)
Good morning, Lady Chiltern!

MABEL CHILTERN (*Aside to* LORD GORING)
I shall be in the conservatory, under the second palm tree on
the left.

LORD GORING
Second on the left?

MABEL CHILTERN (*With a look of mock surprise*)
Yes; the usual palm tree.   200
            Blows a kiss to him, unobserved by LADY CHILTERN,
                                            and goes out

LORD GORING
Lady Chiltern, I have a certain amount of very good news to
tell you. Mrs Cheveley gave me up Robert's letter last night,
and I burned it. Robert is safe.

LADY CHILTERN (*Sinking on the sofa*)
Safe! Oh! I am so glad of that. What a good friend you are to
him – to us!   205

LORD GORING
There is only one person now that could be said to be in any
danger.

196 *Good morning, Lady Chiltern* in BLTS Lord G asks Mabel to leave the room, and
  she complies. The s.d. at ll.197, 198, 199 and 200 first appear in PR. With the
  interview between Lord G and Lady C the printed version and its close antecedents
  (F, BLTS) begin to agree with LC, C and MS.
197 *second palm tree* in l. 382 it has become the third.
201, etc. *Lady Chiltern* . . . LC and earlier versions have a different beginning to this
  sequence, including variant speeches for Lady C. See Appendix I.

LADY CHILTERN
  Who is that?

LORD GORING (*Sitting down beside her*)
  Yourself.

LADY CHILTERN
  I! In danger? What do you mean?   210

LORD GORING
  Danger is too great a word. It is a word I should not have used.
  But I admit I have something to tell you that may distress you,
  that terribly distresses me. Yesterday evening you wrote me
  a very beautiful, womanly letter, asking me for my help. You
  wrote to me as one of your oldest friends, one of your   215
  husband's oldest friends. Mrs Cheveley stole that letter from
  my rooms.

LADY CHILTERN
  Well, what use is it to her? Why should she not have it?

LORD GORING (*Rising*)
  Lady Chiltern, I will be quite frank with you. Mrs Cheveley
  puts a certain construction on that letter and proposes to send   220
  it to your husband.

LADY CHILTERN
  But what construction could she put on it? . . . Oh! not that!
  not that! If I in – in trouble, and wanting your help, trusting
  you, propose to come to you . . . that you may advise me . . .
  assist me . . . Oh! are there women so horrible as that ..? And   225
  she proposes to send it to my husband? Tell me what
  happened. Tell me all that happened.

LORD GORING
  Mrs Cheveley was concealed in a room adjoining my library,
  without my knowledge. I thought that the person who was

---

222 *But what . . . on it?* in F this is followed by a manuscript s.d.: '*They look fixedly at
  each other a moment. Lady C. falls back on chair horrified*'.
225–7 *Oh! . . . happened* texts before PR have a longer version of this, far more
  melodramatic in tone:
      Oh! what have I done? What did you make me do? Why did you let her take it?
      You should have killed her first. Why didn't you kill her? You have killed me
      instead! . . . No, no, what have I to fear? I am innocent of anything . . . Robert
      could not believe such a thing of me, any more than I before yesterday could have
      believed of him what I now know to be true. Ah! he will believe it! It will be his
      revenge! (BLTS, later deleted in manuscript revision.)
  In F there are appropriate manuscript s.ds. for this: she moves '*wildly R. to C. and
  down L.*', sinks on the couch, rises '*with a cry*' ('Ah! he will believe it!') and falls back
  on the couch.

waiting in that room to see me was yourself. Robert came in   230
unexpectedly. A chair or something fell in the room. He
forced his way in, and he discovered her. We had a terrible
scene. I still thought it was you. He left me in anger. At the
end of everything Mrs Cheveley got possession of your letter
– she stole it, when or how, I don't know.   235

LADY CHILTERN
   At what hour did this happen?

LORD GORING
   At half-past ten. And now I propose that we tell Robert the
   whole thing at once.

LADY CHILTERN (*Looking at him with amazement that is almost
terror*)
   You want me to tell Robert that the woman you expected was
   not Mrs Cheveley, but myself? That it was I whom you   240
   thought was concealed in a room in your house, at half-past
   ten o'clock at night? You want me to tell him that?

LORD GORING
   I think it is better that he should know the exact truth.

LADY CHILTERN (*Rising*)
   Oh, I couldn't, I couldn't!

LORD GORING
   May I do it?   245

LADY CHILTERN
   No.

LORD GORING (*Gravely*)
   You are wrong, Lady Chiltern.

LADY CHILTERN
   No. The letter must be intercepted. That is all. But how can
   I do it? Letters arrive for him every moment of the day. His
   secretaries open them and hand them to him. I dare not ask   250
   the servants to bring me his letters. It would be impossible.
   Oh! why don't you tell me what to do?

LORD GORING
   Pray be calm, Lady Chiltern, and answer the questions I am
   going to put to you. You said his secretaries open his
   letters.   255

LADY CHILTERN
   Yes.

LORD GORING
  Who is with him today? Mr Trafford, isn't it?

LADY CHILTERN
  No. Mr Montfort, I think.

LORD GORING
  You can trust him?

LADY CHILTERN (*With a gesture of despair*)
  Oh! how do I know?   260

LORD GORING
  He would do what you asked him, wouldn't he?

LADY CHILTERN
  I think so.

LORD GORING
  Your letter was on pink paper. He could recognize it without
  reading it, couldn't he? By the colour?

LADY CHILTERN
  I suppose so.   265

LORD GORING
  Is he in the house now?

LADY CHILTERN
  Yes.

LORD GORING
  Then I will go and see him myself, and tell him that a certain
  letter, written on pink paper, is to be forwarded to Robert
  today, and that at all costs it must not reach him. (*Goes to the*   270
  door, and opens it) Oh! Robert is coming upstairs with the
  letter in his hand. It has reached him already.

LADY CHILTERN (*With a cry of pain*)
  Oh! you have saved his life; what have you done with mine?
              Enter SIR ROBERT CHILTERN. *He has the letter in*
              his hand, and is reading it. He comes towards his
              wife, not noticing LORD GORING'S *presence*

---

257 *Mr Trafford* earlier versions have 'Mr Montfort' (Cf. note to 'The Persons of the
    Play') and om. l. 258.
268–73 *Then I will go . . . mine!* the present arrangement first appears in BLTS. F, LC
    and earlier versions have Mabel enter at the equivalent of 1.269, overhear the
    reference to a letter on pink paper, and inform them that she has seen Chiltern
    coming upstairs, reading such a letter. Lady C's exclamation (l. 273) is simply 'I
    am lost!'.

SIR ROBERT CHILTERN

'I want you. I trust you. I am coming to you. Gertrude.' Oh, my love! Is this true? Do you indeed trust me, and want me? 275 If so, it was for me to come to you, not for you to write of coming to me. This letter of yours, Gertrude, makes me feel that nothing that the world may do can hurt me now. You want me, Gertrude?

> LORD GORING, *unseen by* SIR ROBERT CHILTERN,
> *makes an imploring sign to* LADY CHILTERN *to accept*
> *the situation and* SIR ROBERT'S *error*

LADY CHILTERN

Yes. 280

SIR ROBERT CHILTERN

You trust me, Gertrude?

LADY CHILTERN

Yes.

SIR ROBERT CHILTERN

Ah! why did you not add you loved me?

LADY CHILTERN (*Taking his hand*)

Because I loved you.

> LORD GORING *passes into the conservatory*

SIR ROBERT CHILTERN (*Kisses her*)

Gertrude, you don't know what I feel. When Montfort passed 285 me your letter across the table – he had opened it by mistake, I suppose, without looking at the handwriting on the envelope – and I read it – oh! I did not care what disgrace or punishment was in store for me, I only thought you loved me still.

LADY CHILTERN

There is no disgrace in store for you, nor any public shame. 290 Mrs Cheveley has handed over to Lord Goring the document that was in her possession, and he has destroyed it.

SIR ROBERT CHILTERN

Are you sure of this, Gertrude?

LADY CHILTERN

Yes; Lord Goring has just told me.

279 s.d. First appears in PR.
285 In versions before PR, the speech begins 'My wife! my wife!'.
287 *without . . . envelope* first appears in PR.

SIR ROBERT CHILTERN
Then I am safe! Oh! what a wonderful thing to be safe! For   295
two days I have been in terror. I am safe now. How did Arthur
destroy my letter? Tell me.

LADY CHILTERN
He burned it.

SIR ROBERT CHILTERN
I wish I had seen that one sin of my youth burning to ashes.
How many men there are in modern life who would like to   300
see their past burning to white ashes before them! Is Arthur
still here?

LADY CHILTERN
Yes; he is in the conservatory.

SIR ROBERT CHILTERN
I am so glad now I made that speech last night in the House,
so glad. I made it thinking that public disgrace might be the   305
result. But it has not been so.

LADY CHILTERN
Public honour has been the result.

SIR ROBERT CHILTERN
I think so. I fear so, almost. For although I am safe from
detection, although every proof against me is destroyed, I
suppose, Gertrude ... I suppose I should retire from public   310
life?

He looks anxiously at his wife

LADY CHILTERN (*Eagerly*)
Oh yes, Robert, you should do that. It is your duty to do
that.

SIR ROBERT CHILTERN
It is much to surrender.

299–301 *I wish . . . before them* cf. the vivid personification of the 'sin' in Act II (ll.
    803–5). At the climax of *Dorian Gray* the hero attempts to kill his past:
        He looked round, and saw the knife that had stabbed Basil Hallward, He had
    cleaned it many times, till there was no stain left upon it. It was bright, and
    glistened. As it has killed the painter, so it would kill the painter's work, and all
    that that meant. It would kill the past, and when that was dead he would be free.
    It would kill this monstrous soul-life, and, without its hideous warnings, he
    would be at peace. He seized the thing, and stabbed the picture with it. (*DG*,
    p. 223 / *CW*, pp. 166–7.)
    The phrase 'in modern life' first appears in BLTS; in versions before PR 'white ashes
    before them' is simply 'ashes'.
308 *I think so* see Appendix I, for an additional passage from texts before PR.

LADY CHILTERN

No; it will be much to gain.   315

> SIR ROBERT CHILTERN *walks up and down the room*
> *with a troubled expression. Then comes over to his*
> *wife, and puts his hand on her shoulder*

SIR ROBERT CHILTERN

And you would be happy living somewhere alone with me,
abroad perhaps, or in the country away from London, away
from public life? You would have no regrets?

LADY CHILTERN

Oh! none, Robert.

SIR ROBERT CHILTERN (*Sadly*)

And your ambition for me? You used to be ambitious for   320
me.

LADY CHILTERN

Oh, my ambition! I have none now, but that we two may love
each other. It was your ambition that led you astray. Let us
not talk about ambition.

> LORD GORING *returns from the conservatory, looking*
> *very pleased with himself, and with an entirely*
> *new buttonhole that someone has made for him*

SIR ROBERT CHILTERN (*Going towards him*)

Arthur, I have to thank you for what you have done for me.   325
I don't know how I can repay you.

> *Shakes hands with him*

LORD GORING

My dear fellow, I'll tell you at once. At the present moment,
under the usual palm tree ... I mean in the conservatory ...

---

315 *No ... gain* in versions before PR this is followed by four additional speeches:
> SIR ROBERT
> It is a just punishment, but all punishment is bitter in one's mouth.
> LADY CHILTERN
> Don't say that, Robert. It seems to me that the people one should pity most
> in life are those who are not punished for the wrong they have done. They
> should be pitied, not the others.
> SIR ROBERT
> Then I shall send in my resignation this afternoon.
> LADY CHILTERN
> My husband! my husband!
> (LC version).

317 *abroad ... country* first appears in PR.

325–8 *Arthur ... conservatory* in texts before PR, Lord G enters with Mabel and begins
to ask permission to marry her. Lord C interrupts.

Enter MASON

MASON
Lord Caversham.

LORD GORING
That admirable father of mine really makes a habit of turning   330
up at the wrong moment. It is very heartless of him, very
heartless indeed.

       Enter LORD CAVERSHAM. MASON *goes out*

LORD CAVERSHAM
Good morning, Lady Chiltern! Warmest congratulations to
you, Chiltern, on your brilliant speech last night. I have just
left the Prime Minister, and you are to have the vacant seat   335
in the Cabinet.

SIR ROBERT CHILTERN (*With a look of joy and triumph*)
A seat in the Cabinet?

LORD CAVERSHAM
Yes; here is the Prime Minister's letter.   *Hands letter*

SIR ROBERT CHILTERN (*Takes letter and reads it*)
A seat in the Cabinet!

LORD CAVERSHAM
Certainly, and you well deserve it too. You have got what we   340
want so much in political life nowadays – high character, high
moral tone, high principles. (*To* LORD GORING) Everything
that you have not got, sir, and never will have.

LORD GORING
I don't like principles, father. I prefer prejudices.

331–2 *It is . . . indeed* (I must remonstrate with him F, LC, C). BLTS om. this line and
    substitutes: 'Fathers should be neither seen nor heard. That is the only proper basis
    of family life'.
335–6 *the vacant seat in the cabinet* in MS Wilde originally had Lord C bring news of an
    under-secretaryship, with the 'promise' of the next vacant cabinet post. He also
    provided a reason for anticipating this as an imminent possibility: a cabinet reshuffle
    was on the way, partly on account of a certain member's being unable to get a wink
    of sleep in the House of Commons and so seeking elevation to the Lords. This was
    deleted from the MS. Wilde evidently felt unsure about Lord C's indiscretion in
    bringing the news, and the convenience of his intimacy with the premier. In F and
    C Sir Robert is told that the Prime Minister 'was very much impressed':
        In fact, I am deputed by him to certain degree, informally, you understand, to
        offer you the vacant seat in the Cabinet.
344 *I don't . . . prejudices* (om. F, LC, C; I am afraid so, father BLTS). Most texts before
    PR include at this point a sequence which incorporates material later redeployed to
    the scene which opens the act in BLTS, PR and the 1st ed. (including ll.22-32). Lord
    G is rebuked by his father for lacking the ambition that drives Sir Robert: 'Look
    at Chiltern; there is where ambition brings man'. The s.d. following the speech first
    appears in PR.

*SIR ROBERT CHILTERN is on the brink of accepting
the Prime Minister's offer, when he sees his wife looking
at him with her clear, candid eyes. He then
realizes that it is impossible*

SIR ROBERT CHILTERN
I cannot accept this offer, Lord Caversham. I have made up　345
my mind to decline it.

LORD CAVERSHAM
Decline it, sir!

SIR ROBERT CHILTERN
My intention is to retire at once from public life.

LORD CAVERSHAM (*Angrily*)
Decline a seat in the Cabinet, and retire from public life?
Never heard such damned nonsense in the whole course of my　350
existence. I beg your pardon, Lady Chiltern. Chiltern, I beg
your pardon. (*To* LORD GORING) Don't grin like that, sir.

LORD GORING
No, father.

LORD CAVERSHAM
Lady Chiltern, you are a sensible woman, the most sensible
woman in London, the most sensible woman I know. Will you　355
kindly prevent your husband from making such a ... from
talking such ... Will you kindly do that, Lady Chiltern?

LADY CHILTERN
I think my husband is right in his determination, Lord
Caversham. I approve of it.

LORD CAVERSHAM
You approve of it? Good Heavens!　　　　　　　　　　　360

LADY CHILTERN (*Taking her husband's hand*)
I admire him for it. I admire him immensely for it. I have
never admired him so much before. He is finer than even I
thought him. (*To* SIR ROBERT CHILTERN) You will go and write
your letter to the Prime Minister now, won't you? Don't
hesitate about it, Robert.　　　　　　　　　　　　　　365

SIR ROBERT CHILTERN (*With a touch of bitterness*)
I suppose I had better write it at once. Such offers are not
repeated. I will ask you to excuse me for a moment, Lord
Caversham.

LADY CHILTERN
I may come with you, Robert, may I not?

SIR ROBERT CHILTERN
  Yes, Gertrude.   370

                          LADY CHILTERN *goes out with him*

LORD CAVERSHAM
  What is the matter with this family? Something wrong here,
  eh? (*Tapping his forehead*) Idiocy? Hereditary, I suppose. Both
  of them, too. Wife as well as husband. Very sad. Very sad
  indeed! And they are not an old family. Can't understand
  it.   375

LORD GORING
  It is not idiocy, father, I assure you.

LORD CAVERSHAM
  What is it then, sir?

LORD GORING (*After some hesitation*)
  Well, it is what is called nowadays a high moral tone, father.
  That is all.

LORD CAVERSHAM
  Hate these new-fangled names. Same thing as we used to call   380
  idiocy fifty years ago. Shan't stay in this house any longer.

LORD GORING (*Taking his arm*)
  Oh! just go in here for a moment, father. Third palm tree to
  the left, the usual palm tree.

LORD CAVERSHAM
  What, sir?

LORD GORING
  I beg your pardon, father, I forgot. The conservatory, father, 385
  the conservatory – there is someone there I want you to talk
  to.

LORD CAVERSHAM
  What about, sir?

374–5 *And ... understand it* first appears in PR.
381 *any longer* texts before PR add: 'I'll go back to the Prime Minister and tell him that
    Chiltern is the damnedest fool I ever knew' ('is off his head' BLTS). At this point
    Mabel emerges from the conservatory, only to be sent back in so that Lord Goring
    might speak to Lady Chiltern alone. (She observes that she doesn't like knowing
    what people say about her behind her back – 'It makes me too conceited'; cf.
    ll.117–8. above).
378 *a high moral tone* cf. *Earnest*, I, 205, etc.: 'When one is placed in the position of a
    guardian, one has to adopt a very high moral tone on all subjects. It's one's duty
    to do so ... '.
385–92 *I beg ... loud* om. F, BLTS. Earlier texts have a longer exchange, incorporating
    material later used in the opening of the act (including ll.77–81), followed by the
    conversation beginning at l.393 of the present edition.

LORD GORING
About me, father.

LORD CAVERSHAM (*Grimly*)
Not a subject on which much eloquence is possible.   390

LORD GORING
No, father; but the lady is like me. She doesn't care much for
eloquence in others. She thinks it a little loud.
   LORD CAVERSHAM *goes into the conservatory.* LADY
      CHILTERN *enters*

LORD GORING
Lady Chiltern, why are you playing Mrs Cheveley's cards?

LADY CHILTERN (*Startled*)
I don't understand you.

LORD GORING
Mrs Cheveley made an attempt to ruin your husband. Either   395
to drive him from public life, or to make him adopt a
dishonourable position. From the latter tragedy you saved
him. The former you are now thrusting on him. Why should
you do him the wrong Mrs Cheveley tried to do and failed?

LADY CHILTERN
Lord Goring?   400

LORD GORING (*Pulling himself together for a great effort, and
showing the philosopher that underlies the dandy*)
Lady Chiltern, allow me. You wrote me a letter last night in
which you said you trusted me and wanted my help. Now is
the moment when you really want my help, now is the time
when you have got to trust me, to trust in my counsel and
judgment. You love Robert. Do you want to kill his love for 405
you? What sort of existence will he have if you rob him of the
fruits of his ambition, if you take him from the splendour of
a great political career, if you close the doors of public life
against him, if you condemn him to sterile failure, he who was
made for triumph and success? Women are not meant to judge 410
us, but to forgive us when we need forgiveness. Pardon, not

---

401 s.d. first appears in PR.
410 *triumph and success* texts before PR add:
   What sort of love will he keep for you when he is soured, disappointed, baffled,
  unhappy? When he sits alone, thinking over a ruined past, mourning over a lost
  future? He will have no love for you. He will grow to hate you. You will be horrible
  in his eyes. (BLTS version, marked for deletion.)

punishment, is their mission. Why should you scourge him
with rods for a sin done in his youth, before he knew you,
before he knew himself? A man's life is of more value than a
woman's. It has larger issues, wider scope, greater ambitions.   415
A woman's life revolves in curves of emotions. It is upon lines
of intellect that a man's life progresses. Don't make any
terrible mistake, Lady Chiltern. A woman who can keep a
man's love, and love him in return, has done all the world
wants of women, or should want of them.   420

LADY CHILTERN (*Troubled and hesitating*)
But it is my husband himself who wishes to retire from public
life. He feels it is his duty. It was he who first said so.

LORD GORING
Rather than lose your love, Robert would do anything, wreck
his whole career, as he is on the brink of doing now. He is
making for you a terrible sacrifice. Take my advice, Lady   425
Chiltern, and do not accept a sacrifice so great. If you do, you
will live to repent it bitterly. We men and women are not made
to accept such sacrifices from each other. We are not worthy
of them. Besides, Robert has been punished enough.

LADY CHILTERN
We have both been punished. I set him up too high.   430

---

416 *in curves of emotions* (on curves of emotions F, etc.). Presumably intended as an
    example of Lord Goring's 'psychology', but in fact a restatement of the classic theory
    of the 'complementarity' of the sexes. Cf. John Ruskin, 'Of Queens' Gardens'
    (*Sesame and Lilies*, 1865):
> The man's power is active, progressive, defensive. He is eminently the doer, the
> creator, the discoverer, the defender. His intellect is for speculation and
> invention; his energy for adventure, for war, and for conquest, wherever war is
> just, wherever conquest necessary. But the woman's power is for rule, not for
> battle, – and her intellect is not for invention or creation, but for sweet ordering,
> arrangement, and decision ... Her great function is Praise: she enters into no
> conquest, but infallibly adjudges the crown of contest. (Section 68.)

    This view had already been challenged by a number of dramatists and novelists, as
    well as by behavioural psychologists (including Havelock Ellis). For a discussion of
    Ruskin's ideas in their context, see Kate Millett, *Sexual Politics* (1971), ch. 3.
418–20 *A woman . . . of them* see Appendix I for additional passage from texts before
    PR.
428–9 *worthy of them* texts before PR add:
> LADY CHILTERN
>   You think that Robert wishes to continue in public life, having done what he
>   has done?
> LORD GORING
>   A strong man thinks only about his future. A weak man about his past.
> (BLTS version, marked for deletion).

LORD GORING (*With deep feeling in his voice*)
Do not for that reason set him down now too low. If he has
fallen from his altar, do not thrust him into the mire. Failure
to Robert would be the very mire of shame. Power is his
passion. He would lose everything, even his power to feel
love. Your husband's life is at this moment in your hands,   435
your husband's love is in your hands. Don't mar both for
him.

Enter SIR ROBERT CHILTERN

SIR ROBERT CHILTERN
Gertrude, here is the draft of my letter. Shall I read it to
you?

LADY CHILTERN
Let me see it.   440

SIR ROBERT *hands her the letter. She reads it,*
and then, with a gesture of passion, tears it up

SIR ROBERT CHILTERN
What are you doing?

LADY CHILTERN
A man's life is of more value than a woman's. It has larger
issues, wider scope, greater ambitions. Our lives revolve in
curves of emotions. It is upon lines of intellect that a man's
life progresses. I have just learnt this, and much else with it,   445
from Lord Goring. And I will not spoil your life for you, nor
see you spoil it as a sacrifice to me, a useless sacrifice!

SIR ROBERT CHILTERN
Gertrude! Gertrude!

LADY CHILTERN
You can forget. Men easily forget. And I forgive. That is how
women help the world. I see that now.   450

SIR ROBERT CHILTERN (*Deeply overcome by emotion, embraces*
her)
My wife! my wife! (*To* LORD GORING) Arthur, it seems that I
am always to be in your debt.

438–9 *Shall . . . you?* texts before PR read:
    Gertrude, here is the draft of the letter I am going to send to the Prime Minister.
    I will see one of the whips this evening and tell him to make arrangements for
    my resigning my seat.
    Lady C takes the letter and tears it up, without speaking. Her husband asks
    'Gertrude, what do you mean?'.
447 *a useless sacrifice* texts before PR add: 'I love you all the same, and not with blind
    eyes now!'

LORD GORING
  Oh dear no, Robert. Your debt is to Lady Chiltern, not to
  me!

SIR ROBERT CHILTERN
  I owe you much. And now tell me what you were going to ask   455
  me just now as Lord Caversham came in.

LORD GORING
  Robert, you are your sister's guardian, and I want your
  consent to my marriage with her. That is all.

LADY CHILTERN
  Oh, I am so glad! I am so glad!
                                    Shakes hands with LORD GORING

LORD GORING
  Thank you, Lady Chiltern.   460

SIR ROBERT CHILTERN (*With a troubled look*)
  My sister to be your wife?

LORD GORING
  Yes.

SIR ROBERT CHILTERN (*Speaking with great firmness*)
  Arthur, I am very sorry, but the thing is quite out of the
  question. I have to think of Mabel's future happiness. And I
  don't think her happiness would be safe in your hands. And   465
  I cannot have her sacrificed!

LORD GORING
  Sacrificed!

SIR ROBERT CHILTERN
  Yes, utterly sacrificed. Loveless marriages are horrible. But
  there is one thing worse than an absolutely loveless marriage.
  A marriage in which there is love, but on one side only; faith, 470
  but on one side only; devotion, but on one side only, and in
  which of the two hearts one is sure to be broken.

LORD GORING
  But I love Mabel. No other woman has any place in my life.

457 *guardian* (natural guardian, her parents being dead F, etc.).
463–6 *Arthur . . . sacrificed!* F and earlier texts have a a longer version, in which Lord
    G reminds Sir Robert that he is under some obligation to him.
468 *horrible* in BLTS he adds 'They are the stain upon our age!' (marked for
    deletion).

LADY CHILTERN
Robert, if they love each other, why should they not be
married?   475

SIR ROBERT CHILTERN
Arthur cannot bring Mabel the love that she deserves.

LORD GORING
What reason have you for saying that?

SIR ROBERT CHILTERN (*After a pause*)
Do you really require me to tell you?

LORD GORING
Certainly I do.

SIR ROBERT CHILTERN
As you choose. When I called on you yesterday evening I   480
found Mrs Cheveley concealed in your rooms. It was between
ten and eleven o'clock at night. I do not wish to say anything
more. Your relations with Mrs Cheveley have, as I said to you
last night, nothing whatsoever to do with me. I know you were
engaged to be married to her once. The fascination she   485
exercised over you then seems to have returned. You spoke
to me last night of her as of a woman pure and stainless, a
woman whom you respected and honoured. That may be so.
But I cannot give my sister's life into your hands. It would be
wrong of me. It would be unjust, infamously unjust to her.   490

LORD GORING
I have nothing more to say.

LADY CHILTERN
Robert, it was not Mrs Cheveley whom Lord Goring expected
last night.

SIR ROBERT CHILTERN
Not Mrs Cheveley! Who was it then?

LORD GORING
Lady Chiltern!   495

LADY CHILTERN
It was your own wife. Robert, yesterday afternoon Lord
Goring told me that if ever I was in trouble I could come to

---

490 F and earlier texts add further expostulation on both sides, ending with a 'false exit'
for Lord Goring.

him for help, as he was our oldest and best friend. Later on, after that terrible scene in this room, I wrote to him telling him that I trusted him, that I had need of him, that I was coming to him for help and advice. (SIR ROBERT CHILTERN *takes the letter out of his pocket*) Yes, that letter. I didn't go to Lord Goring's after all. I felt that it is from ourselves alone that help can come. Pride made me think that. Mrs Cheveley went. She stole my letter and sent it anonymously to you this morning, that you should think ... Oh! Robert, I cannot tell you what she wished you to think ...

SIR ROBERT CHILTERN

What! Had I fallen so low in your eyes that you thought that even for a moment I could have doubted your goodness? Gertrude, Gertrude, you are to me the white image of all good things, and sin can never touch you. Arthur, you can go to Mabel, and you have my best wishes! Oh! stop a moment. There is no name at the beginning of this letter. The brilliant Mrs Cheveley does not seem to have noticed that. There should be a name.

LADY CHILTERN

Let me write yours. It is you I trust and need. You and none else.

498 *later on* texts before PR continue:
    wounded in my pride, wounded in my monstrous pride at what you had said to me in that terrible scene in this room I wrote to Lord Goring, telling him ... (BLTS version, marked for deletion.)
    Wilde removed this and other passages suggesting that her approaching Lord Goring was indeed reprehensible, and motivated by her reaction *against* her husband. Cf. Appendix I for sequence omitted from the interview between Lady C and Lord G (ll. 418–20, above).
507 *wished you to think* F, LC and the BLTS typescript have an additional passage which first appears in revisions to C:
    ... I was afraid. I did not dare to tell you the truth!
    SIR ROBERT
    You should have told me, Arthur.
    LADY CHILTERN
    He wanted to, I would not let him.
    SIR ROBERT
    My child! my poor child! Well, upon my word, Arthur, Mrs Cheveley turns out after all to be an extremely stupid woman. (BLTS version, marked for deletion.)
    The dialogue then continues with 'You can go to Mabel ... '.
511–2 *go to Mabel* a survival from the earliest drafts, in which at this point the proposal had yet to take place.

LORD GORING
  Well, really, Lady Chiltern, I think I should have back my
  own letter.

LADY CHILTERN (*Smiling*)
  No; you shall have Mabel.   520
                    Takes the letter and writes her husband's name on it

LORD GORING
  Well, I hope she hasn't changed her mind. It's nearly twenty
  minutes since I saw her last.
                    Enter MABEL CHILTERN *and* LORD CAVERSHAM

MABEL CHILTERN
  Lord Goring, I think your father's conversation much more
  improving than yours. I am only going to talk to Lord
  Caversham in the future, and always under the usual palm   525
  tree.

LORD GORING
  Darling!   *Kisses her*

LORD CAVERSHAM (*Considerably taken aback*)
  What does this mean, sir? You don't mean to say that this
  charming, clever young lady has been so foolish as to accept
  you?   530

LORD GORING
  Certainly, father! And Chiltern's been wise enough to accept
  the seat in the Cabinet.

LORD CAVERSHAM
  I am very glad to hear that, Chiltern ... I congratulate you
  sir. If the country doesn't go to the dogs or the Radicals, we
  shall have you Prime Minister, some day.   535
                    Enter MASON

MASON
  Luncheon is on the table, my Lady!
                                          MASON *goes out*

LADY CHILTERN
  You'll stop to luncheon, Lord Caversham, won't you?

LORD CAVERSHAM
  With pleasure, and I'll drive you down to Downing Street
  afterwards, Chiltern. You have a great future before you, a
  great future. Wish I could say the same for you, sir. (*To* LORD   540
  GORING) But your career will have to be entirely domestic.

LORD GORING
  Yes, father, I prefer it domestic.

LORD CAVERSHAM
And if you don't make this young lady an ideal husband, I'll
cut you off with a shilling.

MABEL CHILTERN
An ideal husband! Oh, I don't think I should like that. It   545
sounds like something in the next world.

LORD CAVERSHAM
What do you want him to be then, dear?

MABEL CHILTERN
He can be what he chooses. All I want is to be . . . to be . . .
oh! a real wife to him.

LORD CAVERSHAM
Upon my word, there is a good deal of common sense in that,   550
Lady Chiltern.

          They all go out except SIR ROBERT CHILTERN. *He*
          sinks into a chair, wrapt in thought. After a little
          time LADY CHILTERN *returns to look for him*

LADY CHILTERN (*Leaning over the back of the chair*)
Aren't you coming in, Robert?

SIR ROBERT CHILTERN (*Taking her hand*)
Gertrude, is it love you feel for me, or is it pity merely?

LADY CHILTERN (*Kisses him*)
It is love, Robert. Love, and only love. For both of us a new
life is beginning.   555

CURTAIN

551 *Lady Chiltern* (my dear F, LC etc.) In MS the play now moves to its conclusion with
the single line, spoken by Lady C: 'There is love in it, and that is better'. In C this
becomes 'Ah! There is love, and that is everything!' (derived from a manuscript
addition to the typescript acquired by the Clark library at the Prescott Collection
Sale) to which Wilde added 'father', at the same time changing the speaker to Lord
G. The final three speeches appear as an addition to BLTS, and the s.d.
accompanying them first appear in PR. In F a manuscript s.d. following the final
words reads '*Exit* CAVERSHAM - GORING *and* SIR ROBERT *meet* C. *shaking hands as
Curtain falls*'. This may well have been the practice of the first production: it is not
unlikely that Wilde's original intention to give Lady Chiltern the curtain-line was
set aside in the interests of the actor-manager, then modified to give Hawtrey the
'tag', and finally changed in the published edition to return it to Lady C when the
more elaborate and intimate ending was added.

APPENDIX I
Longer Textual Notes

I, 321–5 *She is . . . to make, too* after the report of Mrs Cheveley's opinion of the opera audience, MS and HTC have the following dialogue:

LORD G

Then you and Lady Marchmont could not have been there!

MRS M

Of course we were not. It was not a Wagner night!

LADY B

We only go on Wagner nights.

LORD G

Ah! I only go to talk. Best place for talking I know, the Opera. One can say what one likes!

LADY B

Then you must never come to my box, Lord Goring. You had better go with Mrs Cheveley. I hear she talked the whole time last night at the top of her voice!

MISS C

Who talked the whole time last night at the top of her voice? I am sure I should like her!

LADY B

Mrs Cheveley!

(IITC version, marked for deletion).

I, 471 *You thought that letter had been destroyed* in MS this is part of a long speech, without the interruptions from Sir Robert. It continues:

I know the Baron told you so. How foolish of you to believe him. No sensible person – and in business the Baron was always sensible – ever destroys a dangerous letter, or writes a compromising one. The Baron kept it, not to harm you, but to make himself secure. Now the Baron and I were great friends. I would have done anything in the world for him, except love him. He would have done anything in the world for me, except marry me – so we remained simply friends. For ten years we were great friends. The Baron died quite suddenly as you know. His wealth he left to his nephew. To me he left as a memento a little villa he had in Hungary – with some Boucher tapestries and nice Louis Seize furniture – the sort of background that just suits me. One day in the drawer of an inlaid escritoire I found a large sealed packet marked 'to be destroyed after my death' – you know what a woman's curiosity is – almost as great as a man's. I opened it of course. The secret history of the nineteenth century was in it. Letters from great ladies offering their favours for money. Letters from kings who had lost their thrones. Letters from demagogues who wanted to be kings. And a letter from you on the top of which, in that delicate small hand of his that you must remember, the Baron had written 'The [origin] of Robert Chiltern' – and on the back of it the sum, £50,000.

It is interesting that, at this early stage, Wilde connected the taste for Boucher and Louis Seize furnishings with the desire for power and wealth.

I, 491–521 *My dear . . . this scheme* after 'you would be hounded out of public life' MS continues:

and all the people who had done the same sort of thing themselves, or something much worse, would of course be the loudest against you. When a victim is offered up to public respectability it counts as a general whitewashing all round and every thief has the opportunity of dilating on the enormous importance of honesty.

'You have a splendid position' is elaborated as follows:

you are undersecretary for Foreign Affairs: you will have the next vacant seat in the Cabinet: everybody tells me that you have brilliant social position. You have wealth that you have doubled, trebled by judicious investment: and you have a wife of the highest possible moral principles.

I, 570 *He has had . . . career* in MS and HTC Lady M observes that Lord Radley placed great trust in Sir Robert:

And got him his first seat in Parliament and everything of that kind . . . And I should fancy helped him in other ways, though I don't really know of course. Sir Robert is well born, on one side, at any rate – his mother was Lady Adeliza Gillray, but there was not a penny of money in the family. I remember Lady Adeliza always went about in a plain black silk dress, which is a great confession of failure, and it is said that she used to pay her visits in omnibuses, though perhaps that is only a malicious scandal.

Wilde may have thought this too reminiscent of Mrs Arbuthnot's impoverishment and black dress: the earlier play was too fresh in the public mind for him to risk implying that Sir Robert was a Gerald, come to mature years under Lord Radley's kind (and perhaps fatherly) protection.

II, 91–109 *One night after dinner . . . possessed it* MS1 has a

cancelled opening to this speech in which Sir
Robert's early poverty is referred to:

Arthur, *you* don't know what want of money means. You have
never known it. I have. My father was poor all his life. The result
was that he was an utterly disappointed man. The position he was
entitled to hold he was never able to attain. He was baffled and
trammelled at every point. It soured his nature and [?cramped] his
mind. I grew up in a sordid atmosphere of ways and means where
every penny was counted and every pound haggled over. The rich
people who lived near us laughed at my father for his absurd pride,
at my mother for her shabby dresses – I used to see them do it. It
enraged me. I knew the humiliation of being poor myself when I
was a boy. At school I was always in shabby clothes. At Oxford I
had not enough to live on. I could not accept hospitality that I could
not return. So I lived apart from the others. I was lonely and in my
loneliness and bitterness I determined to be rich. When I left
Oxford Lord Radley who was a cousin of my mother's offered me
the post of his secretary. I accepted it with joy. I felt a chance was
open to me at last.

A number of details were changed in the remainder of the
speech. In MS1 'modern', 'quiet' and 'preached to us' are
absent, and the gospel taught is 'tragic' rather than 'marvellous'. There is no reference to Arnheim's 'jewels' and
'carved ivories' and the sequence moves directly from 'the
luxury in which he lived' (1.104) to 'six weeks later I wrote
him the letter . . . ' (1.139). MS2 gives the development of his
philosophy more or less as printed, including the curious
image of luxury as 'a background, a painted scene in a play'.
The Baron's teaching might be compared with the reflections
of Lord Henry Wotton in *Dorian Gray*, who wonders
whether 'we could ever make psychology so absolute a
science that each little spring of life would be revealed to us'.
To him the hero appears 'like one of those gracious figures in
a pageant or play, whose joys seem to be remote from one, but
whose sorrows stir one's sense of beauty, and whose wounds
are like red roses' (*DG*, pp. 57–8/ *CW*, p. 56).

II, 177 MS and C have the following passage, before 'The
English can't stand . . . ':

Well, a man who know[s] the House of Commons very well said
once that if one of the Members had murdered his mother-in-law,
and got up in the House and asked leave to make a personal explanation, and frankly admitted that in a moment of irritation which
no one regretted more than himself, he *had* brained the aged lady

with the drawing room poker, and threw himself on the mercy of the House, and appealed to other honourable members as to whether his general conduct had not been uniformly courteous and humane – well, the man who knew the temper of the astounding assembly at Westminster said that the member in question would sit down amidst a perfect storm of applause, and that any further reference to the manner in which he had treated his aged relative would be regarded by both sides as being in extremely bad taste.

(marked for omission in C.)

II, 194 etc. *That I will not do* . . . MS1 contains a longer version of this dialogue, including the following cancelled exchanges, after the equivalent of 1.196:

SIR R

But this woman? How can I defend myself against her?

LORD G

She has learned the gospel of gold. Bribe her.

SIR R

I will give her half of my fortune.

LORD G

And how much would that be?

SIR R

Two hundred thousand pounds.

LORD G

And if she asked for all your fortune?

SIR R

Rather than lose my wife's love I would give it all.

LORD G

Then the gospel of gold breaks down sometimes.

SIR R

Rather than lose the woman I love I would strip myself of everything I have. Rather than lose her love I would make myself an outcast. But if she knew of this thing that I have done she would turn from me. Her very virtues make her pitiless. Her perfections mar her –

(Then follows 1.16, in a version slightly different to that published.) It is interesting that this passage, subsequently rejected, includes the notion of self-sacrifice – with its Biblical associations of the naked penitent – that fascinated Wilde. The rearrangement takes away some of the less convincing, melodramatic touches and focusses attention on Mrs Cheveley – with Sir Robert's marriage as background.

III, 387–92 *Pray have . . . discovered* the point of the reference to smoking changed in the course of revision. The BLTS typescript reads:

MRS C

Thanks. May I smoke a cigarette? I can never talk business unless I am smoking a cigarette.

LORD G

Certainly. You don't mind my smoking? Thanks. Well, Mrs Cheveley?

This derives (with one slight alteration) from MS. After revision in manuscript to BLTS, Wilde produced the version in the C typescript:

MRS C

Thanks. I'd sooner walk about. May I smoke a cigarette? I never can talk business unless I am smoking cigarettes. All the pretty women in Vienna smoke cigarettes

LORD G

And half the pretty women in London. Well, Mrs Cheveley?

In revising C, Wilde changed the second speech to:

And half our pretty women in London. Personally I prefer the other half. Well, Mrs Cheveley.

LC is close to the revised C; F has a hybrid of the early drafts and the text as printed.

IV, 54–5 *They will never say that of you, sir* this is added to the BLTS typescript, from which the following passage of dialogue has been deleted:

LORD G

It is quite wonderful, father, I have nothing to say, except that he deserves it all.

LORD C

Mark my words, sir, Robert Chiltern will be Prime Minister some day.

LORD G

I don't mind. *I* am not going to compete, father.

LORD C

You haven't got the necessary ambition.

LORD G

No, that is the only thing that is wanting.

LORD C

It is not the only thing, sir. You have not got the high principles that are requisite.

LORD G

I don't like principles. I prefer prejudices. There is much more to be said in favour of people's prejudices than there is in favour of people's principles.

LORD C

Well, you have got to acquire ambition and principles at once. I am going to put you into politics, sir. You have got to stand for Parliament at the next election.

LORD G

My dear father, that would be quite impossible. Why, only people who look dull ever get into the House of Commons, and only people who are dull ever succeed there.

IV, 175–6 *And it is . . . extravagant* the BLTS typescript om. this, and continues with a passage marked for omission:

LORD G

How nice of you to say so! And now, when shall we get married?

MABEL

Well, today is Thursday, isn't it? I suppose you have any amount of engagements till the end of the season haven't you?

LORD G

Only one that I care twopence about.

MABEL

Dear, how sweet you are! Of course, you have got to see Robert. He is my guardian.

LORD G

Oh! that won't take five minutes, at the most.

MABEL

And I have got to see my dressmaker. That will take about six months at the least, and we must give people time to get their presents. And then I want the thing to be a dead secret for a little while.

LORD G

A dead secret? Why?

MABEL

Oh! how silly you are! Of course I should like to tell everyone about our engagement, and it is not very nice to tell a person anything that is not a great secret. What is the use of telling people things that they know already? One might just as well write for the papers.

LORD G

Well, it will be a dead secret till I get Robert's consent.

MABEL

Yes: and after he has given his consent we will deny the whole thing.

LORD G

Why? I certainly won't.

MABEL

Well, I will. I'll say I've been driven into it. And everybody will be

most sympathetic. I love people to be sympathetic. Ah! but I love
love better.

LORD G

Darling!

The most elaborate of the earlier versions of this scene (all of
which are placed nearer the end of the act, after Sir Robert's
permission has been granted) is contained in the draft
acquired by the Clark library at the Prescott Collection sale
(cf. p. xlii above). The typescript leaves, ff. 27–8, which
include the sequence do not correspond to the subsequent
typescript (C) which otherwise derives directly from the
Prescott version. Mabel's response to Lord Goring's fear of
being refused is more extreme in this draft:

MABEL (*Looking up at him*)

But you never have been refused yet by anybody, have you, Arthur?
I can't imagine anyone refusing you. (*Smiling*) It would create a
sensation. It would give you a sensation. It would give me a sensation. (*Solemnly*) I feel that I am going to refuse you.

LORD G (*Drawing back: showing a human emotion for the first time*)

What! You adore me, and you are going to refuse me?

MABEL (*Sadly*)

That is the trouble. I love you. I adore you. To have you would be
perfect – too perfect. You hate perfection. I fear perfection. It cannot last – it wouldn't be, if it did. (*Rapturously*) It would be nicer to
create a sensation than to have you for a husband. All London
would thank me. The season has been frightfully dull. (*Archly*)
And it would be good for you. (*As if to herself*) I shall miss you . . .
but . . . I shall accept the other proposal. How delightful! that
makes the second today.

This is Tommy Trafford's, made as usual on one of his days
for proposing –

LORD G

Oh! bother Tommy Trafford!

MABEL (*Dismally*)

I shall. I shall marry him. Bother him! Of course! That is the business of wives. But it will improve his manners. Yours are beyond
improvement. They are charming! (LORD GORING *smiles depre-
catingly*) They are perfectly scandalous! Lord Caversham says so.
Every one says so. (*Sighs*) Poor Tommy!

After admitting that he is extravagant, Lord Goring adds that
he has been 'terribly irregular' (implicitly, in his bachelordom).
Mabel counters: 'Dearest! So am I! Irregularity is the thief of
boredom. So we'll never quarrel'. (It should be noted that
these pages are remarkable for the fullness of their stage
directions – rare in Wilde's drafts.)

IV, 201 etc. *Lady Chiltern* . . . in MS this sequence begins as follows:

LADY C

Lord Goring, what can you think of me? I dare not look you in the face. (LORD GORING *approaches and kisses her hand*) In a moment of folly I wrote to you a foolish letter. It was Violet who by telling me what she thought I am, what I know I should be, prevented me from coming to your house at night. Oh why did you, my friend, our friend, suggest so mad, so wrong a thing to me, whom you should have protected rather, knowing what you did about my husband, whom I love, and whose love I fear I have lost[?]

LORD G

I wished to teach you a lesson, Lady Chiltern, a lesson in charity. I wished you to realise how weak we all are, and how kind we should be to those who have done weak or foolish things.

C's version does not imply that Lord Goring's letter was intended to have such an effect, or that anything improper might be thought to have taken place:

LADY C

Lord Goring, I am afraid I must have kept you in yesterday evening, waiting for me. Do excuse me. But at the last moment I felt that no real help comes to any one of us, except from ourselves, and that when we stand face to face with a great tragedy we have to solve it for ourselves and by ourselves. The tragedy that has come on me so suddenly, so horribly, I have solved as I think it should be solved. Whatever public disgrace comes on Robert, I will share with him, if he will let me. It is my duty!

LORD G

How good! how wise you are! But there will be no public disgrace. Mrs Cheveley gave up Robert's letter to me last night, and I burned it. Robert is safe.

This also appears in LC and F, but is deleted in BLTS.

IV, 308 *I think so* BLTS continues with a passage marked for omission:

. . . But, oh! why is it that you women are so much finer than we are? When I look into your eyes, I see truth there. When I kiss your hands, I feel truth in them. Your lips are eloquent of truth. You women are made of finer material than we are. We are soiled with the mire and the battle. You are our proper ideals.

LADY C

Oh, don't say those things to me, Robert. Don't ever say those things to me.

SIR R

What else should I say to the woman I worship?

LADY C

We are not made for worship.

SIR ROBERT

For love, then, which is better. And now, Gertrude, although I am safe from detection . . .

IV, 419–20 *all the world wants of women* BLTS reads 'all we want of women', and continues with a passage marked for omission:

. . . Be content if you can keep your husband's love. Don't sacrifice him to gratify the vanity of a high moral tone!

LADY C

Is this the philosophy you are going to teach your wife when you marry[?]

LORD G

Certainly. I am idle, and my father tells me I am good-for-nothing. That may be so. But I think that women are simply made to love and to be loved, and if I ever do some weak or wrong thing, I will expect from my wife pity, gentleness, kindness, forgiveness.

LADY C

You think me hard and unwomanly, then?

LORD G

I think you hard but not unwomanly.

This may have been removed on the grounds of its prolixity, but it is a purely conventional view of woman as forgiving angel, and may have seemed too blatantly orthodox for a supposedly 'original' speaker. The 'curves of emotion' speech has at least an air of originality.

APPENDIX II
WOMEN'S COSTUMES IN THE PLAY

The extract in this appendix is from an article in *The Sketch*, giving lady readers an account of costume in *An Ideal Husband*. It suggests the elaboration and expense of fashionable dress in the period – effects difficult to reproduce now economically, because of the amount of material involved. It will be seen that Wilde's description of Mrs Cheveley in his stage direction (I, 50) corresponds to the magazine's description of her dress.

From 'Dress at the Theatres' by 'Florence', *The Sketch*, 9 January 1895. (The columnist begins with an account of 18th century costumes in Henry James' play *Guy Domville*.)

So much for these fascinating last-century costumes; and now, if for a change you would like some eminently up-to-date gowns which are full of good ideas, you had better let me tell you about the dresses in the new Haymarket piece, "An Ideal Husband," for they are distinctly worthy of notice. I have nothing but admiration for Miss Julia Neilson's three beautiful gowns; but then, when the wearer is so perfectly and grandly beautiful herself, she makes the gown instead of the gown making her. In Act II, then, Miss Neilson [as Lady Chiltern] wears a white satin gown, brocaded with a large conventional floral design, the skirt and the whole of the long train being bordered with small bunches of Neapolitan violets, set at regular distances apart, while great trails of the same flowers pass over the shoulders and fall on to the loosely hanging sleeves of white chiffon, which fall away from the arm in front in a fashion most becoming to anyone with such lovely arms as Miss Neilson's. The bodice itself is draped across with the chiffon, a great bunch of violets being placed on the right side of the corsage, and another at the left side of the waist, where the chiffon is tied into long, broad sash-ends, sprinkled over with a shower of violets. Miss Neilson wears long strings of pearls, caught up on the bodice in festoons, together with a diamond tiara and sundry diamond ornaments. Her next dress has a perfectly plain skirt of white satin foulard, brocaded with a Pompadour design of shadowy pink roses nestling in tender green leaves, the bodice being veiled with accordian-pleated pink chiffon, held in in front by two broad braces of the brocade, tapering to a point at the waist, which is encircled by a twist of chiffon. Miss Julia

155

Neilson, like Mrs. Patrick Campbell, abjures collars, and the chiffon is softly shirred beneath the throat, which is left perfectly free, the puffed sleeves of brocade having deep transparent cuffs – also of the shirred chiffon. Miss Neilson does not come on in Act III, but she reappears in the last act in a wonderfully handsome dress with a perfectly plain trained skirt of buttercup-yellow satin, the bodice, which is a most elaborately beautiful one, having a vest arrangement of golden tissue, through which there gleams a suggestion of blue, the deep shoulder-capes, which fall in soft, graceful folds and taper to a point at each side of the waist, being of the yellow satin, lined with pinkish mauve. A band of gold passementerie, glittering with stones which reproduce the various colours, outlines the neck and encircles the waist, and the sleeves are composed of draperies of brocade and golden gauze, the cuffs being of blue glacé, covered with the pinkish-mauve chiffon, while at the back, below the neck, there is a butterfly bow of the gauze, edged with jewelled passementerie.

Next comes the turn of Miss Florence West, who, as the scheming adventuress of the piece, has some very striking and elaborate gowns, though two, at least, of them did not by any means meet with my approval. The first – an evening dress – is of dark emerald-green satin, the bodice veiled with gauze of the same colour, glistening here and there with broad streaks of silver and cream. This filmy drapery is continued on the skirt, where it terminates just below the knees in front, and disappears into the long train at the side, beneath a trail of roses in every imaginable shade of pink and crimson. The skirt is bordered in front with festoons of gauze, caught by tiny bunches of pink roses, over each of which hovers a graceful swallow, two more birds being used as trimming, one of them having fluttered on to the centre of the bodice at the back, while the other nestles into the waist in front. I have nothing but disapproval for such a mode of trimming, for, though it may be original and, in a way, effective, it is barbarous and unpleasant, and I only hope that women will show their disapproval of this needless slaughter by refraining from imitation. But to return to the remaining – and unoffending – details of the dress. It is guiltless of sleeves, unless a rope of roses which passes over the shoulders can be said to do duty as such, and a lovely effect is secured by closely set clusters of shaded roses, which line the edge of the skirt and the whole of the enormously long train, every movement disclosing some fresh shade. Certainly a lovely and original gown, but the sight of those birds spoiled it entirely, as far as I was concerned. Miss Florence West's next costume is startling, to put it mildly. It consists of yellow mirror moiré, and has a deep square collar of scarlet velvet, which forms crossed revers in front, fastening over at the left side with a paste button. Both from collar and revers falls a deep frill of mellow-tinted lace, and, in order that there may be plenty of contrast, there is a collar-band of bright-green velvet, with a bunch of violets set at each side. Then the sleeves are of cream-coloured chiné glacé, brocaded with pink roses and foliage, and to crown all there is a hat of green straw, which has masses of orchids in various colours, including purple and red. Then remember that, for this occasion, Miss West has indulged in hair of the fashionable red, or – I apologise – auburn shade, and you may possibly imagine the effect of this combination of colours, which, however, I am bound to say, Miss West carries off exceedingly well. As far as good taste is concerned, her last dress must take first place, for it is simply fashioned of pale tea-rose-yellow satin, brocaded with shadowy roses in the faintest possible shade of pink, the cuffs being turned back with red satin, and a touch of the same colour appearing between the soft falls of lace which adorn the bodice. Round the waist there is a loose golden girdle, the long ends studded with rubies; and Miss West also wears a splendid cloak of black satin, lined with red satin, the cape being cut in battlements over a deep frill of lace, and turned back with red.

Then comes the turn of dainty Miss Maude Millet [as Mabel Chiltern], who has three of the smartest imaginable gowns, in which I immediately recognised a master hand, and eventually found it to be that of Madame Humble, of 19, Conduit Street. The first, which is an ideal evening-gown for a young girl, is of yellow satin, the full skirt perfectly plain, with the exception of a great spray of flowers – white lilac, mauve orchids, and deep-shaded pansies – which is arranged in most artistic fashion at the left side. The bodice is veiled in front with slightly overhanging folds of gold-sequined net, while bands of gold sequins are curved round the sides with excellent effect upon the figure, three diamond buttons being placed down the back. The full puffed sleeves of the satin droop slightly off the shoulders, which are crossed by clusters of the same flowers that adorn the skirt. But for genuine novelty and effectiveness the second dress must take the first place. It is of eau-de-Nil satin, patterned with a tiny spot and an equally diminutive conventional leaf. At each side of the skirt there is a larger bow of orange-coloured velvet, which forms a base for three gracefully curving black ostrich tips – an original method of trimming which is likely to commend itself to most people. The waistband, of black satin ribbon, tied at the back in two smart bows, with a little space between, and the collar, of orange velvet, has two tiny black tips at each side. Then there are square epaulettes of black satin, covered with lace, and, to give a perfect finishing touch, a picture hat of black velvet, the full crown embroidered with steel and trimmed with black ostrich feathers. For the last act, Miss Millett has a pale-tan crépon gown, the skirt having a tiny pointed panel at each side of turquoise-blue mirror velvet, with an appliqué of white cloth, stitched with gold thread and sequins, and fastened in quaintly to the crépon with little gold buttons on one side and black button-holes on the other, and tied at the top with a black satin bow. The bodice has a blouse front of the velvet, with a wide box-pleat down the centre, and neck and waist bands of black satin, the former covered with lace and adorned at the back with lace ruffles and a butterfly bow of satin. But most charming of all is the zouave of blue satin, enriched with its appliqué of cloth and gold, and I think you will allow that Miss Millett's dresses stand out well from all the others.

Then Miss Fanny Brough [as Lady Markby], in a very becoming grey coiffure, has a ruby-coloured velvet evening dress with a berthe of costly lace, and a day dress of grey and terra-cotta brocade, trimmed with satin ribbon to match, grey velvet, and lace; and the list is concluded by Miss Vane Featherstone in green-and-pink striped chiné silk, brocaded with pink roses with a green velvet bodice, and Miss Helen Forsyth, lovely as ever, in a perfectly cut gown of pink mirror velvet.

Women's costume in An Ideal Husband: *Lady Chiltern in Act IV (left) and Mabel Chiltern in Act IV (from* The Sketch, *January 1895)*

APPENDIX III
THE STRUCTURE OF THE PLAY

The numbers in parenthesis indicate the beginning of each section, according to the line numbering of the present edition. Scenes containing major elements of the main plot's development are indicated with an asterisk.

Act I (Octagon Room in Sir Robert Chiltern's House)
a   Party guests (1–).
b* Arrival of Lady Markby, Mrs Cheveley (51).
c* Sir Robert enters: conversation with Mrs Cheveley (in Lady Markby's presence) (86–).
d   Lord Goring enters: conversation with Mabel (199–).
e   Lord Caversham and Goring; then conversations between Goring and Lady Marchmont and Lady Basildon and finally Mabel (257–).
f* Sir Robert's private conversation with Mrs Cheveley: request for help, threat of blackmail (369–).
g   Lady Markby returns (566–).
h* Mrs Cheveley speaks to Lady Chiltern: refers to Sir Robert's intention to support canal project (590–).
i* Conversation between Mabel and Goring: finding of bracelet (619–).
j   Mabel, Goring and Lady Chiltern: leave taking (655–).
k* Lady Chiltern and Sir Robert alone: she insists that he must refuse to support the canal project (678–804).

Act II (Morning-room in Sir Robert Chiltern's House)
a* Goring and Sir Robert: the story of his career (1–).
b   Lady Chiltern returns (274–).
c* Goring speaks to Lady Chiltern: if she ever needs his help, she must contact him (322–).
d   Mabel enters (392–).
e   Mabel and Lady Chiltern: talk of Mabel's suitor Tommy Trafford (437–).
f   Lady Markby arrives with Mrs Cheveley (496–).
g* Mrs Cheveley left alone with Lady Chiltern: the threat made explicit; Sir Robert enters at 746 (496–).
h* Lady Chiltern and Sir Robert alone again: he rebukes her for idealising him (761–814).

Act III (Library of Lord Goring's House)
(N.B. Sections a–d contain elements necessary to set up situation for what follows.)
a   Phipps and Goring. Letter arrives from Lady Chiltern, asking for Goring's help (1–).
b   Caversham arrives: after conversation, is shown into smoking-room. Phipps told to show lady who is expected into drawing-room (57–).

c   Mrs Cheveley arrives and is shown into drawing-room (152–).

d   Caversham leaves (204–).

e* Sir Robert arrives. After discussion with Goring, discovers that Mrs Cheveley is in drawing-room – after Goring, assuming she is Lady Chiltern, has defended her honour (227–).

f* Mrs Cheveley and Goring: confronted with bracelet, she gives up incriminating letter, steals Lady Chiltern's note to Goring (372–617).

Act IV (Morning-room in Sir Robert's House as in Act II)

a   Goring and Caversham (1–).

b   Mabel joins them (85–).

c   Mabel and Goring (124–).

d* Lady Chiltern and Goring (201–).

e* Sir Robert arrives, with 'compromising' letter, but assumes it is intended for him (Goring leaves them alone at 285) (274–).

f   Goring returns, evidently having proposed to Mabel; Caversham brings news of Prime Minister's offer (325–).

g   Caversham and Goring conversation (371–).

h* Goring and Lady Chiltern: he persuades her not to stand in her husband's way (393–).

i* Sir Robert returns; she insists that he must now accept offer (438–).

j* Mabel and Caversham return; Sir Robert refuses to allow Goring to marry her, but Lady Chiltern explains the misunderstanding over Mrs Cheveley's presence in Goring's house. Conclusion, with Sir Robert and Lady Chiltern left alone on stage (523–55).